Racial Experiments in Cuban Literature and Ethnography

UNIVERSITY PRESS OF FLORIDA

Florida A&M University, Tallahassee
Florida Atlantic University, Boca Raton
Florida Gulf Coast University, Ft. Myers
Florida International University, Miami
Florida State University, Tallahassee
New College of Florida, Sarasota
University of Central Florida, Orlando
University of Florida, Gainesville
University of North Florida, Jacksonville
University of South Florida, Tampa
University of West Florida, Pensacola

RACIAL EXPERIMENTS IN CUBAN LITERATURE AND ETHNOGRAPHY

Emily A. Maguire

University Press of Florida
Gainesville · Tallahassee · Tampa · Boca Raton
Pensacola · Orlando · Miami · Jacksonville · Ft. Myers · Sarasota

The publication of this book is made possible by a grant from the University Research Grant Committee at Northwestern University.

Copyright 2011 by Emily A. Maguire
All rights reserved
Published in the United States of America

First cloth printing, 2011
First paperback printing, 2018

29 28 27 26 25   6 5 4 3 2

Library of Congress Cataloging-in-Publication Data
Maguire, Emily, 1972–
Racial experiments in Cuban literature and ethnography / Emily A. Maguire.
p. cm.
Includes bibliographical references and index.
ISBN 978-0-8130-3747-9 (cloth)
ISBN 978-0-8130-6480-2 (pbk.)
1. Cuban literature—History and criticism. 2. Ethnography—Cuba. 3. Blacks—Cuba—Ethnic identity. 4. Identity (Philosophical concept) in literature. I. Title.
PQ7373.M34 2011
860.9'97291—dc23   2011018994

The University Press of Florida is the scholarly publishing agency for the State University System of Florida, comprising Florida A&M University, Florida Atlantic University, Florida Gulf Coast University, Florida International University, Florida State University, New College of Florida, University of Central Florida, University of Florida, University of North Florida, University of South Florida, and University of West Florida.

University Press of Florida
2046 NE Waldo Road
Suite 2100
Gainesville, FL 32609
http://upress.ufl.edu

CONTENTS

Acknowledgments   vii

Introduction: A Folklore for the Future: Race and National Narrative in Cuba   1

1. Locating Afro-Cuban Religion: Fernando Ortiz and Lydia Cabrera   29

2. Beyond Bongos in Montmartre: Lydia Cabrera and Alejo Carpentier Imagine Blackness   63

3. The National Art of Signifyin(g): Nicolás Guillén and Lydia Cabrera   104

4. Gender, Genre, and Ethnographic Authority: Lydia Cabrera and Zora Neale Hurston   143

Epilogue: Textual Straits: Race and Ethnographic Literature since the Cuban Revolution   173

Notes   189

Selected Bibliography   209

Index   227

ACKNOWLEDGMENTS

This book only exists thanks to the help of numerous individuals and institutions. I was able to conduct research for this project in Cuba and Miami thanks to a King Juan Carlos I of Spain Center Summer Travel Grant and a Tinker Field Research Grant. In Cuba, Alexander Pérez Heredia met me upon my arrival in Havana and became not only the best of guides through the city but also a true friend. I thank him and Virgilio López Lemus for facilitating my research at the Instituto de Literatura y Lingüística. At the Biblioteca Nacional José Martí, I was welcomed by Araceli García-Carranza, and helped by Teresa Valladares, Maritza Colón, and Licia Otero. I am indebted to Victor Fowler for a conversation that helped orient me with regard to both the archives and the state of race relations in Cuba, and to María del Rosario Díaz for helping me access the correspondence between Fernando Ortiz and Lydia Cabrera. Natalia Bolívar Aróstegui and Jesús Guanche gave me important insights into Lydia Cabrera's work and ethnography in Cuba today. Ramón Gainza shared his memories of life with Lydia and Titina at the Quinta San José. Juana García Abás, José Luis Fariñas, and Adrían Hernández Diez have helped me in innumerable large and small ways on my multiple visits to Havana. I thank Enrique del Risco Sr., Magda Heredia, and Eric del Risco for their generous hospitality, and Mercedes González, Ignacio Valdés, and Carmen Vargas for opening their homes to me. Yoss and the inimitable Zandra Gómez always make the corner of Jovellar and San Lázaro streets feel like home. Mil gracias también a usted, Juany, por todos sus consejos y bendiciones.

In Miami, Estela Varona and Lesbia Orto Varona helped make my time at the Cuban Heritage Collection the most pleasant and productive of research experiences. I also thank Ángel Lozada and Arnaldo López for introducing me to the Santería communities of Washington Heights, the Bronx, and San Juan, Puerto Rico.

My colleagues at Indiana University, Patrick Dove, Melissa Dinverno, Carl Good, Alejandro Mejías-López, and Steve Wagschal, provided me with friendship and intellectual dialogue in my first years as an assistant professor. Deborah Cohn and Matthew Guterl provided key mentoring advice at multiple points during my time in Bloomington and helped me grow as a scholar and as a human being. This project benefited at a crucial stage from my dialogues with fellow participants in the Variations on Blackness Faculty Seminar held at Indiana University in 2005–2006. I would especially like to thank Eileen Julien for sharing her thoughts on the relationship between Cabrera's politics and her ethnographic methodology. I would also like to thank the graduate students in my class on "Négritude and Negrismo," whose astute questions and comments helped me reframe some of my own readings of texts I explore in this study.

At Northwestern University, I have been lucky to find a community of like-minded colleagues whose friendship and intellectual engagement with my work has been vital to me in the last stages of this project. Nathalie Bouzaglo, Alejandra Uslenghi, Yarí Pérez Marín, and Sacramento Roselló Martínez have been good friends and excellent readers of numerous drafts. Ana Aparicio, Darío Fernández Moreira, Lucille Kerr, Elisa Martí López, Ramón Rivera-Servera, Mary Weismantel, Ivy Wilson, and Dorris Garraway have provided support and helpful advice at various moments. I am indebted to Reginald Gibbons for his detailed and substantive comments on the manuscript, and to Jorge Coronado and Josef Barton, who have been not only the most generous of interlocutors but also the most supportive of chairs.

This book could not have been written without the help of the numerous friends and colleagues who contributed to the conception and realization of this project. I owe Gerard Aching a particular debt of gratitude, not only for introducing me to the work of Lydia Cabrera but also for his astute interventions and unfailing support at various moments during the writing process. The insightful comments of Ana María Dopico, Sylvia Molloy, Mary Louise Pratt, and Sibylle Fischer were also instrumental in shaping this project. Mariana Amato, Barbara Andrews, Natalia Brizuela, Lena Burgos Lafuente, Kahlil Chaar Pérez, Gabriel Giorgi, Francisco-Javier Hernández Adrián, Stephanie Kirk, Christina Kullberg, April Marshall, Urayoán Noel, Néstor E. Rodríguez, Kalpana Shankar,

Laura Tanenbaum, Rebecca Vitz Cherico, and Erna Von der Walde read and commented on earlier versions of this project, and I would like to thank each of them. In the final stages of the book's genesis, Stephen Berrey, Deborah Cohen, Lessie Jo Frazier, Erin Graff Zivin, Eden Medina, and Ellen Moodie were there to offer advice and encouragement, and to read multiple drafts. They know this work almost as well as their own. I am particularly grateful to Jacqueline Loss and James J. Pancrazio for their thoughtful comments on the manuscript, and to Guillermina De Ferrari, who offered numerous helpful insights and suggestions in the final stages of revision. I would also like to thank my editors at University Press of Florida: my acquisitions editor, Amy Gorelick, who believed in this project from the beginning; my project editor, Marthe Walters, who guided this book through its various stages of production; my copy editor, Helena Berg, for her patient and careful editing; and my proofreader, Erin Dougherty.

While not directly involved in the writing process, my parents, James Maguire and Betty Hayzlett, and my brother Stephen kept me going with their unconditional love and support. The Flying M. Coffee House in Boise, Idaho; Atlas Café in Williamsburg, Brooklyn; Soma Café in Bloomington, Indiana; and The Coffee Studio in Andersonville, Chicago, always had a seat and a hot cup of coffee waiting for me on days when I couldn't (or couldn't bear to) work at home. Finally, I thank Lola, who was there at the beginning, and Idaho, who is here at the end.

I wish to thank the following individuals and institutions for permission to reprint or reproduce the following materials in this book:

Nicolás Hernández Guillén and the Fundación Nicolás Guillén in Cuba for their generous permission to reprint Nicolás Guillén's poems "Negro Bembón," "Secuestro de la mujer de Antonio," "El abuelo," and "West Indies, Ltd." in their entirety.

Achy Obejas, for her translations of Nicolás Guillén's "Negro bembón," "Secuestro de la mujer de Antonio," and "West Indies, Ltd."

Kutzinski, Vera M., translator. "El Abuelo (The Grandfather)." Callaloo 10:2 (1987), 191. © 1987 Charles H. Rowell. Reprinted with permission of The Johns Hopkins University Press.

Portions of chapter 3 appeared as "Tracing a Caribbean Sense of Play: Signifyin(g) in Lydia Cabrera and Nicolás Guillén," *Ciberletras* 7 (2002).

In all other cases every effort has been made to locate possible copyright holders or to acquire necessary permissions.

Introduction

A FOLKLORE FOR THE FUTURE

Race and National Narrative in Cuba

> *Somos, aunque no quieren saber que somos.*
> *Somos el músculo;*
> *somos la escencia del eco alegre;*
> *somos un signo tabüizante para las lacras de nuestro rol;*
> *la sombra nos dio pieles con qué abrigar el miedo*
> *y es una piel de sustos saber nuestro color.*
>
> [*We are, although they don't want to know that we are.*
> *We are the muscle;*
> *we are the essence of the joyful echo;*
> *we are a taboo sign for our blighted role;*
> *the shadow gave us skins to cover our fear*
> *and it is a skin of shocks to know our color.*]

In these lines from a 1935 poem entitled "Canción negra sin color" (Black Song without Color), Afro-Cuban poet Marcelino Arozarena captures the paradoxical treatment of black Cubans in Cuba (and Cuban literature) of the time.[1] Black Cubans are present within the national space, he asserts, in both a physical sense—"the muscle"—and as a kind of spiritual presence. This multifaceted existence, however, is met with a lack of acknowledgment—"they don't want to know that *we are*"—as well as by fear and resistance (a "skin of shocks"). These contradictory reactions are what produce a "black song without color," in which blackness is present but unrecognized. Arozarena's description exposes the ambivalent and contradictory function of blackness in the transnational racial politics of the time. While Afro-Cuban culture was in a position to contribute significantly to the idea of Cubanness being constructed by the island's intellectuals, it was also a problematic, stigmatized element.[2]

One year later, in 1936, the literary critic Gilberto González y Contreras published a short article entitled "La poesía negra" (Black Poetry) that presented a very different—and more positive—view of the significance of Afro-Cuban culture. González y Contreras focuses his analysis on what he calls "black Cuban poetry," the relatively large body of literature that had been published in Cuba in the preceding decade (the 1920s) portraying black Cubans, much of it by writers who, unlike Arozarena, were not themselves Afro-Cuban.[3] The "black Cuban poetry" to which his essay refers was part of an artistic movement known as *Afrocubanismo* (Afro-Cubanism), generally understood as a "revalorization of Afro-Cuban culture" in vogue in Cuban literature, music, and visual arts in the 1920s and 1930s.[4] Literary *Afrocubanismo* is most often tied to the poetry of writers such as Ramón Guirao, Emilio Ballagas, and Nicolás Guillén, although it has also been connected to novels such as Alejo Carpentier's *Écue-Yamba-Ó*. González y Contreras argues that this body of work, viewed by many at the time as a literary fad, is in fact a project with profound implications, for the authors of "black Cuban poetry" are involved in an endeavor more complex than mere poetic creation:

> La esteva del entólogo remueve la petrificada arcilla, clasificando los materiales, que luego anima el poeta, dotándolos de agilidad, renovándolos. Pero cuando el folklore no deviene del pasado, cuando no se trata de la resurrección de una verdad poética, sino de algo que flota en el presente, de una sustancia prendida a las raices de la vida popular, la misión del poeta es la de un etnólogo artista. (40)

> [The ethnographer's plow blade stirs up the petrified clay, classifying the materials, which the poet then animates, endowing them with agility, renewing them. But when folklore doesn't come from the past, when one is not dealing with the resurrection of a poetic truth but with something floating in the present, a substance attached to the roots of popular life, the poet's mission is that of an artist-ethnographer.]

Through this unusual figure of the artist-ethnographer, González y Contreras characterizes this new literary production as both art and social science: it involves the recognition and understanding of something already present (if unrecognized) as well as the creative adaptation of that "substance," the coming together of these elements of material culture in a new aesthetic form.

At the time that "La poesía negra" appeared, the term "folklore," particularly in a European context, was often used to refer to elements of a collective past, whether ethnic, regional, or national.[5] González y Contreras, on the other hand, points to the way in which black Cuban culture is not a folk culture rooted in the past but rather a new kind of "poetic truth" operating in the present. Instead of "animating" a substance from a distant historical moment (suggested in his description by the plow blade, more resonant of archaeology than ethnography), he posits that this new poetic process of expressing "the roots of popular life" involves shifting between registers, as elements of "popular culture" are absorbed and then transformed into what came to be termed "high" culture, implicitly understood as literature and the fine arts. González y Contreras does not explicitly connect the artistic and intellectual project he describes to ideas of nationhood; yet his use of the term "folklore," coupled with the importance he gives to this new method of creation—the idea of a poetic "mission"—implies that the kind of textual production and the images of black Cubans it presents are more closely related to a concept of national culture than might first appear.

Arozarena and González y Contreras approach the representation of blackness in Cuban letters from opposing positions. As an Afro-Cuban, Arozarena is concerned that black Cubans be fully acknowledged and accepted within the national space. (He also implicitly desires greater possibility for Afro-Cuban self-representation.) "We are," his poem declares: know us, recognize us. His poem's paradoxical title makes visible this "absent presence" and implicitly critiques those who would condone this marginalization.[6] González y Contreras, on the other hand, is interested in understanding the creative potential of Afro-Cuban culture as a material substrate of Cuban culture. The artistic process of the writers he identifies as artist-ethnographers involves navigating a "living" folklore, studying and adapting it. While González y Contreras does not explain the extent to which the articulation of this "poetic truth" needs to be faithful to its subject, nor just how this creative-scientific process should work, his essay nonetheless identifies a significant strain of interdisciplinary experimentation that informs Cuban literary and artistic production of the time.

What is the significance of the cultural production around black popular culture that González y Contreras describes? What does it really mean to transport and transform these racialized elements of "popular life" into texts that form part of what Angel Rama has termed the "republic of letters"—both the production and the discursive and intellectual space of the literary (and political) elite?[7] And what ways of writing are necessary to effect this transformation? This book looks at how writers in Cuba attempted to answer these questions in the country's first half-century of its existence as an independent nation. Following the lines of investigation suggested by González y Contreras's provocative observations, it argues that writers in Cuba in the first half of the twentieth century forged a unique literary space in which to imagine the nation precisely through diverse creative experiments that borrow elements from both ethnographic and literary discourses. To explore the potential of this encounter between established literary forms, developing ethnographic methodologies, and popular culture and to show how the texts it produced were employed to create and buttress a particular idea of Cuba as a nation, it analyzes the work of four such "artist-ethnographers": Fernando Ortiz (1881–1969), seen as the founding father of Cuban anthropology; the novelist Alejo Carpentier (1904–1980); the Afro-Cuban poet Nicolás Guillén (1902–1989); and Lydia Cabrera (1898–1991), a self-taught ethnographer and short-story writer whose work epitomizes the discursive impulses of this moment. Their textual experimentation was necessary to negotiate what—for elite intellectuals and political leaders—were potentially problematic elements of what could viably be posited as Cuba's national identity, in particular race.

As a Caribbean island that only gained full independence in 1901, Cuba was not the only nation in the region to struggle with the question of how to interpret, represent, or incorporate a (majority) nonwhite population. Yet the particular circumstances of Cuba's history make it a fascinating case study for examining how the relationship of blackness to nation has been constructed in a postcolonial context. For Cuba, blackness was both the problem and the solution: just as the Afro-Cuban presence was part of what made Cuba unique, in a world in which progress and modernity were associated with the Western (European) idea of the nation, the presence of black Cubans threatened to relegate Cuba to the status of non-modern. Through their creative use of literary techniques and ethnographic viewpoints, these artist-ethnographers attempted to navigate this crucial balance.

The 1920s was not the first time that Cuban writers had considered race an issue of cultural and political significance. Cuban writing in the nineteenth century frequently alluded to race, often through its depictions of slavery. So-called antislavery novels such as Gertrudis Gómez de Avellaneda's *Sab* (1841), Antonio Zambrana's *El negro Francisco* (1873), and Cirilo Villaverde's *Cecilia Valdés o la Loma del Ángel* (1882) focused on the violent, cruel, and degrading aspects of slavery in an attempt to show their readers that the system itself was uncivilized and should be abolished. These writers relied on the narrative form of the novel to disseminate their political message; they believed that readers would come to understand the extent of slavery's inhumanity through their empathic identification with the texts' enslaved characters. William Luis asserts that these novels "create a permanent space for blacks in a literature of foundation" (2), yet the space that these novels allowed their black and mulatto protagonists was limited to their position as victims of the slavery system.

Political theorist Benedict Anderson posits that the nation is an "imagined community," fashioned in large measure from shared rhetoric and constructed via print culture. In her study of the nineteenth-century Latin American novel, Doris Sommer builds on Anderson's concept to argue that the narrative form becomes a textual stage on which national tensions are played out or resolved through romance. In these novels, a unified national imaginary is achieved and national differences such as race or class are resolved "through reconciliations and amalgamations of national constituencies cast as lovers destined to desire each other" (*Foundational Fictions* 24). In the case of Cuban antislavery novels such as *Sab*, Sommer has shown that while these "foundational fictions" condemn slavery, they often reaffirm unbridgeable social divisions between black and white Cubans.[8] It is important to keep in mind, however, that unlike the other Latin American novels that Sommer analyzes, written in the late nineteenth and early twentieth centuries (decades past independence for much of Latin America), Cuban antislavery novels were written and published while the island was still a Spanish colony; while they could grapple with issues of race relations, Cuban writers did not yet have a new national identity to narrate. It was only with Cuban Independence that the fledgling nation needed to create new ways of talking about race.

As Partha Chatterjee and Mary Louise Pratt (among others) have argued, the very idea of an "imagined community" carries within it ideas of Western (European) superiority, given that colonizing powers are the ones doing the imagining; the Western model of the "nation" is often assumed by postcolonial nations to be a hegemonic template.[9] In this study, I make an intervention into the relationship between nation building and literature by challenging the notion that narratives (like those that Sommer analyzes) are required for enacting the abstract idea of nationhood. Nations need imaginaries, yet the Cuban case—and Cuba's particular situation as a new nation in the twentieth century—suggests the limits of narrative as a means of configuring a coherent, stable, homogenized, and inclusive image of nationhood. While not rejecting such genres as the novel, the writers I analyze here work to disentangle and reexamine the coupling of nation and narration, opening up the potential of other kinds of writing in order to posit an idea of nation that takes into account the paradoxical exigencies of the Cuban situation.

The methods and means of Cuba's artist-ethnographers were more innovative in form, challenging in their inclusion of cultural references, and transgressive in their use of marginal discourses—and their representations of Afro-Cuban culture thus more varied—than González y Contreras's description of *Afrocubanista* poetry would imply. The creative process he describes can be seen in texts written both before and after those decades, including texts that have not traditionally been identified as "literature" such as the "ethnographic" writing of Fernando Ortiz and Lydia Cabrera. Indeed, I contend that their very in-between-ness, the incorporation of multiple literary and ethnographic textual strategies, is both what makes *all* of these texts difficult to categorize according to traditional discursive or disciplinary frameworks and what provides a key to their intended function: the creation of a literature designed to harness and at the same time neutralize cultural blackness on the island in order to identify Cuba as a modern nation, where modern is understood to mean industrial, urban, "civilized"—as manifested through the arts—and white (European).[10]

Cuba in Black and White

The growth of Cuba's economy in the nineteenth century was due in large part to the Haitian Revolution (1791–1804). Prior to Haiti's independence, the French colony had been the largest producer of sugar in the Caribbean; after the Revolution, international ostracism of Haiti (in addition to the resettlement of a large number of Haitian colonists in Santiago and other parts of eastern Cuba) allowed Cuba to take its place as the top exporter of sugar in the Caribbean. As the nineteenth century advanced, Cuba's economy thus became increasingly centered on the plantation system, whose modern capitalist division of labor had been sustained by a workforce made up largely of African slaves, even as sugar production—and the corresponding use of slave labor—was declining elsewhere in the Caribbean (López Valdés 15).[11] This economic and social shift—in which Cuba came to more closely resemble pre-independence Haiti in social organization—meant that the specter of the Haitian Revolution (understood as a slave rebellion) was never far from Cuban minds. Michel-Rolph Trouillot asserts that the Haitian Revolution was silenced in histories and accounts of the time because it was an "unthinkable" event; white colonists could not conceive that black people would not only carry out a successful rebellion but also would be capable of self-governance (*Silencing* 70–107). Similarly, Sibylle Fischer observes that Haiti was central to the battle over ending slavery that emerged in the Caribbean, "although often only as the unspeakable, as trauma, utopia and elusive dream" (2). Haiti continued to haunt the Cuban imagination as the possibility of black uprising (one carried out in a Creole vernacular), a fear that, even if unstated, fueled tensions around the issue of slavery throughout the nineteenth century.

Cuba was one of the last of Spain's colonies to gain independence, and both slavery and racial divisions on the island played a crucial role in the war for independence. As historian Ada Ferrer has shown, the conflict was as much a fight over "the boundaries of Cuban nationality" (and the racial contours of those boundaries) as it was a struggle for the end of colonial rule (17). In the first act of Cuban rebellion, the "Grito de Yara" of October 10, 1868, sugar planter Carlos Manuel de Céspedes gathered the slaves on his plantation La Demajagua, declared them free, and invited them to join him in taking up arms for Cuban independence (Ferrer 15). Like Céspedes, the white Creole elites who initially supported the rebellion came largely from the Eastern part of the island, which produced less sugar (and was thus less reliant on slave labor as a means of production). Western sugar planters and others who opposed independence often described the conflict in racial terms, casting it as a black rebellion akin to the Haitian Revolution and warning that it would result in a moral degradation of Cuban society (Ferrer 47–54). The fact was that many Afro-Cubans did participate in the War for Independence, and a number of high-ranking officers—among them national heroes Antonio Maceo, Rafael Serra, Prudencio Martínez, and Pedro Díaz—were black.

Despite the large numbers of slaves who won their freedom in the Ten Years' War (1868–78), the first stage of the Cuban struggle for independence, the end of slavery was a gradual process; the Moret Law, enacted in 1871, declared free any child born to a slave mother, but slavery as a whole did not end until 1886. Nevertheless, the island's African-descended population at the end of the nineteenth century was large and heterogeneous. Larger Cuban cities such as Havana, Santiago, and Puerto Príncipe (now Camagüey) had a sizeable free black and mulatto population. Afro-Cubans were artisans and craftsmen, dock workers and day laborers. The descendents of slaves (often house slaves who had earned their freedom), they formed the beginnings of an Afro-Cuban working class (Brown, Palmié).

Cuba's economic dependence on plantation agriculture meant that Africans continued to arrive in Cuba long after the slave trade had been declared officially ended in 1862. At the time of Cuba's independence from Spain in 1898, a significant number of black Cubans had a parent or grandparent who had come from Africa. Thanks to the Spanish practice of permitting slaves to form *cabildos*, cultural organizations for Africans (often from the same tribe or region) that also served as mutual aid societies (and semi-clandestine religious centers), many African cultural and linguistic traditions survived into the post-Independence period.[12] These included both religious practices—*Regla de Ochá* (also known as Santería), Palo Monte, and Abakuá traditions—as well as African languages such as *Lucumí* (Yoruba) or *Congó* (Bantu in origin), which were still spoken in both religious and secular contexts, in addition to *bozal*, an African-influenced Spanish Creole.

Cuba emerged as a nation with the arrival of the twentieth century; after curtailed independence struggles between 1868 and 1878 (known as the Ten Years' War), Cuban insurgents again went to war with Spain in 1895, and in 1898 finally succeeded in defeating the Spanish and securing Cuba's independence. However, independence from Spain was achieved only through North American intervention; the United States, interested in ending Spain's control of the island (and hoping to claim Cuba), pronounced the defeat of the Spanish a U.S. victory and began a military occupation of Cuba (Pérez, *Cuba* 137–8). Upon winning the war, the United

States declared the island a U.S. protectorate, and it remained so until the signing of the Platt Amendment to the Cuban Constitution in 1901. The Platt Amendment further constrained Cuban Independence, given that it included a clause that allowed the United States to intervene again in Cuba should it deem it necessary. The large nation ninety miles to Cuba's north exerted its influence over the island in both overt and subtle ways. North American–owned businesses dominated Cuban agriculture and would also come to control major elements of the island's infrastructure, such as railroads and electricity suppliers (Pérez, *Cuba* 146–53). At the same time, the U.S. occupation had opened Cuba as a market for North American products and exposed Cubans to North American customs and ideas.[13]

Cuba thus entered the international arena in a paradoxical situation: it was a modern nation emerging from four centuries of Spanish colonialism, but one in which North American interests were gaining increasing control over the island's economy. Cuba was caught between its past as a Spanish colony and the heavy weight of U.S. influence; even as it aspired to full political autonomy it was entering a new situation of economic dependency. In addition to the destruction of private property and public infrastructure resulting from the war for independence, Cuba had to contend with aspects of a colonial heritage that could not be assimilated as modern, in particular the relatively recent (and late) end to chattel slavery (in 1886) and the presence of a racially mixed population. Despite an influx of Spanish immigrants towards the end of the nineteenth century, in the 1899 census by the U.S. War department, roughly 33 percent of the Cuban population was listed as "colored," a number that would have included Chinese immigrants, free blacks and mulattoes, and large numbers of former slaves.[14] Both U.S. politicians and the North American press had used Cuba's mixed-race population to create an image of Cuba as an inferior nation on racial grounds, an idea that Cuban intellectuals and politicians would need to combat to identify Cuba as modern.[15]

Thanks to Spanish colonialism, U.S. intervention, and its long independence struggle, Cuba in 1902 was a country in which several opposing and contested narratives of race were present. Many Cubans saw independence as having been achieved by the Cuban population as a whole, one in which a desire for—and a belief in—national unity transcended race.[16] Cuban writer José Martí, who had worked tirelessly for Cuban independence before dying in 1895 in one of the war's first battles, had declared in

"Nuestra América" ("Our America," 1891), his proscriptive essay on the necessity for Latin American unity, "No hay odio de razas, porque no hay razas" (22). [There is no racial hatred, for there are no races.][17] However, Martí's belabored insistence on the absence of racial difference, which he would go on to elaborate in essays such as "Mi raza" ("My Race," 1893), hints at a continued anxiety, at a fear of the divisive power of race and the need to negate race (and with it blackness) in order to control it.

Despite the unifying cause of the independence struggle, race had been, and would continue to be, a volatile political issue. As Ferrer observes, even before the war began in 1895, within the pro-independence community, "Calls for racial unity and racial silence overlapped with the rise of political mobilization on the basis of race," a lobbying largely centered on an early civil rights campaign advocating for the desegregation of public spaces and the creation of an active black press (132–34). In the first decade following the Platt Amendment, many of the political debates centered around the political participation of black Cubans in Cuban politics, and the ability of "Cubans of color" (as they were then identified) to achieve political or socioeconomic equality with white Cubans. Thanks in part to the American occupation of the island, North American Jim Crow policies and accompanying racist stereotypes had entered Cuban practice and speech. Influenced by U.S. racist ideologies, some Cubans argued that centuries of slavery had produced a morally abject population that was incapable of self-leadership (Ferrer 129). Nevertheless, the Constitutional Convention of 1901 went on to grant Cubans universal male suffrage, an act that conceded political participation irrespective of race (de la Fuente, "Myths," 54).

Black intellectuals such as Juan Gualberto Gómez and Rafael Serra had been lobbying for creating a political voice along racial lines since the early 1890s.[18] Following Cuban Independence, their work intensified. Feeling that Cubans of color were not achieving adequate representation within existing political parties, Evaristo Estenoz founded the Independent Party of Color (Partido Independiente de Color, or PIC) in 1908. The decision to create a racially identified political party was strongly criticized, both by white members of the Liberal Party (who feared losing their black electorate) and by Afro-Cuban politicians such as Gómez and Martín Morúa Delgado, who argued that racial divisions would lead to social and political instability, a dangerous situation for a nation that was barely a decade old (de la Fuente, *Nation* 69–74). Thanks to Morúa Delgado's lobbying, the Morúa Law, enacted in 1911, outlawed the existence of any political organization that limited membership by race or color. When the PIC actively protested the Morúa Law, the government's attempt to repress the protests in 1912 led to an island-wide white backlash against black Cubans that rapidly deteriorated into what has been characterized as a race war. Even after the infamous "Guerrita del '12" (Little War of 1912) had ended, sporadic incidents of racial violence continued to occur throughout the island over the following decade (de la Fuente, *Nation* 78).

The Morúa Law, and violence of 1912 that followed it, effectively ended political organizing along racial lines. The results of this were varied. The absence of a racially identified political voice strengthened the discourse that Cuba was a racial democracy and that Cubanness was fundamentally racially inclusive. This "myth of racial democracy" dramatically reduced the conditions of possibility for black Cubans to gain political and material access to full participation in the new Republic, as any mention of racial struggle was now criticized as promoting national discord and fragmentation. Yet this myth had positive as well as negative consequences for black Cubans themselves; as de la Fuente argues, as much as it limited race-identified political participation, "the integrationist ideal also opened up opportunities for [blacks'] participation in republican society" (*Nation* 14). In concrete terms, however, Cuban society in the succeeding years in many ways became increasingly segregated. Black Cuban men could vote, but blacks were barred from many exclusive restaurants, hotels, and elite social establishments such as the Havana Yacht Club. In response, middle- and upper-class Cubans of color formed their own sports teams and social clubs, such as the *Club Atenas*.[19] Some of the Afro-Cuban mutual-aid centers that in the colonial era had been known as *cabildos* became *sociedades de color* (colored societies), in the process losing their emphasis on preserving African-derived cultural and religious practices but remaining racially identified social organizations.

Social class was one of the strongest factors in determining racial boundaries in post-Independence Cuba. Middle-class black Cubans emulated the social practices of their white peers, emphasizing the cultivation of European-influenced literature and fine arts and condemning anything markedly Afro-Cuban in origin as "uncivilized."[20] Black social organizations actively discouraged African-derived social and religious practices; as Robin Moore notes, many of the *sociedades de color* prohibited the use of Afro-Cuban musical forms at their social gatherings (*Nationalizing*

Blackness 39). Although as Moore has shown, thanks in part to the vogue of *Afrocubanismo,* musical forms such as the *son* gradually found their way into acceptance in middle-class society by the middle of the 1930s, other African-derived musical genres, such as the carnival *comparsa,* continued to be limited by both official and unofficial regulation.[21]

Afro-Cuban religious traditions such as Santería and Palo Monte found themselves in a similarly tenuous position with regard to the law. Police frequently raided Afro-Cuban religious celebrations and confiscated the religious objects being used (Bronfman, Brown, Palmié). The first decades of the twentieth century also witnessed the birth of a new social panic: a fear of black *brujos* (witches), who were believed to rob graves and abduct white children to use in their rituals.[22] As a result of both official policing and the fanning of popular fears, Afro-Cuban religious practices continued to be criminalized well into the twentieth century, and much of the general knowledge of these religions came from the sensationalizing pages of Cuban daily newspapers.

Divergent Imaginaries

Cuban intellectuals at the beginning of the twentieth century felt constrained by the nation's attenuated sovereignty, and many expressed dismay over what they saw as the country's social and political inadequacies. In the first decade of Cuba's independence, books such as *La convulsión cubana* (*The Cuban Convulsion,* 1906) by Roque E. Garrigó, Manuel Márquez Sterling, and Francisco Figueras and *Alrededor de nuestra psicología* (*Concerning Our Psychology,* 1906) by Manuel Márquez Sterling, produced a severely pessimistic portrait of the fledgling nation, characterizing Cuban society as corrupt and immature, and arguing that the nation's attempts at self-governance were destined to fail.[23] Political theorist Tom Nairn has pointed out that the idea of the (Western) nation as synonymous with future-oriented development and progress grounded in a historically organic relation between nation-state (with a particular territory) and people (with a unified "culture") is by definition a "metropolitan fantasy," an ideal never achieved by even the most "developed" nations (12). According to Nairn, nationalism is "Janus-faced," looking to both the future and the past in order to construct the nation as modern (18). Thanks to the country's colonial history, early Cuban writers, in a rush to measure up to European or North American standards, saw their nation as "already behind." Yet despite the fact that these essayists were primarily concerned with the political state of the Cuban nation—and specifically, with Cuba's (in)ability to govern itself, they expressed their concerns and doubts in cultural terms. They saw Cubans as weak and decadent, incapable of self-governance because of biological and cultural formation—what literary critic Rafael Rojas has termed *cubanidad negativa*, negative Cubanness (*Isla* 158).[24] While they did not all explicitly state that this inferiority was based on race, many of these texts implied or indicated that this was the case. This discourse thus saw Cuban society as doomed to failure thanks to the island's political history and its social composition.

Yet while republican Cuba's early essayists bemoaned Cuba's postcolonial situation, other writers began to search for literary material with which to shape alternate—and more positively unifying—narratives of Cubanness. Building on Anderson's concept, Homi Bhabha observes that the idea of "nation" often functions itself as a "narrative strategy," one that can cover for an absence of concrete commonalities. For Bhabha, the term nation " . . . produces a continual slippage into analogous, even metonymic, categories, like the people, minorities, or 'cultural difference' that continually overlap in the act of writing the nation" ("DissemiNation" 292). Cuban intellectuals looked to the idea of "nation" as just such a strategy: one that would allow them to write their way out of the country's colonial past and resolve the contradictions of its (neo)colonial present, in particular its diverse and heterogeneous population. Cuban writers thus accorded print culture an added responsibility in the nation's first decades: it was an opportunity for Cuban artistic and literary production to legitimate the island's status as a modern nation.[25]

Cuba was not alone in its anxiety to create a legitimating national narrative. Even if Cuban Independence had arrived over half a century later than that of most of Spain's former colonies in the region, the early twentieth century saw writers in many other Latin American countries also struggling with the question of national culture, a question they sought to resolve by trying to identify what was distinctive about both popular culture and artistic production. Following European Romantic models, evidencing the natural existence of a given nation necessitated the recovery of ostensibly national (and/or regional) traditions and practices, that is, elements of popular culture that could be showcased in the creation of modern "civilized" artistic productions, especially literary narratives.[26]

This search for "national culture" was a search for what Martinican writer Édouard Glissant refers to as "filiation": a (real or mythic) linear history anchored in a "root," a physical territory and/or a moment of origin (*Poetics* 47). As Glissant observes, filiation speaks only to the history of one particular group; myths of filiation fail to include "the other as an element of relation" (50). The search for filiation is thus inherently problematic for young, postcolonial nations whose histories are based on the uprooting and encounter of multiple peoples.[27] Glissant's solution for this is "relation," which emphasizes the processes of these encounters and which produces literature "as an effort or passion of memory" (68). Yet writers in Latin America and the Hispanic Caribbean felt the pressure to measure up to European models. As a result, they employed various strategies as a way to create—artificially, if necessary—a kind of filiation, or at least an idea of the locally "authentic."

Writers in countries such as Mexico, Peru, and Bolivia, all of whom had large indigenous populations, chose to look to these ethnic groups as the source for an idea of "authentic" culture. In these countries, *indigenista* (indigenist) discourses were able to make use of their Indian populations symbolically, without representing or giving voice to indigenous individuals.[28] The Indian past was put forth as part of the nation's original cultural essence, even while contemporary Indians themselves were viewed as primitive and socially and politically marginalized. As Estelle Tarica puts it, "Indians were denied coevalness in order that the nation might be brought into being as itself a relation of coevalness among individuals" (5). The appropriation of indigenous peoples as national folk also temporally identified them as "the past," a strategy that allowed intellectuals to make symbolic use of indigenous culture—to carry the nation forward into the future—while marginalizing indigenous people and preventing them from participating in the nation as political actors.[29]

When it came to fashioning elements of a national folk culture, Cuba's circumstances were different from those of countries such as Mexico, Peru, or Bolivia. Like its fellow Caribbean islands, Cuba had no significant indigenous population from which it could borrow, as most of the existing *Taíno* (Arawak) population had been nearly obliterated in the early years of the Spanish conquest.[30] Afro-Cuban culture was the only thing that might occupy the place of a "folk" in the Cuban context, yet as González y Contreras's observations on black Cuban poetry indicate, Afro-Cuban culture could not be made to represent a deep mythical past, as it always pointed to a colonial and neocolonial present.[31] Since Africans had arrived in Cuba via the slave trade, a reference to blackness was inextricably linked to a recent—linear—understanding of history, and more specifically to colonialism and to race-based slavery. Additionally, as Sidney Mintz, Michel-Rolph Trouillot, and Stefan Palmié have observed, Afro-Caribbean cultures were in fact the result of modern systems, the encounter between African cultural traditions and the "highly rationalized agroindustrial order" of the plantation system.[32] By the time of Cuba's independence, Afro-Cubans were not a geographically isolated group but a well-integrated part of both Cuba's urban and rural populations. While Cubans could (and did) declare many African-derived cultural practices to be "primitive," the fact that black Cubans were not confined primarily to rural spaces made a denial of coevalness difficult.

The challenges of this situation help to explain why Cuban writers came to employ both emergent ethnographic and literary textual strategies in their revalorization of Afro-Cuban culture as the source for an idea of Cubanness. Africanness had been the basis for organizing and legitimizing slavery; to have it now form the basis for generating an idea of nation required a discursive sleight of hand to navigate between the country's historical circumstances—the actual black bodies inhabiting the island's diverse spaces—and an idealized version of the imagined community these writers were trying to envision, one in which Afro-Cuban practices were summoned to stand in for the nationally authentic. Both ethnography and literature offered specific possibilities for negotiating these constructions. Nonetheless, the history of these discourses, and their relationship to race in an international context, also presented particular challenges.

Developing Ethnography

When González y Contreras, the critic from the 1930s with whom I began this discussion, speaks of Cuban writers as "artist-ethnographers," it is important to understand that his conception of ethnography was very different from a twenty-first-century definition of the term. As the close study of human societies through their rituals, practices, and belief systems, ethnography was a methodology that in its origins was linked to colonialism and imperialist expansion, to the desire of Europeans (and the colonial bureaucracies that often employed them) to understand the cultures that they had "conquered" and that they deemed "primitive." Trouillot argues that the Renaissance creation of "the West" as an idea required the simultaneous creation of the West's other, what he refers to as "the Savage slot." According to Trouillot, the fact that anthropology arose specifically "as a separate discipline specializing in the occupants of the Savage slot" not only implicates it in the creation of this concept of otherness, but also makes it "part of the very geography of the imagination that it seeks to understand" (*Global Transformations* 2). In this way, according to Michel de Certeau, ethnography functions as a kind of "exegesis" through which the "modern West" seeks to understand the relationship between self and other.[33] A desire to understand (and categorize) the occupants of the Savage slot had sparked anthropological endeavors in the nineteenth century, and it continued to do so well into the first decades of the twentieth, often with the expression of an additional nostalgic opinion that "backwards" cultural practices should be documented before they were destroyed, obliterated, or simply phased out as "primitive" peoples were educated in the Western concept of progress and brought into the modern era. As Johannes Fabian has shown, a "denial of coevalness"—"a persistent and systematic tendency to place the referent(s) of anthropology in a Time other than the present of the producer of anthropological discourse"— was one way in which ethnography enforced a definition of the primitive (understood as "non-modern"), thus establishing a distance between the ethnographer and his subject (31).

When it first emerged as a subfield of anthropology in the late nineteenth century, ethnography distinguished itself from other branches of social science through its identification with the methodological practice of fieldwork. Thanks to the work of pioneering cultural anthropologists such as Franz Boas and Bronislaw Malinowski, ethnographic fieldwork was anchored in the idea of extensive observation of the culture or community of study in situ. As James Clifford has shown, the idea of fieldwork itself became an increasingly professionalized one, anchored in academic discipline.[34] Renato Rosaldo half-jokingly refers to the image of the professional in the first half of the twentieth century as that of "the Lone Ethnographer" (31), the dedicated scientist who gained an insight into another culture thanks to his time spent observing it.

As Rosaldo notes, ethnographic texts produced in the first decades of the twentieth century themselves appeared to be "a transparent medium" (31). It was not until the 1980s that ethnographers came to develop an awareness of both the literary nature of the ethnographic text and the ways in which ethnographers themselves are implicated in systems of exchange.[35] Ethnographies produced since then have articulated, and often explored, the ways in which these texts themselves are, in the words of Clifford, "multivocal exchanges occurring in politically charged situations," communications embedded in a situation with frequently unequal power dynamics (*Predicament of Culture* 10).

Pratt identifies the "politically charged" space of ethnographic encounter as a "contact zone," which she defines (in a much-cited passage) as "[a] social [space] where disparate cultures meet, clash, and grapple with each other, often in highly asymmetrical relations of domination and subordination" (*Imperial Eyes* 4). The contact zone refers most directly to the experience of colonialism, but it also describes the negotiations that take place in an encounter between an ethnographer and his or her subjects and informants. Contact zones are also not limited to the experience of colonialism; in Cuba, social asymmetries and cultural clashes remained equally (if not more) intense in the contact zone of post-emancipation, neocolonial society, in which class, race, and gender continued to operate in concert to produce unequal relationships.

While Cuban writers exploring Afro-Cuban culture in the 1930s and 1940s cannot be said to be "self-conscious" in the sense that later generations of ethnographers would be concerned with the literary specificity of the ethnographic genre, as Cubans and as scholars they were keenly aware—some to a greater extent than others—of the close position in which they found themselves situated with regard to Afro-Cuban culture. Their position shares something with the concept of autoethnography, which Pratt defines as "a text in which people undertake to describe themselves in ways that engage with representations others have made of them" ("Arts" 35). Yet here I suggest that autoethnography needs to take into account the predicament of postcolonial nations, in which multiple fields of power operate simultaneously. On the one hand, social class and race separated writers such as Cabrera and Carpentier from their subjects; on the other hand, their writing seeks to represent aspects of Cuban culture for a public that was implicitly international (not to say imperial), and their texts seek to find local uses for (and local responses to) dominant metropolitan paradigms.[36]

The presence of ethnography in Cuba and its adoption by Cuban intellectuals must be understood in the context of the country's postcolonial situation and the presence and influence of a number of different social-science methodologies. Cuban interest in the emerging discipline of anthropology had begun while the island was still a colony; the Cuban Anthropological Society had actually been founded in 1877 (Bronfman, *Measures of Equality* 28). Yet it was during the U.S. occupation (1899–1902) that the University of Havana consolidated the Department of Anthropology and Anthropometric Exercises. At that time, the preferred anthropological methodologies were not participant-centered ethnography, but eugenics and criminology. Influenced by the evolutionary theories of Darwin and Lamarck, eugenicists argued that human identity was profoundly shaped by biology and heredity, and that inherited traits had as much or more of an effect on society than learned behaviors. Similarly, criminology, as advanced by Italian scientist Césare Lombroso, argued that criminal tendencies were hereditary and that criminality was most pronounced in "inferior peoples," races that had not yet fully left behind a primitive evolutionary state (Bronfman, *Measures of Equality* 31). Proponents of eugenics and criminology concluded that social and racial hierarchies were biologically determined, that some individuals (and races) were biologically superior, and that the best way to "improve" society was through selective breeding. These theories of biological racial hierarchies went hand in hand with colonialism, since those peoples recognized as "racially inferior" were—almost without exception—nonwhite colonial subjects.

As Nancy Leys Stepan has shown, the eugenicist belief in the biological superiority of the white race had a significant impact on nations throughout Latin America, where the racial make-up of the population was cause for anxiety among national elites.[37] For Latin American scientists and politicians who believed in them, these racial theories were more than intellectual abstractions; they called for shifting the terms of eugenics—or altering the racial make-up of their populations—in order to forge modern states capable of progress. In Cuba, Luis Montané, founder of the Cuban Anthropological Society and later director of the Museum of Anthropology, and Arístides Mestre, head of the Department of Anthropology at the University of Havana and later also the director of its Museum, were supporters of Darwinian/Lamarckian ideas of biological, and particularly racial, determinism (Bronfman, *Measures of Equality* 28–29). Eugenics was more formally advanced by Eusebio Hernández and Domingo F. Ramos, who proposed the concept of "homiculture," the idea that society as a whole could be improved by cultivating the health of the individual.[38] Given the popularity of these ideas in the first decades of the

Cuban Republic, writers who chose to reject eugenics and criminology in favor of the fieldwork techniques of cultural anthropology as a means of understanding Afro-Cuban cultural practices can in many ways be seen as taking a radical stand for the time.

Race and the Metropole

Even as the ideas of biological racial superiority put forth by eugenics and criminology were enjoying popularity among some Latin American social scientists, they were in direct contrast to the prevailing fascination with culture as a construct and with ideas of the primitive in vogue among literary and artistic avant-gardes in the early twentieth century.[39] The 1920s, notes historian George Stocking, was a moment when "many intellectuals had begun to question these [cultural] values and the idea of civilization in which they were embodied" ("Ethnographic Sensibility" 214). Apart from their desire to create a radical—and radically new—aesthetic, avant-garde artists and writers were drawn to African culture precisely because it had come to stand for the primitive Other; more than "non-modern," primitiveness in this context thus assumed an aesthetic as well as a cultural otherness. In France, Guillaume Apollinaire and Paul Guillaume cultivated an interest in African art that was taken up by members of the Dada and Surrealist movements. Visual artists such as Pablo Picasso and Constantin Brancusi began to utilize elements of African design in their painting and sculpture. As art historian Petrine Archer Straw observes, in signifying difference from a European aesthetic and social status quo, black imagery "became an artistic device for distinguishing avant-garde art, and a conceptual tool for signifying anarchy and transgression" (51). Embracing the primitive, in an artistic sense, was viewed as a way to simultaneously reject current social norms (and the trajectory of Western civilization) and to return to something that could be identified as a kind of essentialized, instinctual human nature (Pavloska).

As Trouillot and others have shown, ethnography as a discourse had emerged to identify the West's others and to solidify their position of otherness. This relationship was easily adapted by European avant-garde writers, who were attracted to blackness precisely because it articulated an idea of exotic difference. For European avant-gardes, this was a time when the arts and this budding branch of anthropology were mutually influential in their deployment of a public desire for the primitive. As a still-developing genre, ethnography was easily adapted for use by the Surrealists and others. *Documents,* a Surrealist journal, published accounts by ethnographers such as Marcel Mauss and Michel Leiris together with African and African-influenced photographs and drawings by artists such as Alberto Giacometti. Clifford argues that *Documents* reveals "how ethnographic evidence and an ethnographic attitude could function in the service of a subversive criticism" (*Predicament of Culture* 129). Just as ethnographic texts helped inform the production of the metropolitan conception of the primitive (and the primitive African in particular), the vogue of "things African" and a reconceptualized African aesthetic helped shape the ethnographic gaze and the kinds of ethnographic texts that were produced.

The European fascination with blackness could be problematic for Caribbean writers, but it also created a productive space for them. Europe, and Paris in particular, provided a key place for transnational and cross-cultural encounters for artists and writers from across Africa, Latin America, and the Caribbean. The dialogue between black intellectuals around representations of blackness contributed to what Brent Hayes Edwards calls a "black internationalism," and produced texts such as Aimé Césaire's *Cahier d'un retour au pays natal* (*Notebook of a Return to the Native Land,* 1939), which introduced the idea of Négritude, a radical black subjectivity grounded in an anticolonial spirit. These exchanges shifted the meaning of blackness within a transnational context, even as Cuban writers were working to locate it within the space of the nation.

Cuban writers' treatments of blackness were certainly shaped by these international interventions in racial discourse and black subjectivity. Yet both the avant-garde use of blackness and the perspective of ethnography, in which white ethnographers studied colonized and/or non-Western subjects, presented certain challenges in a Cuban context. While they might be separated from (what they identified as) Afro-Cuban culture—and from black Cubans themselves—by divisions of race or class, Cuban writers who chose to explore Afro-Cuban culture in their texts were nonetheless writing about national subjects with whom they shared public and private space. Both the areas of daily living and the narrative space of the nation were contact zones, in which these writers had to navigate positions of distance from and also situations of intimacy with their subjects. As they explored a new literary idea of the nation, these writers had to find a way to incorporate Afro-Cuban culture into a narrative of Cubanness that would define these elements of popular culture as uniquely Cuban without constituting Cubanness *itself* as black or primitive, without fully relegating Afro-Cubans to the position of the Savage slot. They had to produce "a folklore for the present," as González y Contreras puts it, without the advantage of a temporal separation; and their experimental and hybrid texts—and the sometimes contradictory representations of blackness that emerge from these experimentations—reveal the ways in which the use of both the ethnographic and the literary was necessary for their purposes.

Hybridities

Fredric Jameson, in *The Political Unconscious*, argues that there have generally been two ways in which literary criticism has approached the study of genre: the "semantic" approach, which attempts to capture a genre's "existential experience" or "spirit," and the "syntactic" approach, which looks to understand and define a genre through an analysis of its "mechanisms and structure" (108). Previous studies of the relationship between anthropology and Latin American literature have focused—from a largely "syntactic" perspective—on the ways in which anthropology (approached broadly) has served as a metanarrative or framing technique for the modern Latin American novel.[40] I contend, however, that the use of these two discursive practices (in a Cuban context) was not limited to novelistic borrowings of ethnographic description. This study walks the difficult line of trying to approach this corpus of Cuban writing from both a semantic and a syntactic perspective. On the one hand, I am interested in diagnosing what one might call an "ethnographic spirit" in writing from this period—a moment that, thanks to ethnography's own development, was necessarily experimental. On the other hand, I seek to understand the experimental sensibility of this moment through an analysis of the structural mechanics of the texts in question: the use (or absence) of symbolism, the role of wordplay, the authority of the narrative voice. I am not interested, however, in identifying which elements are "ethnographic" and which are "literary." Given both the moment in which they were writing and the postcolonial contact zones they inhabited, the writers I analyze in this study approached ethnography from a perspective that was both more "limited" (i.e., less self-reflexive) and more flexible, since as María Eugenia Cotera notes, ethnography in this period was still developing as both a practice and a discourse (27). The term I arrive at for these varied Cuban texts that explore blackness and its connection to nation is "ethnographic literature," a label that hints at the multiple directions from which discursive cross-fertilization can (and did) occur.

While understanding these texts as hybrid in both "spirit" and "letter," I am interested in the ways in which they position themselves, the other texts—and scholarly figures—that their authors reference, and the discourses with which they identify. I thus pay special attention in this study to the prefaces and forewords that accompany the texts I analyze. Edwards observes that a preface "speaks double": "[I]t is outside, it marks what is not within the book, it precedes the book's 'speaking,' but it is also the very force that animates the book, that opens it for us and shows its contents" (45). Prefaces tell us how to read, not just in terms of describing what will be said, but also by indicating how to organize or categorize what is said. In the case of the experimental texts I analyze, prefaces can be used to define that particular text with regard to a discursive tradition, or to legitimate or professionalize the work of a particular scholar. In these cases, the preface becomes another technique with which to identify (potentially peripheral) Cuban texts as central to a broader, Western intellectual tradition. I read the prevalence of forewords and prefaces in these examples of ethnographic literature as a reaction to the experimental nature of the texts themselves. They betray the contradictory impulses at the heart of these works both to position race (and discourse) in a fixed way and to reach a place that escapes that kind of fixedness.

While this study explores the hybrid strategies of the texts themselves, racial discourse in twentieth-century Cuban literature is also dominated by discourses of hybridity.[41] Literary critics frequently identify discourses of *mestizaje* (racial mixing) as the dominant paradigm for understanding Cuba's racial make up (Duno Gottberg, Kutzinski, Miller, Morejón). Luis Duno Gottberg refers to this process as "solventando las diferencias" (resolving differences); the construction of a mixed-race Cuban identity responds to racial tension by symbolically uniting black and white populations. Vera Kutzinski asserts that since the 1890s, "*mestizaje* has been perhaps the principal signifier of Cuba's cultural identity" (*Sugar's Secrets* 5). Certainly, discourses of *mestizaje* were (and are) an important method of creating a symbolically unified "Cuban people."

Of the writers I focus on in this study, Ortiz and Guillén in particular made notable contributions to a uniquely Cuban language of hybridity.

Guillén speaks in a visionary, utopian tone in the introduction to his collection *Sóngoro cosongo* (1931) of a day when there would be no divisions between black or white Cubans, only what he calls "color cubano" (Cuban color) (*Obra poética* 85). Ortiz, on the other hand, is best known for coining the term "transculturation," a concept of cultural hybridity that describes encounters between cultural groups as a process of give and take (even between groups where there is an unequal balance of power). Transculturation—understood both as cultural mixing and as the ongoing process of the same—has now come to be recognized as a defining process for the Caribbean region as a whole. Edward Kamau Brathwaite's idea of "creolization" and Patrick Chamoiseau, Raphaël Confiant, and Jean Bernabé's concept of *créolité* both borrow from transculturation in viewing Caribbean culture as a process of struggle and negotiation between different racial and cultural groups.[42]

Guillén's and Ortiz's ideas of hybridity, although significant for the ways in which they envisioned an ultimate solution to Cuba's racial contact zone, leave important elements unresolved. While I shall delve more fully into these concepts in subsequent chapters, it is important to point out here that both the idea of a racially mixed "color cubano" and a culturally mixed "transculturated Cuba" gesture toward a fully realized national *future*. What happens in the space of the present (and thereby, by implication, what has occurred in the space of the past) has less to do with hybrid products—racial or cultural—and more to do with the elements (and events) that make up this process. This symbolic ideology of racial mixing elides the actual social and historical conditions that bring about racial miscegenation and the real range of racial distinctions displayed in everyday life. Afro-Cuban cultural attributes become useful only for the purpose of constructing a racially hybrid Cuban subject. Hybridity risks gesturing towards a black presence (and again, we might think of Arozarena's "absent presence") while hiding black subjects. While it is important not to ignore these discourses on hybridity, I contend that they are a way to make palatable a reality—a black population in Cuba, and a history of slavery—that, as Trouillot has shown, has been characterized as "unthinkable" (*Silencing* 70–107). This intention makes discourses of racial and cultural mixing not merely aesthetic choices but also political ones. In this study I am thus interested in how these visions of a utopian *mestizaje* coexist with (and sometimes contain) other representations of Afro-Cuban culture. The treatment of Cuban blackness by these writers—even when blackness is deployed to construct narratives of hybridity—reveals how narratives of a once-and-future hybridity do not fully erase the (racial) anxieties of a colonial past. In fact, I argue that the manipulation of temporally structured narratives—the insistence on a transcendent future—becomes one of the ways in which these writers attempt to ameliorate the racial anxiety produced by attempts to represent blackness.

Although Ortiz, Carpentier, and Guillén have been consistently recognized in Cuban criticism for their contribution to a dialogue on race in Cuba, no writer better exemplifies the use of discursive experimentation in the treatment of race than Lydia Cabrera. Born into one of Havana's elite literary families—her father was the poet and newspaper editor Raimundo Cabrera—Cabrera has always been a difficult writer to categorize. Like Carpentier, she spent time in France and Spain in the late 1920s and 1930s and was exposed to European and Latin American avant-garde artists in Paris. Yet her large body of work, which includes texts characterized as "ethnographies" along with those identified as literary fiction, focuses almost exclusively on Afro-Cuban culture. Recent criticism has tended to view her as an exceptional figure, both in her mixing of genres and literary styles and in her treatment of race.[43] Critics such as Edna Rodríguez-Mangual and Flora González Mandri characterize her as someone whose work contests the hegemonic cultural narratives—and the dominant methodologies—of the time.[44] This study, however, contends that the presentation of blackness in her work is not radical or exceptional but central to the understanding of the relationship between race and nation during this period in Cuba's history. Rather than struggling to categorize her as "an ethnographer who also wrote fiction" or "a short-story writer who also published ethnographies," we need to view her diverse corpus as emblematic of the experimentation with genre in which she and her contemporaries were engaged. At the same time, as a woman writing in a male-dominated intellectual space—not only anthropology as a profession but the Cuban "republic of letters" as a whole—she shares something with other women writers, such as Zora Neale Hurston, Ruth Landes, and Ella Cara Deloria, who were negotiating issues of gender as well as those of race and class in their writing.[45]

This book is constructed as a series of counterpoints that place Cabrera's work in dialogue with that of four other contemporaries: Fernando Ortiz, Alejo Carpentier, and Nicolás Guillén, and the African American writer Zora Neale Hurston. Using Cabrera's texts as interlocutors serves two purposes. First, it reveals Cabrera's centrality to the use of discursive experimentation to construct race in Cuba. Second, it shows the ways in which these texts complement or dialogue with each other, even when their authors were not writing as part of an explicitly understood movement or even at the same moment. When viewed together rather than individually, texts by Cabrera, Ortiz, Guillén, and Carpentier illuminate the dynamic, sometimes contradictory—rather than static or unified—dialogue around race in republican Cuba. I show how their constructions of blackness posit the usefulness of discursive exploration as a way of resolving, or attempting to resolve, the challenges inherent in crafting national narratives in which Afro-Cuban culture becomes the basis for the cultural heritage of the Cuban people as a whole. Seen in this light, their textual strategies can be understood as political stances as much as aesthetic ones. A comparison of the work of these Cuban writers with that of Hurston reveals the uniqueness of this Cuban dialogue in a transnational context, despite a shared interest in using black culture to construct an idea of the "folk."

The first chapter of this study explores the ways in which narrative structure itself shapes and is shaped by the presentation of race—specifically, how Cuban writers use ideas of time (historical and textual) and space (physical and textual) to present blackness. I turn to a text traditionally recognized as one of Cuba's first ethnographies, Fernando Ortiz's *Hampa afrocubana: Los negros brujos* (*Afro-Cuban Underworld: Black Witches*, 1906), to show how Ortiz constructs this text—and with it his idea of a national project—via a temporal framework that privileges positivist ideas of evolution. Ortiz's desire to create a coherent national narrative creates a constant tension in his work between defining Afro-Cuban culture and subsuming the question of blackness into a narrative of hybridity. I argue that the tension visible in this early text extends into his later work, including his better-known *Contrapunteo cubano del tabaco y el azúcar* (*Cuban Counterpoint: Tobacco and Sugar*, 1940). That Ortiz's early work should stand in stark contrast with Lydia Cabrera's later monograph *El monte* (*The Bush*, 1954)—curiously the only other significant ethnography on Afro-Cuban religious traditions—is understandable. Yet I show how Cabrera's use of a spatial, rather than temporal, framework of analysis allows her, unlike Ortiz, to posit a national space in which different races and cultural narratives coexist.

While Ortiz and Cabrera utilize the narrative structure of their texts as a way to negotiate the presentation of actual Afro-Cuban religious practices, my second chapter explores the encounter between an ethnographic perspective and avant-garde aesthetics through a reading of the symbolic function of blackness in the work of novelist Alejo Carpentier and Lydia Cabrera's short fiction. Caught between the desire to portray (and define) an essential Cubanness while still proving himself to be aesthetically avant-garde, Carpentier's solution is the creation of what he himself identifies as a "hybrid" product: a text set in Cuba, dealing with a particularly Cuban subject matter, yet stylistically indebted to European Surrealism. Carpentier's first novel *Écue-Yamba-Ó* (1933) uses an ethnographic perspective to characterize Cuba as "primitive" in an avant-garde sense; that is, blackness stands in as symbolic of both exotic otherness and a rejection of western social norms, even as it is also portrayed as an authentically Cuban element that counters foreign threats to the national space. I argue that a similar (racialized) national anxiety is present but displaced in his later novel *El reino de este mundo* (*The Kingdom of This World*, 1949). In contrast, Cabrera's first volumes of short stories, *Cuentos negros de Cuba* (*Afro-Cuban Tales*, 1936) and *Por qué . . . cuentos negros de Cuba* (*Why . . . Afro-Cuban Tales*, 1948) creates a textual world in which race does not function allegorically by practicing a strategy of containment, turning the reader into a participant-observer of an environment in which blackness is not exceptional. While Cabrera locates blackness in the realm of the "folk," her emphasis on class structures—and other kinds of social boundaries—ensure that this racialized strata of the popular is never confused with Cuban society as a whole.

Having analyzed the symbolic function of blackness in texts by Carpentier and Cabrera, in chapter 3 I examine the ways in which race is explored rhetorically and structurally in the short stories of Lydia Cabrera and the Afro-Antillean poems of Nicolás Guillén. Building on Henry Louis Gates Jr.'s concept of Signifyin(g), referring both to African-derived wordplay and to strategies of literary intertextuality, I show how Cabrera and Guillén improvise on Afro-Cuban culture at a structural level, playing with genres such as the *son* and the folktale, to make Signifyin(g) function not just as a racial strategy, but also as a national one. For both Cabrera and Guillén, play—understood as linguistic and rhetorical devices, and as narrative strategies of inclusion—serves as a way of mediating race in their texts in the name of cultural authenticity. As texts that mix Afro-Caribbean-influenced language structures with elements of avant-garde writing, Guillén's *Motivos de son* (*Son Motifs*, 1930), *Sóngoro cosongo* (1931), and *West Indies, Ltd.* (1935), and Cabrera's *Cuentos negros de Cuba* utilize a hybridization of high-culture literary style with popular linguistic styles to augment existing elements of wordplay, improvisation, and humor already available in language production in the Caribbean in order to foreground Afro-Cuban expression within Cuban cultural production as a whole. While Guillén's poetry uses Signifyin(g) to critique racist stereotypes and postcolonial structures of economic and social domination, Cabrera's stories subvert, contest, and play with contemporary assumptions of literary and cultural authority, disrupting the cultural norms inherent in traditional reading practices.

This study centers on how race is written into the space of nation in the Cuban context; yet the issues that these Cuban writers were addressing are also meaningful within other transnational and/or neocolonial contexts elsewhere in the Americas. My fourth chapter thus returns to the question of ethnographic authority to look at the ways in which the positioning of the figure of the ethnographer within the text becomes a strategic tool for negotiating the power differentials involved in talking about race. It interrogates the nature of ethnographic authority in Cabrera's *El Monte* (1954) and African American writer Zora Neale Hurston's *Mules and Men* (1935), showing the ways in which these two writers modify the construction of the ethnographic narrative voice to navigate racial and gender differences and to interweave ethnographic, autobiographical, and fictional narratives. By comparing how Cabrera and Hurston position themselves within the text, I emphasize the importance of gender in Cuban writing and the uniqueness of the Cuban situation with regard to race, even in the context of a broader, transnational experimentation with genre conventions. Even as Hurston and Cabrera comply with the genre's professional imperatives, they use an awareness of both the freedoms and limitations of their position as women (both in the profession and in their communities of study) to make their work open to more subversive readings. Their experiments with the formal elements of ethnography, I argue, allow them to highlight the limits of ethnography as a discourse for negotiating otherness within the space of the nation.

The fertile textual dialogue around the relationship of race and nation in Cuban writing prior to 1959 resulted in a range of experimental textual strategies made visible in a broad corpus of texts. With the triumph of the Cuban Revolution in 1959, the island—and its writers—entered a new moment of national redefinition. In the wake of the Revolution, both the encounter between the ethnographic and the literary and the discourse surrounding blackness in Cuba underwent significant shifts, in keeping with the other radical changes underway in Cuba's social and economic realms. In the Epilogue, I trace the ongoing life of the kinds of multiple textual strategies I explore here and the heated valence of race in Cuban and Cuban diasporic politics since the Revolution. The leaders of the Revolution declared racism to be a thing of the past; the new revolutionary society was making social equality a reality, and to talk about racial difference was to focus unnecessarily on divisions of the past. As this revolutionary rhetoric closed the space for discussing race, the space for discursive encounter also changed. Among writers on the island, encounters between ethnography and literature, while still innovative, moved in ways that bolstered the larger narrative of the Cuban Revolution. In an effort to contest the Revolution's cooptation of earlier texts, Cabrera, in exile in Miami, returned to a more conservative—and more nostalgic—form of ethnographic narration. What in the course of this book's analysis I come to call ethnographic literature may have taken multiple forms as Cuban intellectuals struggled with the politics of nation formation in a neocolonial, racialized world, yet these textual experimentations continue to impact narratives of race and nation in Cuba today.

1
LOCATING AFRO-CUBAN RELIGION
Fernando Ortiz and Lydia Cabrera

When thinking of how Cubanness came to be defined, perhaps no voice is as consistently (and insistently) present as that of Fernando Ortiz. Ortiz was a public intellectual in the full sense of the term. Born into a well-to-do Creole family in Havana, he was raised in Cuba and Spain, completing his education, including a PhD in law, in Madrid.[1] Upon his return to Cuba in 1902, he both studied and wrote broadly—on politics, literature, music, folklore, and anthropology—and taught sociology and anthropology courses at the University of Havana. He was a founding member of the journals *Surco (Track)*, *Ultra*, *Estudios Afrocubanos (Afro-Cuban Studies)*, and *Archivos del Folklore Cubano (Archives of Cuban Folklore)*, and the author of numerous scholarly articles and close to two dozen books (Pamies, xiv). His lengthy and productive career began with the twentieth century and lasted into the first decades after the Revolution of 1959. Throughout Ortiz's wide-ranging scholarly investigations, his primary interest was (and remained) the formation of Cuban culture and Cuban identity. Gustavo Pérez Firmat notes that Ortiz's life and work "are synonymous with Cuba" (17). Ortiz's daughter, María Fernanda Ortiz Herrera, remembers him as saying he "fought for... '*cubanidad*' [Cubanness]" (Ortiz Herrera 7). He aimed through his scholarly and intellectual work to improve the understanding of Cuban culture and promote its celebration.

Given Ortiz's passionate interest in (and, some might say, obsession with) Cubanness, it should come as no surprise that he has come to be considered the founding father of Cuban ethnography. Ortiz was also one of the first Cuban scholars to undertake a study of Afro-Cuban culture, and to explore the question of how to incorporate blackness within the space of the nation. His interest in Cubans of African heritage and his progressive attempts to identify and understand various aspects of what he came to identify broadly as Afro-Cuban culture profoundly affected Cuban ideas about race and the way Cubans came to define their society as a whole. In addition to founding the journals *Archivos del Folklore Cubano* (*Archives of Cuban Folklore*, 1924–1930), and *Estudios Afrocubanos* (*Afro-Cuban Studies*, 1939–1945), the first—and only—journal to focus exclusively on the study of Afro-Cuban culture, Ortiz was the author of one of the earliest ethnographies of Afro-Cuban religion, *Hampa afrocubana: Los negros brujos* (*Afro-Cuban Underworld: Black Witches*, 1906). He continued to write about Afro-Cuban history and culture in subsequent books such as *Los negros esclavos* (*Black Slaves*, 1916), *Glosario de afronegrismos* (*Glossary of Black-African Vocabulary*, 1924), *La africanía de la música folklórica de Cuba* (*The Africanness of Cuban Folkloric Music*, 1950), and *Los instrumentos de la música afrocubana* (*Instruments of Afro-Cuban Music*, 1952–1955), while studies such as *El engaño de las razas* (*The Lie of Races*, 1946) analyze the concept of race (and the origins of racism) more generally. His best-known work, *Contrapunteo cubano del tabaco y el azúcar* (*Cuban Counterpoint: Tobacco and Sugar*, 1940), is an exploration of the role of tobacco and sugar in shaping Cuban history and society that also highlights the relationship of race to these commodities. Despite the apparent focus on Afro-Cuban culture undergirding many of his publications, an interrogation of the construction of national culture lies at the heart of this corpus, as it does the rest of Ortiz's work. Even as he investigates Afro-Cuban culture, he is most centrally concerned with what composite of factors makes a culture—and Cuba's in particular—unique, and thus the basis for nation.

Lydia Cabrera, coincidentally Ortiz's sister-in-law, has often been seen as the inheritor of Ortiz's work on Afro-Cuban culture.[2] Born into a well-to-do literary Havana family (her father, Raimundo Cabrera, edited the journal *Cuba y América*), Cabrera found her way to Paris in 1927, where she became involved with the Venezuelan writer Teresa de la Parra. In later interviews, Cabrera declared that she began to write stories based on Afro-Cuban tales to entertain de la Parra, who was ill with tuberculosis. Yet Cabrera's interest in Afro-Cuban culture did not end with these literary interventions. Shortly after publishing one of the first collections of Afro-Cuban short stories, *Cuentos negros de Cuba* (*Afro-Cuban Tales*, 1936) in France, she began a serious—and lifelong—study of Afro-Cuban religious practice. Although she had not been formally educated in the social sciences, Cabrera spent nearly two decades doing ethnographic research among Afro-Cuban communities in the Havana area, and in 1954 published one of the most significant and comprehensive monographs on Afro-Cuban religion, El Monte: Igbo Finda, Ewe Orisha, Vititi Nfinda (*Notas sobre las religiones, la magia, las supersticiones y el folklore de los negros criollos y el pueblo de Cuba*) (*The Bush: Notes on the Religions, Magic, Superstitions and Folklore of Black Creoles and the People of Cuba*, hereafter El Monte), in addition to a number of other important studies of Afro-Cuban religion, most notably *La sociedad secreta abakuá narrada por viejos adeptos* (*The Abakuá Secret Society Narrated By Old Experts*, 1959).

This chapter traces the representation of Afro-Cuban culture in two ostensibly ethnographic texts—Ortiz's Hampa afrocubana: Los negros brujos (hereafter Los negros brujos), and Cabrera's El Monte, while considering them in the context of other texts by these writers. Ortiz's and Cabrera's work can be seen as book-ending the study of Afro-Cuban culture in Cuba during the Republic; the nearly fifty years separating El Monte from Los negros brujos include some of the most significant changes in racial discourse for Cuba as an independent nation, and also some of the greatest moments of textual experimentation, as writers struggled with how to define Afro-Cuban culture and how to incorporate images of blackness into Cuban artistic and literary production. Yet Ortiz's and Cabrera's work seems to be further connected when one considers that between the appearance of Ortiz's first Afro-Cuban texts and the publication of El Monte, few other studies of Afro-Cuban religious tradition were produced.[3] Ortiz and Cabrera were interested not only in explicating Afro-Cuban religion, but also in positioning it as constitutive of Cuban culture as a whole.

As they undertook to explain Afro-Cuban religious practices to a reading public that viewed them as stigmatized and/or other with respect to the nation, Ortiz and Cabrera were faced with the challenge of using a discipline that inherently positions its subjects of study as other—locating them within what Michel-Rolph Trouillot terms the "Savage slot"—to describe the practices of fellow Cuban citizens (*Global Transformations* 9). Unlike poets such as Emilio Ballagas and Ramón Guirao, who were free to create stylized images of black Cubans in the *negrista* poetry they began to publish in the late 1920s, in producing texts drawn from fieldwork with living subjects, Ortiz and Cabrera had the challenge of navigating the distance between living Afro-Cuban subjects (and their cultural practices) and the representational space of the printed page. Both authors construct polyphonic narratives that incorporate a variety of material—informant testimony, ethnographic description, and the reproduction of newspaper articles, letters, and other texts—to present an understanding of Afro-Cuban culture as fundamental to an understanding of Cuban culture more broadly.

While little evidence exists of explicit collaboration between the two scholars, there is no doubt that Ortiz to some extent facilitated Cabrera's entrance into the field, accompanying her to rituals, writing the preface for her first book of short stories, and ensuring that her work was published and reviewed in scholarly journals such as *Estudios Afrocubanos*.[4] As a result, readers of Ortiz and Cabrera over the past decades have tended either to consider Cabrera a protégée of Ortiz, or to see her as writing against the work of the senior scholar. Taking the latter position, Edna Rodríguez-Mangual views the writers' perspectives and methodologies as diametrically opposed. She argues that Ortiz confines Afro-Cuban culture to the realm of the mysterious, in contrast to Cabrera, who "dismantles the hegemonic discourse of Cuban culture" in order to "[create] the fiction of a space of resistance for the marginal subject" (64). According to Rodríguez-Mangual, Ortiz's distanced approach to Afro-Cuban religion in *Los negros brujos* identifies and isolates Afro-Cubans as a negative other, ultimately at the expense of the voice and agency of Afro-Cubans themselves (47). This may, indeed, be a valid assertion in the case of Ortiz, as his texts approach Afro-Cuban culture through methodologies very different from Cabrera's. Yet I argue that Cabrera's text, despite the radical centrality it gives to the voices of ethnographic informants, ultimately reaffirms certain hegemonic discourses, particularly those of class.

Cabrera and Ortiz articulate their different portrayals of Afro-Cuban religious culture in part through the ways that they construct their texts, and the structuring devices themselves provide Ortiz and Cabrera with ways of locating Afro-Cuban practices—and through them, blackness—within the national space. Within these "ethnographic" texts, I argue, Ortiz and Cabrera use time and space as both literary tropes and structuring devices, but to very different effect. Thanks to the influence of positivist thought, Ortiz views Western, modernizing societies as engaged in a process of historical evolution. As a result, his analysis emphasizes historical development and makes use of a temporally structured narrative. At the same time, as Alfredo Cesar B. de Melo has observed, the most prevalent rhetorical strategy that Ortiz makes use of is antithesis (124). His text is organized around ideas of conflict and movement, such that space itself comes to be viewed as a struggle between metropole and periphery (Europe vs. Cuba), between point of origin and place of arrival (Old World vs. New), and between different strata of society (the "underworld" vs. acceptable—"healthy"—social spheres). These structuring dialectics create a tension in *Los negros brujos* that extends into Ortiz's later texts, such as the *Contrapunteo cubano del tabaco y el azúcar* (*Cuban Counterpoint: Tobacco and Sugar*, hereafter *Contrapunteo*), and explain why even when Ortiz's opinion of Afro-Cuban culture shifts from a desire to understand it in order to encourage Afro-Cuban assimilation to a celebration of Afro-Cuban contributions to Cuban culture more broadly, an anxiety over the presence of blackness in Cuba, first visible in this early text, is still apparent.

Beginning her ethnographic investigation several decades after Ortiz, Cabrera structures her study (and her ideas about race) around ideas of space and containment, centering her text both organizationally and thematically on *el Monte* (the Bush), the physical and symbolic center of Afro-Cuban religion. In addition to being the location of many plants and herbs in the Afro-Cuban pharmacopeia, *el Monte* was also traditionally the place in which maroons—escaped slaves—sought refuge. It is thus the location of the material elements of an Afro-Cuban religious practice, and a zone whose isolation from Cuban society (the plantation system) makes it representative of freedom. Cabrera's analysis of *el Monte* as a metaphorical space extends to an exploration of other concrete spaces within the text—both centers of religious practice and the corresponding spatial (and racial) organization of Cuban society. Her mapping of these spaces of Afro-Cuban religion enables her to simultaneously incorporate radical ethnographic methodologies and to uphold conservative ideas of social structure, painting a portrait of Cuban society in which different races and cultural narratives coexist in relations of unequal power. Her texts accord Afro-Cuban culture its own place, but they also trace the limiting social boundaries that serve to contain it.

Introducing Race: *Los negros brujos*

What motivated a young Fernando Ortiz to investigate Afro-Cuban religion? Certainly it was not an intimate familiarity with his subject. Prior to the publication of *Los negros brujos,* Ortiz had spent a significant part of his life (and education) in Europe, particularly in Spain.[5] He showed an early interest in various branches of social science, including folklore and criminology, and his studies prior to 1906, carried out largely in Europe, had focused primarily on the documentation of European folk traditions.[6] *Los negros brujos* is notable not only for being Ortiz's first foray into Afro-Cuban religious practice; it was also one of the first attempts at a comprehensive study of Afro-Cuban religion, and as such a very different approach from prior general studies of black Cubans.

With the exception of nineteenth-century travel narratives and historical descriptions of African slaves in Cuba, prior to Cuban independence there existed little scholarship dealing with Afro-Cuban religious traditions.[7] While Cuba was still a colony, black Cubans, as (former) slaves and "inferior peoples," were doubly marginalized subjects of empire. Once Cuba became an independent nation, this positioning shifted, as the new narratives of identity that were being constructed came into contact (and conflict) with the documentation of actual racialized cultural practices. Cubans had been interested in anthropology since before the country's independence; the Cuban Anthropological Society was founded in 1887, significantly just after the ending of slavery (in 1886). Early interest in Afro-Cuban culture, however, was often driven by ideas of racial superiority, in particular eugenics. In arguing that human identity was profoundly shaped by biology and heredity, eugenics supported the belief that social and racial hierarchies were biologically determined, that some individuals (and races) were biologically superior. Eugenics and criminology were popular among white intellectuals in Cuba, beginning in the nineteenth century and extending into the first decades of the twentieth.[8] However, the relegation of Cubans of African or mixed-race heritage to the category of inferior peoples was problematic for Cuban scholars. White and black Cubans had shared both public and domestic space during the colonial era, often in situations of significant intimacy. Once Cuba achieved independence, Cuban anthropologists found themselves studying people who were now their fellow citizens. In making Afro-Cuban cultural practices the focus of their research, Cuban intellectuals' principal concern was not merely one of understanding but one of interpretation: how should these practices be viewed—and where should they be located—relative to the dominant (European-derived) Cuban society?

Los negros brujos reflects the shift in discussions of race (and social science methodology) that these concerns for national narrative produced.

Edward Mullen refers to the text as a "bridge" between nineteenth-century investigations of race and the renewed interest in Afro-Cuban culture of the 1920s and 1930s (Mullen, "*Los negros brujos*" 114). At the moment in which Ortiz's study appeared, ethnography—as a social science methodology centered on participant observation—was not yet a widespread practice. Those social scientists who were not taking biometrical measurements in accordance with the research practices of eugenics were often "armchair anthropologists," scholars who compared the practices or cultural narratives of various civilizations.[9] Ortiz's text anticipates modernist ethnography in the specificity of its focus and his use—however limited—of informants. Yet unlike many early ethnographic monographs written by European or North American scholars (which tended to focus on distant and "exotic" cultures), Ortiz chose to center his investigation on a culture which, however unfamiliar, was (perhaps uncomfortably) close to home.[10] In the large body of criticism produced on Ortiz, critics have tended to focus on his later work, such as the *Contrapunteo* (1940). Ortiz's early work has been seen as maintaining a starkly different perspective, largely because of his use of a criminological methodology that in the later decades of the twentieth century came to be understood as outmoded and racist (Rodríguez-Mangual 30–32). It is my contention, however, that the narrative of Cuban culture that Ortiz will develop in his later texts is already visible in *Los negros brujos*.[11]

Ortiz's ostensible focus on the *hampa afrocubana* (Afro-Cuban underworld), visible in his title, suggests that he will confine his analysis (and Afro-Cuban culture itself) to this particular space. As in his later texts, however, his concern in this first study is the creation of a narrative that will adequately serve to simultaneously link and yet separate Cuban and Afro-Cuban identity.[12] In investigating, compiling, and interpreting information about Afro-Cuban culture for his educated audience, Ortiz initiates his own kind of myth-making—an attempt to narrate, explain, and understand the elements making up Cubanness, both for the benefit of Cubans themselves and for the world beyond the island. Yet his anxiety over how to conceptualize Cuba as a nation—and the place of race within it—reveals itself in the tensions between temporal and spatial modes of narration that run through *Los negros brujos*. His desire to create a coherent national narrative creates a conflict in his work between subsuming the question of blackness into an idea of racial hybridity and recognizing and understanding the uniqueness of Afro-Cuban culture itself.[13]

The way that Ortiz chooses to introduce his text (and his subject) shows how his anxiety over visibility (both personal and national) produces a rhetorical strategy. On the first page of *Los negros brujos*, Ortiz includes a 1905 letter from Cesare Lombroso in Turin, Italy addressed to Ortiz himself. Lombroso, today known as the father of criminology, was one of the most famous social scientists of his day, at a time when criminology was seen as an important branch of anthropological practice.[14] Lombroso's tone in the letter is respectful and collegial. He writes, "Distinguido abogado: He recibido su manuscrito, lo he leído y lo juzgo de un interés extraordinario, tanto, que debo rogarle se digne cederme para mi revista, el *Archivio de Psichiatría, ecc.*, su estudio acerca del suicidio en los negros, el de la criminalidad afro-cubana y también el del delito de violación de sepulturas" (1). [Distinguished lawyer: I have received your manuscript, have read it, and judge it to be of extraordinary interest, so much so that I beg you to allow me to use your studies on suicide in blacks, Afro-Cuban criminality, and the crime of grave-defiling in my journal *Archives of Psychiatry*.] After offering a few suggestions for future research, Lombroso signs his letter, "your admirer," a closure that suggests that he and Ortiz are colleagues on equal footing, rather than a master social scientist and his admiring disciple.

Ortiz clearly includes Lombroso's letter as a preface to his own study not only because it legitimates his project and his methods, but also because in establishing the existence of a relationship between the older Italian expert and the young Cuban writer, it affirms that Ortiz's work has something in it of value for scholars and scholarship in Europe. Lombroso's letter portrays Ortiz as a scholar already engaged in a conversation with European criminology. As an expert, and a European expert, Lombroso validates Ortiz's scholarly credentials and endorses his investigations. As he affirms the intellectual significance of Ortiz's study, his European gaze identifies Cuban culture, and Afro-Cuban culture in particular, as a subject worthy of investigation by scholars beyond Cuba's borders.

The presence of Lombroso's letter introduces one of the central dialectics at work in Ortiz's text: here versus there; the local (periphery) versus the international (the metropole, conceived of as Europe and North America). *Los negros brujos* was published just five years after the Platt Amendment (barely) released Cuba from being a U.S. protectorate. In these first early years of the Republic, Ortiz was not alone in his desire to make Cuba a nation that could measure up to any nation in Europe.

Other scholars of Ortiz's generation, such as Jorge Mañach and José María Chacón y Calvo, many of them educated in Europe and still looking to Europe for their intellectual models, saw it as vitally important that Cubans themselves should begin to produce scholarly work of interest to Europeans that could contribute to the ongoing intellectual debates on the Continent. In an article written in 1910, Ortiz argues that Cuba's problem is precisely one of production: "No es, pues, la falta de exhibicionismo lo que impide volar a nuestros hombres. Es que, por lo general, no producimos materia exportable a Europa" ("A Unamuno," *Entre cubanos* 12).[15] [Well, it's not a lack of exhibitionism that prevents our men from flying; it's that, in general, we don't produce material worthy of exporting to Europe.] In Ortiz's mind, the production of literature or scientific studies that would be read in Europe is clearly the kind of production that "matters."[16]

Despite their view that Cuba had to be seen as significant by Europeans before it could be deemed of interest, many intellectuals in the island's first years as a republic viewed Cuba as fundamentally unable to compete with European and American intellectual (and artistic) production. Rafael Rojas labels this crisis of inferiority "insularismo negativo" (negative insularity); for writers such as Francisco Figueras, Manuel Márquez Stirling, Jorge Mañach, and even Ortiz himself, Cuba's inferiority was brought on by its weakness as a nation and as a people (Rojas, *Isla* 160). This was, in part, the result of centuries of colonialism, which had engineered both the country and its population to be dependent on Spain. Yet these writers also saw Cubans themselves as morally weak, indolent, and self-indulgent. In his essay *La crisis de la alta cultura en Cuba* (*The Crisis of High Culture in Cuba*, 1925), Jorge Mañach argues that his countryman have not taken their artistic or intellectual development seriously: "Se han ido cultivando superficialmente las inteligencias; pero no se ha organizado la cultura intelectual en forma de que cada inteligencia dé, merced a los estímulos oportunos, su cabal rendimiento. El resultado es que hoy, a los ventitrés años de vida republicana, estamos todavía en una estado de estancamiento respecto de anteriores apogeos" (29). [We have been slowly cultivating our intelligences, but intellectual culture has not been organized so that every mind can achieve, thanks to opportune stimulation, its greatest yield. The result is that today, after twenty-three years of republican life, we are still in a state of stagnation with respect to previous heights.] Mañach, like many of his contemporaries, felt that Cubans were not only at an initial disadvantage, but were squandering the talents they did have. Cubans would have to work together for the nation's intellectual and cultural advancement.

As it reveals Ortiz's attempts to interest both European and Cuban intellectuals in Afro-Cuban religious and cultural practices, Lombroso's letter also suggests some of the chief tensions driving Ortiz's text. As a Cuban writing for Cubans, Ortiz views Afro-Cuban culture as important for the ways in which it can be used to illuminate a particular understanding of national identity. Yet because he is also an anthropologist implicitly writing for other scholars (North American and European), he locates Afro-Cuban culture as "primitive" and worthy of scientific study by virtue of its difference from modern society. These seemingly mutually exclusive intentions explain Ortiz's need to characterize Afro-Cuban culture as primitive while yet recognizing it as making a fundamental contribution to the construction of Cuba as a modern nation.

By viewing Afro-Cuban culture through the lens of European scientific progress, Ortiz, like other Latin American writers before him, locates Cuban identity and, along with it, Cuban modernity within the dialectic of civilization and barbarism.[17] As Lombroso's presence indicates, Ortiz's intentions in this, his first work, are influenced by the Latin American strain of positivism, which viewed national development from an evolutionary perspective.[18] Ortiz's use of Lombroso's name, far from being a trivial gesture, connects his study to what was then a prominent social science methodology centered around racial anxiety, and identifies racialized cultural practice as a problematic element—something to be "dealt with"—as much as it is part of what has made Cuba unique. Whatever his conclusions about Afro-Cuban *brujos* (sorcerers/witches), Ortiz's ultimate goal is the "improvement" of Cuban society as a whole (by approaching it from a criminological perspective): "Observemos con escrupulosidad microscópica y reiterada—*cum studio et sine odio*—nuestros males presentes, que la consideración de su magnitud nos producirá la pesadilla que ha de despertarnos más prontamente de nuestra modorra y nos ha de dar valor y fuerzas para alcanzar la bienandanza futura" (7). [Let's observe our present evils with microscopic and reiterated scrupulousness—*cum studio et sine odio*—since our consideration of their magnitude will produce the nightmare that must wake us from our stupor and give us the strength and valor to reach future good fortune.] This description indicates the tension in Ortiz's work between Cuba as a space and Cuba's need to develop over time, between Cuba (and specifically its criminal underworld) as petri dish, and the work towards a "future good fortune" that implies a temporal narrative of evolutionary progress. Lombroso's criminological approach argued that there were certain biological factors that predisposed an individual toward criminal behavior. Following Lombroso's lead, Ortiz's exploration of Cuba's underworld (and the racialized elements of this environment) is thus no superficial endeavor; consideration of these "present evils" is intended not only to aid in their eradication, but to stimulate all of Cuban society to forge ahead, a process to be achieved by both force of will and intellectual work.

Process and Product in Cuban Encounters

Several elements of the first sections of Ortiz's text maintain this tension between space and time, showing how he chooses to make what could be a narrowly focused work into a commentary on the development of the Cuban social landscape. Afro-Cuban *brujería* (witchcraft) becomes the vehicle through which he interrogates the ethnic formation of Cuban society and introduces tropes of hybridity that he will develop more fully in later texts. He states in the prologue, "Pero mi trabajo es de muy limitadas pretensiones, y si bien inicia el estudio metódico y positivista de la poliétnica delincuencia cubana, el modesto nombre que por esto pudiera ganarme únicamente se debería a la concomitancia de factores circunstanciales" (1). [But my work is of very limited ambitions, and if it initiates a methodical, positivist study of polyethnic Cuban crime, the modest name that this could earn me is only due to the coinciding presence of circumstantial factors.] What stands out in this brief characterization of his study is the word "polyethnic." In a text that titles itself a study of *black* witchcraft, this word is significant, for it was the concept of Cuba as a society formed from encounters between different cultures that would become the central focus of Ortiz's later work, particularly in texts such as the *Contrapunteo*.[19] For Ortiz, no part of Cuban society is exclusively black; blackness is always mediated by the presence of other races and ethnicities. However, Ortiz's use of "polyethnic" here speaks not to cultural encounter but to the existence of separate groups. It is different from Ortiz's later term transculturation, which refers specifically to *culture* (not race) and to *process* (rather than product or state of being). The idea of polyethnicity is at the heart of Ortiz's anxiety surrounding his enterprise (the need to define the limits of blackness within Cuban society) and the process of containing both the multivalent nature of this descriptive term and the anxiety it produces is at the heart of both this text and his larger project.

Another indication that Ortiz's intended scope reaches beyond an understanding of Afro-Cuban *brujería* is that he does not actually initiate any discussion of witchcraft itself until his second chapter. He begins by sketching out the large historical context into which he will insert his own observations, and within which he can place and develop his look at Afro-Cuban culture, choosing to begin with a description of the various racial and ethnic elements that make up the Cuban underworld and distinguish it from its European counterparts. He sketches the historical development of Cuban society from a racial perspective, from the first Spanish colonizers to the present day. While on the one hand legitimating (for a second time) his choice of study, situating the study within a historical context gives Ortiz the opportunity to narrate the genesis of Cuban culture from a racial/ethnic perspective. He discusses the arrival of each of the different races—white (the Spanish), black (the African slaves), and "yellow" (largely Chinese laborers)—and identifies what each of these groups contributed not only to the Cuban character in general but specifically to the criminal element of Cuban society.[20]

Into what would appear to be a temporally organized historical narrative, Ortiz inserts another spatial reference as he moves to talk about racial encounter:

> Pero todas estas razas encontraron en Cuba un ambiente tan nuevo y tan radicalmente distinto de aquél del cual eran originarias, que les era de todo punto imposible desenvolver su actividad y energías bajo las mismas normas que en sus países de procedencia, por lo que al factor antropológico se unieron otros sociales para determinar las características de la mala vida cubana. (13)

> [But all these races found in Cuba an environment so new and so radically different from their place of origin that it was impossible for them to develop their activities and energies under the same norms as in their countries of origin. In this way, anthropological factors combined with social factors to determine the characteristics of Cuban criminal life.]

For Ortiz, it is not only the ethnic composition (and commingling) that has made Cuban society what it is, but also the particular conditions of Cuba as a place. This attitude has in it something of the "negative insularity" voiced by Mañach and others, who saw the island environment itself as somehow degrading or unhealthy. It is clear from this description that Ortiz's ideas of criminology were influenced by Italian criminologist Enrico Ferri, who argued for the importance of social conditions in producing criminals. What stands out in this statement, however, is the centrality of Cuba; the island as a space of encounter seems to take precedence over cultural or racial attributes in shaping Cuban (criminal) society. Cuba's particular cultural space is derived not from its ethnic origins (which it shares with several continents), but from the way in which these cultures have combined with the island environment under specific historical circumstances. By narrating the historical origins of Cuban underworld culture, Ortiz highlights the way in which Cuban culture is interconnected to other cultures, again reinforcing that an interest in his study should extend beyond a Cuban readership.

Ortiz's first chapter thus gives us a short foundational myth on the nature of Cuban society well before we are introduced to any of the specific characteristics of Afro-Cuban culture. Minus the criminological lens, this proposes the foundational narrative that Ortiz will continue to develop and refine, culminating in his view of Cuba, expressed in a later essay explicitly titled "La cubanidad y los negros" (Cubanness and the Blacks, 1939) as an *ajiaco*, a ceaselessly changing (typically Cuban) cultural stew: "Mestizaje de cocinas, mestizaje de razas, mestizaje de culturas. Caldo denso de civilización que borbollea en el fogón del Caribe" (6). [Mixing of foods, mixing of races, mixing of cultures. A dense stew of civilization bubbling on the Caribbean hearth.] For Ortiz, Cuban racial and cultural identity is a dish that is forever still cooking: "[N]o es un guiso hecho, sino una constante cocedura" (6). [It is not a finished dish, but rather a constant stewing.] The emphasis in this description is on the process itself, with the (racially mixed) product in a state of suspended expectation, its arrival seemingly forever postponed. By the time "La cubanidad y los negros" was published, however, Ortiz's focus had shifted, and in the transformative process he describes, it is no longer race that matters, but rather culture: "Para comprender el alma cubana no hay que estudiar las razas sino las culturas" (8). [To understand the Cuban soul one must study cultures, not races.] By focusing on cultural blending, Ortiz is able to elide a discussion of racial miscegenation.

In the first chapter of *Los negros brujos,* Ortiz has not yet made the full shift from talking about race to talking about culture, but he takes pains to ensure that his readers will remain aware of the nature of Cuban culture as a whole, even as they read about certain of the more sensational aspects of one of its parts. He points out that one reason for choosing to focus his study on Afro-Cuban crime is that Afro-Cuban culture has given the Cuban underworld some of its most distinguishing characteristics: "La raza negra es la que bajo muchos aspectos ha conseguido marcar característicamente la mala vida cubana, comunicándole sus supersticiones, sus organizaciones, sus lenguajes, sus danzas, etc. . . ." (19). [The black race is the one that in many aspects has marked the characteristics of Cuban criminal life, passing on its superstitions, its organizations, languages, dances, etc. . . .] Significantly, Ortiz only observes Afro-Cuban culture's high profile in the criminal world; by focusing only on this lower stratum of society, he neatly avoids having to discuss how Afro-Cuban culture has affected Cuban society more generally.

The first chapter of *Los negros brujos* thus focuses on Cuba as a site of racial mixing (and cultural encounter). Cuba is the stewpot, the metaphorical site of this process. Just when it appears that Ortiz will begin a focused discussion of *brujería,* in the second chapter, he again chooses to locate it within an historical narrative, this time within the context of African "fetishism," as he labels it, and the relocation of fetishistic practices to the New World through the slave trade. Ortiz traces the development (or maintenance) of fetishism in its travels with the African slaves to the New World, presenting Africa as a kind of "pre-history" for Afro-Cuban culture: "Sería pueril pretender que el negro nativo de Africa, que llegó a Cuba trayendo impresas en su cerebro primitivo las aberraciones fetichistas, y que fue precipitado apenas llegó (y para ello fue traído) al abismo de la esclavitud, tan profundo en lo económico como en lo intelectual, se hubiese despojado de sus propias creencias religiosas para vestir el ropaje del catolicismo" (23). [It would be naïve to suppose that the black native of Africa, who arrived in Cuba bringing in his primitive brain these fetishistic aberrations and who was thrown (having barely arrived) into the abyss of slavery, as deep economically as it was intellectually, should have thrown off his own religious beliefs to don the robes of Catholicism.] A positivist tone is readily apparent in the description of these practices as "aberrant," but what Ortiz manages to communicate in this brief description is the force of history in the persistence and transformation of fetishism. Africa is a point of origin (and will also serve as a point of comparison throughout his study), and Ortiz presents fetishism in Cuba as having followed a historical trajectory marked by both slavery and the trans-Atlantic journey. It is thus a practice that has survived both the influences of other cultural (and religious) expressions, and the forces of historical circumstance: war, exile, and the trauma of slavery. Even if time and hardship have failed to alter its practices, Ortiz locates the arrival of fetishism in Cuba within a historical narrative. Its origins are not only in another continent, but also in another time. This keeps Afro-Cuban religious practice fundamentally, temporally tied to the "primitive" past, even while black Cubans themselves are granted the potential to "evolve" (and, implicitly, to mix). Johannes Fabian argues that anthropologists frequently create a separation between the scientist and his or her human subjects through a "denial of coevalness"—a process whereby the subject is defined as "primitive" or other by being relegated to the temporal space of the past (26–31). In his description of fetishism, however, Ortiz does something slightly different. He identifies the religious *practices* as primitive by virtue of their temporal isolation (and failure to adapt and progress), while presenting Cuba as a unique space distant from the origins of those practices, where Afro-Cubans may implicitly progress. The distinction between people and practices allows Ortiz to uphold a positivist vision of progress for Cuban society while describing a people who are other within the nation.

Despite his insistence on the uniqueness of the social, historical, and cultural factors that have helped to make Cuban society what it is, Ortiz portrays Cuban culture—and Afro-Cuban culture in particular—as intelligible primarily when viewed through other cultures, both African and European. One reason that Ortiz chooses to construct a historical narrative within which he can situate his discussion of *brujería* may be that his approach is a comparative one somewhat by necessity, given that he is one of the first scholars to undertake a study of the specifics of Afro-Cuban religion.[21] No doubt in part as a result of the scarcity of firsthand fieldwork and other previous work on Afro-Cuban culture (Palmié 237), (the young) Ortiz frequently consults the work of experts on other areas of the African Diaspora, such as the Brazilian scholar Raimundo Nina Rodrigues, and those whose work focuses on the cultures of Africa itself, most notably the work of British and American scholars such as A. B. Ellis, Thomas Jefferson Bowen, and Samuel Crowther.[22] Ortiz's references to these now-classic texts of early anthropology make it clear that he was well read on the subject of the religious practices of Africa and the African Diaspora, a gesture that intimates the legitimacy of his project within Western social science. Yet while the findings of these writers add the weight of more established scholarly voices to Ortiz's own discoveries and theories, his use of these sources means that many parts of his text—the early sections in particular—are actually less about particular manifestations of Cuban traditions than they are about differences between Cuban traditions and those of Brazil or Dahomey. In describing the individual *orichas* (Afro-Cuban gods), for example, we learn not only about the nature of these deities within Cuba, but also the equivalent saints of each *oricha* in Brazil. Ortiz takes many of the origin myths of the *orichas* from A. B. Ellis's work on the Yoruba in Africa. The text moves back and forth between Ortiz's own descriptions of Afro-Cuban religious practice and the interpretation of similar practices by these "experts," as if Ortiz were seeking validation or corroboration for his own observations. This use of other sources further acts to shore up Ortiz's authority as a scientist, distancing Ortiz from the subjects of his inquiry.

In choosing to paint a historical picture of the African roots of Cuban witchcraft, Ortiz's style owes a great deal to nineteenth-century notions of anthropology and folklore and to scholars, such as James Frazer (author of *The Golden Bough*), who viewed the study of cultures as a comparative process whose goals were to recognize commonly shared patterns or trace inherited characteristics, thus creating a history of cultural evolution and diffusion based on developed differences. The English folklorist Andrew Lang, writing in 1885, argues that a comparative approach was even more important for so-called "primitive" cultures. Differentiating between the monotheistic Judeo-Christian tradition and polytheistic religions, which he collectively terms "fetishism," he observes, "As religions become developed they are differentiated; it is only fetishism that you find the same everywhere" (225). Ortiz's exploration of the shared traits of African religious practices in other parts of the Caribbean and Latin America emphasizes the common African origins of these traditions. But the dominance of these other cultural (and scholarly) voices in the narrative in some sense undermines both his focus on Cuba and his broader intention to assert Cuba's cultural uniqueness and significance. His comparative approach locates the genesis of Afro-Cuban religion within a narrative of world history and cultural development, but it also makes his enterprise a doubly translative one, since many of the conclusions that he draws about the practices of Afro-Cubans are in fact speculations about the Cuban context based on the observations of scholars working in different cultural environments, no matter what their similarities.

Beyond this narrative of cultural origins, Ortiz approaches Afro-Cuban religious tradition as a system of practices, and he proceeds to explain the system by describing the relationship of its parts to each other and to the whole. Once he has described how the religion came to be, he moves on to a basic discussion of each of the *orichas,* their relationship to each other, and the rituals and ritual objects associated with each one. Like someone attempting to record the grammar of a language, he is concerned with the accuracy of detail, since each detail will relate to the whole in a specific way. His third chapter, which focuses specifically on the workings of *brujería,* begins by describing the material accoutrements of witchcraft: altars, ritual dress, the *collares,* the foods used for ritual offerings, etc.[23]

Ortiz's attention to material detail and his solidly anthropological interest in these cultural practices stand in contrast to the positivist narrative for Cuban progress that he articulates in his introduction. This historical-comparativist narrative is also at odds with other, more intimate scenes in the text that return us to the particularities of the Cuban environment. Moments of intense description, literary in both their creative use of language and the subjective perception they display, surface suddenly, seeming to burst through the developmental trajectory he wishes to establish. Take, for example, this description of dancing during religious ceremonies:

> No transcurre mucho tiempo, una vez empezado el baile, sin que la excitación erótica se manifieste en toda la crudeza africana. Los movimientos lascivos del baile están sometidos al son de los tambores y a menudo se oye la voz de un negro gritando ¡iebbe! o ¡iebba! y pidiendo que el *llamador* haga oir su toque para dar el *golpe de frente* . . . No es raro que los negros sudorosos se despojen de la camisa, mostrando sus bustos lustrosos y sus bronceados brazos, que ciñen con febril abrazo el cuerpo de la bailadora. Llegados a este

momento, los bailadores se alocan por la irritación sexual, el *chequeteque*, la música, la danza, etc., y la orgía corona frecuentemente la festividad religiosa. (83)

[Not much time passes, once the dancing has begun, before an erotic excitation appears in all of its African crudeness. The dance's lascivious movements are in time to the sound of the drums, and often one hears the voice of a black man shouting, ¡iebbe! or ¡iebbe!, asking that the *caller* let his beat ring to begin the *golpe de frente* dance.... It's not uncommon for the sweaty black men to take their shirts off, revealing their lustrous chests and bronzed arms, which feverishly grip the bodies of the female dancers close. Having arrived at this moment, the dancers give themselves up to the sexual irritation, the rhythm, the music, the dancing, etc., and an orgy frequently tops the religious festivities.]

Even while Ortiz emphasizes the sexual nature of the dancing in this description as illustrative of the need to assimilate its practitioners into the more acceptable forms of Cuban society, the exoticizing, voyeuristically intimate tone of his narration is unmistakable. Jossianna Arroyo observes a tension (not infrequent in Ortiz's writing) between the stated need to discipline black bodies and "una atracción inevitable hacia ese mismo cuerpo que causa horror" (167) [an inevitable attraction towards that same body that horrifies]. The language lingers on the dancers' bodies— "lustrous" and "bronzed"—using a congregation of the sweat, the beat of the music, and the cries of the participants to recreate not only the emotions of the dancers but to initiate a sense of desire within the text itself. Placed against passages such as this one, Ortiz's insistence on the immorality of *brujería*, and the need to introduce morality into Afro-Cuban religious practice, seems to stem from a need to counterbalance the attractiveness (albeit exoticized) of the religion as portrayed by his own descriptions. Although his original intent may have been to communicate the way in which belief and praxis intersect in the performed rituals of Santería, what Ortiz communicates most effectively in descriptions like this one is the sensual experience of a moment; even if he fails to explain the significance of what it *means* to be there, his text produces a sensation of what it *feels like* to be there, an experience that, from the point of view of Ortiz's ambivalent narrative voice, is one fraught with repressed desires.

While Ortiz uses a first-person narrative voice in *Los negros brujos* to link parts of his own text or to comment on sources he has mentioned previously, he makes almost no references to himself as an investigator, to interactions between himself and Santería practitioners, or to his own experiences as an observer. In *Los negros brujos* this is in part a result of the fact that Ortiz had done very little of his own research, yet if we look at his later texts, written after Ortiz had had ample opportunity to interview informants, the same tone and textual persona can be observed. *Los bailes y el teatro de los negros en el folklore de Cuba* (*Black Dance and Theater in Cuban Folklore*, 1951), a comprehensive look at Afro-Cuban musicality published over four decades after Ortiz's first ethnography, is, like *Los negros brujos*, structured around comparisons between musical traditions in Africa and those in Cuba. Ortiz sketches a broad panorama, full of generalized declarative statements about "black" culture or music, beginning with his observation, "El arte del negro es un arte transido de socialidad" (27). [The black man's art is one permeated by sociability.] He cites the work of several recognized scholars on Africa before narrowing his focus to Cuba, and his tone of voice rarely departs from the third-person detachment of a scholar. Although accounts by students and fellow scholars confirm not only Ortiz's participation in Afro-Cuban ritual but also his use of informants, he rarely if ever mentions informants, and never by name.[24] Despite the fact that this is a return to the same scene of religious dancing visited in *Los negros brujos*, in this later study Ortiz has separated the authority of his scientific narrative from his personal (emotional) response as a witness.

While *Los negros brujos* alternates principally between historical overview and descriptions of the kind discussed above, there are in fact several secondary narratives that run through the text: the stories of accused *brujos* (both male and female witches) who have been prosecuted by the Cuban legal system for crimes committed in conjunction with their religion. These stories form the bulk of the last third of the book and are the main source of Ortiz's direct information about Afro-Cuban religious practice. These newspaper excerpts are carefully separated from the main body of the text, and although he makes reference to certain of the more sensational cases within his own description of *brujería*, Ortiz is largely content to let these documents stand on their own as evidence for the immorality of the religious practices he is documenting. As a result, the reader is left with very little to help him or her interpret the stories that may be behind these arrests. It is impossible to know what was actually taking place, what was being observed, etc. To a modern reader, aware of the heavy extent to which *any* kind of Afro-Cuban religious practice was prosecuted at the time Ortiz was writing, these clippings reveal less about *brujería* than they do about social repression and the ways in which white Cubans, especially the police and legal system, were inclined to view all Afro-Cuban activities as immoral and potentially dangerous. In sketching out a clear discussion of the origins of Afro-Cuban religion and faithfully detailing both oral literature and material artifacts, Ortiz seems to feel that he is giving as clear as possible a presentation of these cultural practices. But both his descriptions and these newspaper articles point to how much remains unsaid, and imply the wealth of stories, beliefs, and experiences that are waiting to be interpreted.

Ortiz's narrative of Cuban culture as a process of constant encounter, negotiation, fusion, and re-encounter culminates in his introduction of the idea of "transculturation," a term whose meaning he first elaborates in the *Contrapunteo* (1940), perhaps his best-known work. Ortiz introduces this neologism as a new way to accurately explain the processes of cultural exchange, adaptation, and synthesis that happen in an encounter between two cultures. Even when one culture occupies a "dominant" position with respect to another, Ortiz argues, the cultural encounter involves not only the loss of culture (deculturation) and the taking up of aspects of another (acculturation) but "la consiguiente creación de nuevos fenómenos culturales que pudieran denominarse de neoculturación" (260) [the consequent creation of new cultural phenomena, which could be called neoculturation (103)]. Transculturation is the term that Ortiz creates to describe the simultaneous interactions of all of these processes; as Pérez Firmat observes, it is a theoretical apparatus that more fully articulates his earlier, sensual metaphor of the *ajiaco* (Cuban stew). Now, instead of a stew, we get a detailed accounting of the various stages and kinds of mixing, as transculturation highlights the process—the action—rather than the resulting product. Given this emphasis, Pérez Firmat observes, "[I]t might not even be appropriate to speak of a Cuban 'culture,' since the term implies a fixity of configuration that is belied by the fluidity of the Cuban situation" (23). As a concept, transculturation indicates the probable operations in a cultural encounter, but not the possible outcomes.

Significantly, the *Contrapunteo* is not a study of Afro-Cuban culture; it is a comparative exploration—a counterpoint—of tobacco and sugar, and their role in the agricultural, economic, political, and cultural development of Cuba. Following the allegorical model of the "Pelea que tuvo Don Carnal con Doña Cuaresma" (Fight Between Sir Flesh and Madam Lent), which appears in the late medieval *Libro de buen amor* (*The Book of Good Love*) by Juan Ruiz, Archpriest of Hita, Ortiz introduces tobacco and sugar as "los personajes más importantes de la historia de Cuba" (137) [the most important figures in the history of Cuba (4)].[25] Fernando Coronil argues that as Ortiz traces the birth and history of these two "personages," he makes them into true social actors by showing that "they are in fact social creatures, that is, the products of human interaction within the context of capitalist relations of production" ("Introduction" xxviii). Ortiz begins by establishing what appears to be a series of dichotomies: tobacco is masculine, sugar is feminine; sugar is uniform (in taste, color, etc.), while tobacco varies according to character and quality. Yet these contrasts and separations begin to give way to gray areas, as these qualities seem to mix, change, and double back on one another:

> El tabaco es oscuro, de negro a mulato; el azúcar es clara, de mulata a blanca. El tabaco no cambia de color, nace moreno y muere con el color de su raza. El azúcar cambia de coloración, nace parda y se blanquea; es almibarada mulata que siendo prieta se abandona a la sabrosura popular y luego se encascarilla y refina para pasar por Blanca, correr por todo el mundo, llegar a las bocas y ser pagada mejor ... (143)

> [Tobacco is dark, ranging from black to mulatto; sugar is light, ranging from mulatto to white. Tobacco does not change its color; it is born dark and dies the color of its race. Sugar changes its coloring; it is born brown and whitens itself; at first it is a syrupy mulatto [who, being dark, abandons itself to] the common taste; then it [bleaches and refines itself] until it can pass for white, travel all over the world, reach all mouths and [be paid more] ... (9)]

Ortiz employs racial terminology in a surprising way, seemingly privileging "black" tobacco over lighter sugar. Yet what he emphasizes here is purity; as Elizabeth Russ astutely observes, Ortiz privileges native tobacco over sugar who, by lightening herself to become more desirable, "is imitative of all that is foreign" (32). Cuba's "exportable material" must be its own, not a mere imitation "passing" for something original. However, even this metaphorical dichotomy does not last. What seemed at the beginning to be two very different products with vastly different histories, by the end of the first section have become intimately connected; the "marriage" of tobacco and sugar ends with the birth of alcohol, producing a "Trinidad cubana" (Cuban Trinity): sugar, tobacco, and alcohol.

Ortiz does not present a formal introduction of and definition for transculturation until the beginning of the book's second section. Yet by this point, he has already staged a kind of literary, metaphorical demonstration of the ways in which transculturation operates through his description of the changes in the production and consumption of tobacco and sugar. His more detailed ethnographic descriptions of the sociohistorical contexts of these two products in the book's second half merely serve to bolster this schema. Literary critic Antonio Benítez Rojo argues that in the way that Ortiz uses the theoretical section on transculturation to effectively stage a commentary on its own construction, the *Contrapunteo* is a postmodern text *avant la lettre* (*Isla* 153). Yet the *Contrapunteo* also shares many aspects of its approach and structure with *Los negros brujos*. A historical narrative that sets the scene, followed by an ethnographic text that interweaves other scholarly sources with a focus on material culture, are elements present in Ortiz's early text. Both texts begin by emphasizing a historical narrative, and by sketching a broad panorama, before moving on to detail the specificities of particular aspects of material culture.

By focusing on the ways in which material products can travel and change, Ortiz avoids a direct discussion of racial miscegenation, of saying what happens to racially identified groups of people. While race and racial difference are certainly present in the *Contrapunteo*'s narrative, they are primarily mentioned in the context of the historical development of the use or production of tobacco and sugar: the importation of black slaves as labor for the sugar mills, the role of blacks in introducing tobacco smoking to the Creole population. Ortiz also speaks of race metaphorically, as when he compares the variation in tobacco types to the variation in color of Cuban women (*Contrapunteo* 161; *Counterpoint* 22), or when he speaks of a "mestizaje de sabores" (163) (mixture of flavors, 23). Only when he finally comes around to detailing transculturation does he give another brief narrative of the various racial and ethnic encounters at different moments in Cuban history. Furthermore, despite Pérez Firmat's assertion that Ortiz was not obsessed with Cuban "origins" (32), the focus on tobacco as one of these "important personages" allows Ortiz to spend a significant amount of time discussing the indigenous *Taínos* and the role of tobacco in their culture. The *Taínos* themselves may have vanished, but tobacco thus emerges as an explicitly authentic Cuban product, intimately connected to the island's "natural" flora. Cuban culture may be the product of synthesis, but Ortiz's literary and metaphorical counterpoint thus sidesteps having to identify the specific nature of the relationship between blackness and nation in the Cuban narrative.

A Second Introduction

In the same year that he published the *Contrapunteo*, Ortiz found himself writing the introduction to a different kind of presentation of Afro-Cuban culture. In 1940, Lydia Cabrera, then a young art student in Paris (and, somewhat coincidentally, Ortiz's sister-in-law) published a Spanish edition of her first collection of short stories, *Cuentos negros de Cuba* (*Afro-Cuban Tales*, hereafter *Cuentos negros*), which, although written in Spanish, had in fact first been published in a French translation in 1936 by Gallimard press. The Havana edition included an introduction penned by Ortiz, who took credit for some of her interest in Afro-Cuban culture. Just as the letter from Lombroso in *Los negros brujos* legitimated Ortiz's scholarship as worthy of international scholarly interest, Ortiz uses his introduction to *Cuentos negros* to highlight the positive reception a Cuban's work has received in European intellectual circles.

Ortiz views the stories in *Cuentos negros* less as fiction than as ethnographic primary texts directly representative of their "exotic" African cultural origins—as original documents "filtered through" Spanish. He states, "No hay que olvidar que estos cuentos vienen a las prensas por una colaboración, la del folklore negro con su traductora blanca" (8). [We must not forget that these stories arrive at the press through a collaboration, that between black folklore and its white translator.] In his eyes, Cabrera's achievement is the creation of a comprehensible portrait of African culture in Cuba through her rendering in Spanish of existing (African) folktales. This view is highlighted by his use of the word "leal" (loyal, faithful) to describe her work, a word that implies that Cabrera had an original "text" to which she was (and needed to be) faithful.

That Ortiz would write the preface for Cabrera's book further illustrates the importance he places on the legitimating function of prefaces. His introduction insists on identifying Cabrera's fiction as folklore because he wants to see her work as engaged in the construction of a national project similar to the one he himself is intent on creating. Few examples of black folklore had been published prior to *Cuentos negros*, none intended for a mainstream audience.[26] As Ortiz himself points out in an article published in 1929, "[L]os cuentos africanos se ignoran totalmente en Cuba. No sabemos de *uno solo* que haya sido publicado como tal en nuestra tierra" ("Cuentos afrocubanos" 97). [African stories are almost completely unknown in Cuba. We know of none that have been published as such in this country.] Ortiz connects Cabrera's stories to his own scholarly enterprise, in which position they function more as "primary material" than as the result of investigative scholarship. At the same time, Ortiz's paternalistic attitude towards Cabrera's creation intends to locate her work as subservient to his own national project.

As I show later in this study, Cabrera's texts themselves escape this characterization. *Cuentos negros* is very much Cabrera's own creation, although Cabrera herself later admitted that her first creative efforts drew on a knowledge of Afro-Cuban culture acquired through personal and ethnographic contacts. Yet Ortiz's preface establishes a professional connection between his work and Cabrera's own that she does not reject. When she published *El Monte*, her own comprehensive look at Afro-Cuban religious practice and her first long ethnographic study, fourteen years later, she dedicated her book to Ortiz, "con afecto fraternal" (with sisterly affection).

By 1954 when Cabrera published *El Monte*, the study of Afro-Cuban culture occupied a more central (and, to a certain extent, more accepted) position in both the academic and the national imaginary, even if Afro-Cubans themselves were still socially and politically marginalized. Thanks in large part to the work of Ortiz, articles dealing with Afro-Cuban topics regularly appeared in *Estudios Afrocubanos, Revista Bimestre Cubana,* and other scholarly journals. The study of Afro-Cuban culture could also be linked to a larger corpus of work on the African Diaspora in the Americas.[27] While the amount of agency that this increasing cultural visibility afforded black Cubans is debatable, certain elements of Afro-Cuban culture had clearly come to be acknowledged as vital to the idea of Cubanness. Images of Afro-Cubans and Afro-Cuban culture were more numerous and more varied. At the same time, the debates over the nature of Afro-Cuban religious culture, and the role and place of Afro-Cubans in Cuban society, were far from resolved. One could argue that the shift to symbolic discourses of hybridity (brought about in part precisely by texts such as the *Contrapunteo*) and Cabrera's response to them reveal the lasting nature of the undercurrent of anxiety first expressed by Ortiz in *Los negros brujos*.

The contrasting points of view that Cabrera and Ortiz bring to their enterprise can be easily observed by comparing Ortiz's introduction to *Los negros brujos* (and his preface to Cabrera's *Cuentos negros*) with the preface that Cabrera herself provides for *El Monte*. Although several decades divide them, the first lines of Cabrera's prologue seem to echo Ortiz's commentaries on *Los negros brujos*. Like her predecessor, Cabrera identifies her text as a collection of "notas" (notes), opting to downplay the revised and polished character of a finished text. Ortiz's prologue, with the letter from Lombroso, establishes Ortiz as a legitimate scholar with a worthy project, but Cabrera seems reluctant to professionalize her own project, choosing to downplay her talents. It is interesting to observe, however, that whereas Ortiz used his preface to explain the value that could be found in studying Afro-Cuban practices, what Cabrera is actually doing in these first pages is detailing her methodology. Writing several decades after Ortiz, Cabrera does not feel a need to justify her subject. What she does want to explain is the genesis of her text, in terms of both her own motivation and the factors that contributed to its form. While Ortiz hints at attending rituals, it is never clear from his texts how he has acquired information from primary sources. In these first paragraphs, Cabrera is clear about how she has chosen to deal with the ambiguities naturally present in gathering material from informants: "No omito repeticiones ni contradicciones, pues en los detalles, continuamente se advierte disparidad de criterio entre las 'autoridades' habaneras y las matanceras" (1). [I do not omit repetitions or contradictions, since in these details one can continually observe the disparity of criteria between the 'authorities' from Havana and those from Matanzas.] This quote is somewhat shocking in its implications from an ethnographic perspective; it suggests that the text itself cannot serve as an ethnographic authority, and, in fact, that there may not be an authoritative voice available in certain instances. The reference to generational conflict also presents the culture as living and changing, in contrast to the view espoused by earlier ethnographers that primitive cultures were largely static. Finally, it emphasizes the place-specific nature of authoritative knowledge; rather than seeking expertise in previous ethnographic studies—and in so doing, looking for a temporal narrative of cultural development or change, Cabrera identifies authority as profoundly local.

Rituals of Race: Cabrera's Narrative Strategies

In the construction of his text, Ortiz is careful to move from the general to the specific, from known history to the relatively unknown cultural practices that his study wants to explain. In tackling much the same material forty years later, Cabrera approaches the material in *El Monte* in an entirely different way. Rather than working from the outside in, she begins her study by moving in precisely the opposite direction, placing her reader directly at the most vital site of Afro-Cuban religious practice:

> Persiste en el negro cubano, con tenacidad asombrosa, la creencia en la espiritualidad del monte. En los montes y malezas de Cuba habitan, como en las selvas de Africa, las mismas divinidades ancestrales, los espíritus poderosos que todavía hoy, igual que en los días de la trata, más teme y venera, y de cuya hostilidad o benevolencia siguen dependiendo sus éxitos o sus fracasos. (7)

> [There remains in the black Cuban, with surprising tenacity, a belief in the spirituality of the bush. As in the jungles of Africa, there live in the forests and thickets of Cuba the same ancestral deities, the same powerful spirits that still today, as in the days of the slave trade, he most fears and venerates, and on whose hostility or benevolence his successes and failures continue to depend.]

The careful setting of the story within a broader historical context and a more generalized discussion of Cuban society are not apparent in Cabrera's text. In beginning a book about *el Monte* (which operates as the bush, the accumulation of religious knowledge that these places represent, and the powerful magical and medicinal plants found there), she places the reader in *el Monte*, as if making him or her an active witness to a ritual. The reader may not yet have a clear idea of just exactly what *el Monte* represents, but from these first lines he or she gains a clear idea of the strong significance of this space for Afro-Cubans. Cabrera may have chosen to do away with many of Ortiz's introductory strategies, but this is not to suggest that her text lacks a narrative framework; she simply chooses to present this framework differently, performing her methodology rather than explaining it. One cannot hope to know *el Monte* by talking around it; one must *go there*, enter into it, in order to understand it. So after briefly showing us what we are about to enter, the second paragraph actually stages a physical entrance into *el Monte*: "El negro que se adentra en la manigua, que penetra de lleno en un 'corazón de Monte,' no duda del contacto directo que establece con fuerzas sobrenaturales que allí, en sus propios dominios, le rodean" (7). [The black man who enters the thicket, who completely penetrates the "heart of the Bush" does not doubt the direct contact he establishes with the supernatural forces that surround him there, in their own domain.] In following this man's entrance into the physical and spiritual realm of *el Monte*, the reader opens another kind of ritual space by entering the text. The reader is not necessarily identified as a practitioner; Cabrera's description of the journey to *el Monte* conveys an atmosphere—the feeling of a power beyond rational explanation—more than it attempts to explain how the ritual operates. Once we have followed this man into the forest, we can begin to understand the significance of *el Monte* as the place from which all things originate, not only the location of the *orichas* and the source of spiritual power—"los Santos nacen del Monte y nuestra religión también nace del Monte" (7) [the Saints (*orichas*) are born in the Bush and our religion is also born of the Bush]—but even, in the Afro-Cuban cosmology, the origin of life itself.

It is important to observe the extent to which Cabrera's choice of *el Monte* as both central symbolic space and as structuring device centers her narrative in Cuba. Despite the lack of a detailed discussion of Afro-Cuban history, the above description manages to highlight or suggest many of the main points of Ortiz's first chapter: the importance of Africa as the place of origin, the role of the slave trade, and the persistence of these practices despite factors working in their opposition. Yet Cabrera's description identifies *el Monte* as an unconditionally Cuban space, and furthermore a space that proliferates—it can be any of "las montes y malezas de Cuba" (13) [the forests and thickets of Cuba], even, as she says later, "el matorral más próximo" (18) [the closest thicket]. Ortiz talks about the ways in which African religious practices have been adapted within a Cuban environment, but Cabrera takes us to the site of religious power itself.

In Ortiz's temporally focused narrative, as different races and ethnicities in Cuba formed a hybridized society, so Afro-Cuban religions, cut off from their African roots, became modified versions of the original fetishistic practices.[28] In contrast, while Cabrera agrees with the symbolic importance of Africa for Afro-Cubans, she is not interested, in this first section, in debating whether these beliefs can be seen as "original." Even as she explains that belief in the spirituality of *el Monte* can be traced to a system of African religious practices, she places Cuba at the center of her discussion of these traditions, as she communicates the vitality of these practices as they exist on the island. This does not mean that she maintains a solely synchronic view of Afro-Cuban religion; a historical context is important for her narrative, particularly in the later chapters of the book as she begins to distinguish between Santería, Palo Monte, and Abakuá practices, explaining their diverse origins and development in Cuba. Yet by and large, any diachronic view Cabrera gives of Santería or Palo Monte takes as its comparison the religious practices in colonial Cuba and those practices as they appear in the Cuba of 1954. Ortiz's study is dominated by his focus on the foundation of cultural traditions and the presence of Africa in Cuba; historical background is a very minor presence in Cabrera's text compared to the importance she places on the general belief systems themselves.[29] For her, details such as the names of the *orichas* and their powers will mean nothing if we cannot grasp the force of spirituality at the core of these religious beliefs. It is for this reason that for every practice that she herself lays out descriptively she provides either a *patakí* (religious tale) or an anecdote from one of her informants that illustrates the way in which this belief has become incorporated into everyday life, closing the gap (which Ortiz's work seems to maintain) between theory and praxis. It is not enough to know that the palm tree is associated with Changó, the *oricha* connected to lightning and thunder. When we read a description of the ritual offering that "L. modesto empleado del estado, hijo de Changó" [L., humble state employee and "son" (initiate) of Changó] performs "para afianzar su situación en estos tiempos 'traicioneros'" (253) [to situate himself in these dangerous times], a complex ritual that involves submerging a nail in a blessed "syrup" for four days before burying it at the foot of a sacred palm tree, this belief ceases to be something to be viewed in the abstract and begins to assume concrete forms.

Cabrera's discussions of aspects of Afro-Cuban religious practice move from general to specific, but not in a historical or concept-oriented way, as does Ortiz's text. Rather, the performative, experiential elements of the text alternate with the discursive. *El Monte* is Cabrera's central scenario, but after we have entered, the text begins to share opinions, anecdotes, and stories about this space. A reader with no previous knowledge of Santería would still have no idea of what is involved in the basic beliefs and practices of Afro-Cuban religion. As the text itself states, it is only after moving in the shadowland of the forest for a little while that we are gradually able to pick out elements and forms: "El clarividente, solitario en la manigua enmarañada, apercibe las formas estrambóticas e impresionantes que para el ojo humano asumen a veces estos trasgos y demonios silvestres que el negro siente alentar en la vegetación" (7). [The clear-sighted person, alone in the tangled thicket, perceives the strange and awesome forms that these woodland demons and spirits, who the black man feels breathe in the vegetation, sometimes take on for the human eye.] Unlike Ortiz's description of a *tambor* (dance and drumming ceremony), which creates a voyeuristic atmosphere through its exoticized depiction of the bodies of the participants, Cabrera's text allows the reader to witness this ritual setting almost as if he or she were the participant. She identifies the black man as able to read the signs of this magical environment, a space whose power she does not attempt to explain away. Cabrera's text proceeds almost in the form of a ritual itself. The first *oricha* she focuses on, for example, is Elegguá, the first *oricha* to be invoked in any ceremony, since he is, among other things, the god of the crossroads, without whose good will no ritual can proceed. Structurally, her text offers itself to the *oricha* of the crossroads, so that the other chapters of the study can follow.

In a description in tune with Cabrera's own writing, Cuban novelist Lino Novás Calvo has remarked, "Toda la obra de Lydia Cabrera es una intricada manigua de realidad y fantasía. *El Monte* se lee como una biblia, un milyunanoches, un decamerón negro; y los cuentos se leen como páginas escapadas del *Monte* . . ." (19). [Lydia Cabrera's entire oeuvre is an intricate thicket of fantasy and reality. *El Monte* reads like a bible, an *A Thousand and One Nights*, a black *Decameron*; and the stories read like loose pages from *El Monte*.] Comparing *El Monte* to the Bible makes sense on a certain level; not only is it a compilation of beliefs and oral texts of comparable density and significance, Cabrera's text is designed so that even small sections can stand alone. At the same time, Novás Calvo's comparison of *El Monte* to a "thicket of fantasy and reality" is also significant. Ortiz's study is organized via a sense of historical time, both through his interpretation of what he has seen and read and through the newspaper reports detailing the arrest of black Cubans for ostensibly religious reasons. Cabrera's narrative often seems to serve as a framework to link the interrelated stories that form the dense network of text. José Quiroga has observed that in *El Monte* Cabrera "privileges coherence over intelligibility."[30] Her "collection of notes," as she describes her book, is not an attempt to explain the system, but rather an attempt to present the system in its complex functioning, to see these practices as they are performed.

Spaces of Morality

Cabrera's lack of a predetermined narrative allows her a significant freedom in her depiction of Afro-Cuban religion. Although there are moral and ethical judgments expressed at various points in both her short stories and the informant narratives of her ethnography, she herself rarely expresses an explicitly moral opinion on what she describes. She is able to present Afro-Cuban religious tradition as a system with its own internal coherence precisely because she makes no overarching moral judgments. She states at one point:

> También los "cristianos, blancos y negros," somos mezcla de bien y de mal.... La moral circunstancial de nuestros paleros y santeros y la de su numerosa clientela, es el reflejo de un concepto natural de la vida que no han perdido nuestros negros. Conviene tenerlo siempre presente para juzgar la amoralidad, tan característica, del sacerdocio afrocubano; y no pasemos del sacerdocio afro-cubano al resto de la colectividad en todas las esferas. Punto. ¡Dáke! (142)

> [We, the "Christians, white and black," are also a mixture of good and bad.... The circumstantial morality of our *paleros* and *santeros* and that of their numerous clientele is the reflection of a natural concept of life that our blacks have not lost. It's important to keep that in mind when judging the amorality that is so characteristic of the Afro-Cuban priesthood; and let's not take the priesthood for the rest of the Afro-Cuban collectivity in all spheres. Period. Agreed!]

Cabrera's willingness to stand back and not proffer judgments allows her text to take the unusual hybrid form it does. Rather than presenting a central argument, as Ortiz does in his early ethnographic work, and using the information, both primary and secondary sources, to bolster that argument, Cabrera allows the stories and field notes she has gathered to shape the reader's understanding of Santería, Palo Monte, and Abakuá traditions. She reveals Afro-Cuban culture in her short stories in the same way that she allows the reader to enter *el Monte* in an almost physical sense in her ethnography; the reader is thrust into the ritual enactment of culture through the action of the text, rather than through Cabrera's explanation or analysis. Note, however, that her observation above about morality indicates that Afro-Cuban practice is a clearly delimited space, legitimate in its own right, but by no means constitutive of morality (or society) in a more general way.

Cabrera seems less concerned that the reader come away with a complete understanding of Afro-Cuban religious practice after a reading of her work than that the reader get a sense of its integrity as a cultural system. She is careful to establish her own ethnographic voice in her concise introduction, and there are several points in the early sections of *El Monte* when she seems eager to differentiate her methodology from the positivist thrust of Ortiz's work. If, as I discussed earlier, Ortiz states in his preface to *Los negros brujos* that he wishes to expose the mysteries of Afro-Cuban religion in order to help its practitioners be better integrated into "modern society" (as Ortiz defines it), Cabrera's text does the opposite, showing how well practitioners have adapted themselves and their religion to a modern, urban environment such as Havana: "Y en el negro capitalino, a pesar de su innegable adaptabilidad a un progreso material que aquí como en ninguna otra parte, solemos confundir orgullosamente con la cultura, situado en el mismo plano de igualdad que el blanco, disfrutando en todos los órdenes de los beneficios de la civilización, el atavismo africano no es menos fuerte e irreductible que en el negro campesino" (12). [And in the black man from the capital, in spite of his undeniable adaptability to a material progress that here, as nowhere else, we tend to proudly mistake for culture, situated in the same space of equality as the white man and enjoying all of the benefits of civilization at all levels, the African atavism is no less strong and irreducible than in the black peasant.] Santería and Palo Monte are not the fetishistic "remains" of African religious systems, they are dynamic religions in their own right that have adapted to modern and urban life, where the bush may be the few plants growing in one's backyard. One of the central messages that Cabrera demonstrates in her text is that integration is not the issue; these beliefs already exist in a well-integrated way within Cuban society. Early on in the text she discusses the nature of the word *brujo*, as if in direct response to Ortiz: "Brujos son nuestros negros, muchas veces, en el sentido individual que reprueba, teme y condena la magia ortodoxa, cuyas prácticas y ritos se encaminan a obtener el bien de la comunidad . . . [S]iguen reaccionando con la misma mentalidad primitiva de sus antepasados en un medio, como el nuestro, impregnado de magia hasta lo inimaginable . . ." (10–11). [Our blacks are witches, many times, in the individual sense that rejects, fears and condemns orthodox magic, whose practices and rites go towards obtaining the good of the community . . . They continue to react with the same primitive mentality as their ancestors in an environment such as ours, impregnated with magic to an unimaginable extent. . . .]

When Ortiz talks of Cuba's "polyethnic" character, his early work seems to suggest that the only place where any kind of cultural exchange occurs is at the lower rungs of society. Cabrera does not deny that Afro-Cuban practice involves what white culture would recognize as traditional witchcraft; but she also argues that these practices find a convenient fit with an urban Cuban environment.

Cabrera's use of the phrase "nuestros negros" in the above description is important here. In its paternalistic (and racist) overtones, it shortens the distance separating both the reader and Cabrera herself from the culture of study, yet it erects a class barrier that allows Cabrera to maintain a safe distance. Ortiz's study does its best to corral Afro-Cuban religion within the carefully established parameters of certain parts of Cuban society. Cabrera can bring the contact zone home to the houses and neighborhoods of her readers, because with her use of the pronoun "our" she continues to solidify the social and class structures that keep these cultures separate. Afro-Cuban religion is prevalent in the cities, but its presence is controlled by class.

In the Forest of the Text

Despite Ortiz's demonstrated interest in Afro-Cuban culture, in both *Los negros brujos* and his later works such as the *Contrapunteo* this interest is subservient to the creation of a more generalized (and more unified) notion of Cuban culture, one in which the "polyethnic" nature of Cuban society will take a back seat to more unifying narratives of cultural synthesis. The parts, for Ortiz, will always be subservient to the whole, and the whole is nothing less than a Cubanness in which there are encounters and exchanges rather than separate (and potentially conflictive) elements. Ortiz's early focus on Afro-Cuban culture helped legitimate it as an object of study, but his texts suggest that this interest must always remain historically contextualized, subservient to the Cuban society that is emerging from (and defying) its colonial past.

While there are clearly some important differences between the two writers and their attitudes, I think that it is treacherously facile to position Cabrera and her work as essentially "anti-Ortiz." As I have shown, while there are significant differences in both their methodological and narrative approaches, the work of these two writers maintains a more complicated and murkier relationship than critics such as Rodríguez-Mangual would have it. The fact that Cabrera seeks to undermine Ortiz's positivist methodology by granting space to her informants does not automatically afford Afro-Cubans themselves more agency. Indeed, the voices of her informants operate within the carefully defined and maintained space of the text, just as the magic of Afro-Cuban religion operates in the carefully delineated space of "the bush" (whether that wilderness is situated in the Cuban countryside or in a Havana backyard). Despite the radical ceding of ethnographic authority to her informants, some of Cabrera's attitudes toward race are fundamentally conservative; her interest in the space of Afro-Cuban culture is shaped through (rather than in defiance of) an attitude of paternalism typical of white Cubans of her time and social class. *El Monte* is present within the national space as a separate site, one that carefully identifies and demarcates racial (and class) differences. Cabrera allows this sacred space its own magical and unexplained qualities precisely *because* racial and class differences keep it safely other. Rather than rejecting Ortiz's national paradigm, she approaches it another way—positing the existence of separate, individually coherent systems within the same national rubric. I do not believe that in doing this Cabrera is providing an alternative national model; she has simply found a way to acknowledge the integrity of Afro-Cuban culture without affirming it through white (or African) culture. Nor is Ortiz alone in describing the formation of Cuban society; Cabrera's work also has at its center a certain kind of national project, but her vision allows for the existence of a separate racialized cultural practice, rather than feeling a need to find a "safe" way to insert it into a single overarching understanding of Cubanness.

In *Los negros brujos*, but also in his later texts such as *Contrapunteo*, Ortiz sees his work, in a most basic sense, as an attempt to clarify the hidden and distinguishing elements of Afro-Cuban culture. Ortiz's first investigative effort is more rigidly ideological (and more racist) than his later work. At the same time, in the movement between a linear view of colonial history and a process-centered, melting-pot view of Cuban culture, Ortiz's failure to entirely control his narration in this early text also paradoxically offers more space for understanding cultural translation as an imperfect exercise. It is possible to view Ortiz's development of the term "transculturation" as an attempt to renegotiate his original failure to "translate" Afro-Cuban culture; once all the separate cultures are transculturated, fused into the big *ajiaco* that is Cuba, they are no longer safely separate, nor dangerously untranslatable.

The lesser degree of anxiety that Cabrera demonstrates about the location of Afro-Cuban culture within Cuban society gives her greater freedom to represent Afro-Cuban culture more fully within the text. Ortiz argues for a Cuba in which Afro-Cubans are recognized as having had an impact on the wider Cuban culture at a historical moment in which this was subject to wide debate. He emphatically presents both his text and himself as scholarly authorities. Privileging experience over intelligibility, on the other hand, Cabrera shows the reader the oral history of this culture almost in the process of being performed, demonstrating the coherence of the culture through the active nature of the narration and the presence of the voices of Santería practitioners, her informants. Taking the untranslatable nature of Afro-Cuban culture as a basic characteristic of the ethnographic enterprise, she paradoxically allows us access to aspects of Afro-Cuban culture that would otherwise be inaccessible. It could be argued, however, that Cabrera is able to center her narrative in this particularly Afro-Cuban space precisely because Ortiz's previous efforts to establish the importance of Afro-Cuban culture within a narrative of national formation give her the freedom to do so.

2

BEYOND BONGOS IN MONTMARTRE

Lydia Cabrera and Alejo Carpentier Imagine Blackness

"Tata Cuñengue, . . . simiente del Solar del Arará donde más de un nieto de capitanes generales fue a pedir que le confeccionaran un *embó* en tiempos de la colonia, vive ahora, con todo esplendor, en el mismo corazón de Montmartre" ("La Rue Fontaine" 295). [Papa Cuñengue, . . . founder of the Arará House where more than one captain general's grandson went to ask for a magical potion in the time of the colony, now lives, in complete splendor, in the heart of Montmartre.][1] So writes the young Alejo Carpentier, Cuban expatriate in Paris, in an article for the popular Cuban weekly *Carteles* in 1932. In exile from the dictatorship of General Gerardo Machado (1925–1933), Carpentier was a frequent correspondent for the Cuban magazine on the cultural and artistic tastes of the French capital. In this article, he discusses, with pleasure and some surprise, the French vogue for things Cuban, and more specifically, for things Afro-Cuban. (After all, few folk characters from Cuban music could be as Afro-Cuban as Tata Cuñengue, as a Santería-practicing descendent of the Arará people.) As Carpentier notes, once French women discover he is Cuban, their first request of him is, "Teach me to dance the *rrrumba*."[2] While the Afro-Cuban *rumba* was still considered an "indecent" dance in the Cuban capital, it was the height of fashion in France, to Carpentier's amused astonishment.

Less than a year after Carpentier's article declared that Cuban music had conquered the French capital, Jean Cassou, critic and editor of the Marseilles journal *Cahiers du Sud*, wrote to his friend Francis de Miomandre, the editor of the publishing house Gallimard, to thank him for two short stories he had sent him.[3] "Ces deux contes nègres sont délicieux," [These two black stories are delicious,] Cassou raved. "Non seulement la fantaisie la plus réjouissante y circule, mais encore, comme vous le dites, on y sent la présence d'une poésie primitive indiscutible." [Not just the most joyful and rounded fantasy, but also, as you say, one feels in them the presence of an inarguable primitive poetry.]⁴ The two stories were by a young Cuban student at the Sorbonne, Lydia Cabrera. Although Cabrera would go on to spend a good portion of her life researching and writing about Afro-Cuban culture, like Carpentier, she herself was not Afro-Cuban, and these were the first short stories she would publish. Three years later, de Miomandre would translate and publish a French edition of an entire collection of Cabrera's "black stories," entitled *Contes negres de Cuba* (*Afro-Cuban Tales*, 1936). Apparently, Cabrera's French readers shared Cassou's interest in her portrayal of black Cuban culture.

In the previous chapter, I show how writers such as Fernando Ortiz, dealing with the portrayal of black Cubans in the first decades of Cuba's existence as a nation, relied on the techniques of ethnographic narrative to frame blackness.⁵ Despite his connections to European social science, however, Ortiz was writing about black Cubans from Havana. In this chapter, I explore the relationship between Cuban textual constructions of blackness and the broader context of Western portrayals of race. In particular, I analyze the representation and the function of blackness in the work of Carpentier and Cabrera, both of whom developed as writers in the artistic environment of Paris in the 1920s and '30s. I argue that blackness created a locus through which these Cuban writers negotiated their mandate to build a national literature in the context of European neocolonial primitivizing of what was by necessity Cuban "folk" culture. From within the metropole, a space that provided both a liberating and a problematic distance, Carpentier and Cabrera write themselves out of this predicament through the different meanings they give to blackness in their texts, allowing it to signal a sense of Cuban difference (from Europe) and at the same time create a border between a general Cubanness and a black racial identity.

Primitives vs. Folk: Blackness in France, Blackness in Cuba

As Cuban expatriates in the Paris of the 1920s and '30s, Alejo Carpentier and Lydia Cabrera found themselves in an artistic and intellectual environment in which images of blackness were everywhere. This was not, of course, the first time that African imagery had appeared in the French capital. France's colonization of Africa and the slave trade in the Caribbean had initiated the circulation of African images (and black bodies); in the late nineteenth and early twentieth century an interest in things African was further sparked by the Universal Exhibitions, which put Africans on display for a European public, as well as by the arrival of American minstrelsy (blackface performance) and African American performers.[6] Yet from the end of World War I, writers and artists in Paris (and elsewhere) began increasingly to employ images of African and African-Diasporic culture in new and inventive ways. By 1925, France was in the full grip of *la vogue nègre*; music played by African American jazz musicians could be heard throughout the neighborhood of Montparnasse, and African American performer Josephine Baker's dance performance as the banana-skirted Fatou in *La Revue nègre* was the talk of the town. Art historian Petrine Archer Straw labels this fascination with things African "Negrophilia," a fetishization of blackness that began towards the end of the nineteenth century but in many ways reached its peak in the 1920s and '30s. As Archer Straw notes, the images of blackness produced by these movements were a more accurate representation of white Europeans' ideas of blackness (and race more broadly) than they were of actual black culture or of the experience of black people, whether in Europe or elsewhere (21). Indeed, artists and intellectuals were less interested in gaining an understanding of different African (or African American) cultures than they were in images of black people and the meanings that they themselves could fashion from those images.

European avant-gardes were drawn to things African in this post–World War I period precisely because they saw them as standing in contrast (or even in opposition) to European society. Thanks in large part to the history of European imperialism and the colonization of Africa and the Caribbean, African people—and thus, by extension, blackness itself—had come to be identified as "primitive." As Susanna Pavloska has observed, primitiveness is implicitly comparative, in that it identifies one culture or group of people as superior and another as providing a "baseline measure of primal innocence or primal wickedness" (xxviii). The "primitive" quality of blackness was precisely what drew European artists and writers to blackness. It offered not only the lure of the exotic, the other, but it contained a certain shock value in its symbolic rejection of the norms (visual, aesthetic, and, implicitly, social) of European society.[7] For many of these artists, blackness was attractive because it was constructed as different or transgressive (Archer Straw 11). They saw it as providing an antidote to the complacency and conformity that in their opinion were the ailments of modern society.

The literary and artistic renderings of blackness that appeared in the Paris of the 1920s and '30s—and the definition of blackness as primitive—owed a great deal to ethnographic methodologies. Ethnography, used as an imperial tool for cataloguing and categorizing colonized peoples, had been largely responsible for the creation of the idea of the primitive.[8] Ethnographic expeditions had helped to disseminate images of African culture, first through photographs and travel narratives, then through the exhibiting of Africans themselves in Universal Exhibitions (Smalls 351–53). In the hands of the avant-gardes, ethnographic techniques were put to new ends. While ethnographers sought to illuminate unfamiliar and radically different beliefs and social practices in order to assimilate them to Western rationality, the Surrealists explored the unknown or the not-yet-understood precisely to immerse themselves in the new, the strange, and the forbidden. James Clifford calls surrealism "ethnography's secret sharer," a companion discourse (through many of the literary explorations in which avant-garde writers were engaged) to ethnography's focus on the role of myths and the symbolic in "primitive" cultures (*Predicament of Culture* 121–22). One concrete expression of the relationship between ethnography and Surrealism was the journal *Documents*, an "ethnographic surrealist collaboration," to which Carpentier contributed a number of articles (Clifford, *Predicament of Culture*, 129; Birkenmaier, *Alejo Carpentier*, 55–57).[9] *Documents* juxtaposed ethnographic accounts with photographs of African people or African-inspired imagery, often produced by European artists. In the Surrealist approach employed by the journal, the ethnographic elements (both visual and textual), which often served not as descriptive explanation but as elements of collage, emphasized the violent, the disturbing, and the disjunctive rather than rendering these elements more comprehensible.[10]

Robert Desnos's short introduction to Carpentier's first published article in *Documents*, "La musique cubaine" (1929), provides an example of this construction of blackness as transgressive and exotic. Desnos, who had met Carpentier on a trip to Havana, was one of the young Cuban's closest friends in Paris. In contrast to Carpentier's scholarly overview of the African influences in Cuban music, Desnos's "preface" is an evocative rendering of his own experience in Cuba, listening to music and watching dancers on the beach. He speaks of the "belle nègresses" (beautiful negresses) and "l'odeur des ténèbres" (the smell of shadows), and sighs, "Je n'oublierai jamais ces musiciens noirs que je devais revoir, débardeurs le jour, sur le port, et, la nuit, dansers magnifiques et obscènes" (324). [I will never forget the black musicians that I would see, stevedores during the day at the port, and at night, magnificent and obscene dancers.] For Desnos, the perceived freedom of these black bodies both highlights and provides a contrast to the restraints of bourgeois European society. His description renders blackness fully other, and connects it to both uninhibited sensuality and the exotic.

Yet even as European writers and artists such as Desnos were engaged in reading blackness as aestheticized and exoticized, African, Afro-Caribbean, and African American writers were exploring the representation of a black literary subjectivity from within the same city. As Brent Hayes Edwards, Jody Blake, Edward Said, and others have shown, Paris during the interwar years was an important site for the development of the discourses of black internationalism, as it allowed for meeting between black artists, writers, and performers from the United States, Africa, and the Caribbean. As Edwards puts it, the French capital "provided a special sort of vibrant, cosmopolitan space for interaction that was available neither in the United States nor in the colonies" (4). These encounters allowed black intellectuals to engage in conversations about race and racial identity that crossed geographic, national, and even linguistic boundaries. Despite the fact that French colonialism had contributed to the repression of African and Afro-Caribbean peoples, the French capital ironically served as the stage for a number of literary gestures of racial solidarity. In 1930, for example, a group of Caribbean students in Paris, including Martinican writers René Menil, Etienne Léro, and Maurice-Sabas Quitmas, published an anticolonialist manifesto entitled "Légitime défense." Identifying themselves (and their target audience) as "young French Caribbeans," and "children of the black bourgeoisie," they propose the use of Surrealist attitudes and techniques to combat the repressive nature of both French and French-colonial social systems.[11] Similarly, Martinican writer Aimé Césaire published his long poem *Cahier d'un retour au pays natal* (*Notebook of a Return to the Native Land*, 1945), in which he introduces his concept of Négritude, an anticolonial black subjectivity, in the Paris journal *Volontés* in 1939. In an autobiographical gesture, the poem features a poetic speaker who achieves a radically reborn racialized consciousness in part as a result of his experiences as an Afro-Caribbean in France.

Carpentier and Cabrera were thus only two of the numerous writers and artists from Latin America and the Caribbean who were caught up in the excitement of artistic rebellion and renovation in the French capital, and the Paris of the 1920s and '30s became a kind of intellectual incubator for them, thanks to these international crosscurrents.[12] As white Cubans representing blackness for both Cuban and European audiences, both Cabrera and Carpentier drew on ethnographic material in their textual construction of blackness, as ethnographic research was to some extent a basis for their knowledge of Afro-Cuban culture.[13] The understanding of Afro-Cuban practices that they gained through personal fieldwork experiences is given new meaning and significance through the ways in which each writer interpolates these actual encounters with black Cubans to represent and re-create blackness within their texts. As I show in the previous chapter, Fernando Ortiz, faced with the need to describe and portray black Cubans, employs a series of ethnographic narrative techniques in his early ethnography *Hampa afrocubana: Los negros brujos* (1906) that temporally displace these bodies from the space of the nation. Carpentier and Cabrera, in creating literary representations of Cuban blackness, had greater freedom to employ their ethnographic knowledge and material to different aesthetic or symbolic ends. In this way both writers explore the deeper potential meanings of ethnographic allegory, yet they do so within texts that are not, strictly speaking, ethnographies.

Carpentier, son of a French father and a Russian mother, was active as a journalist and in avant-garde literary circles in Cuba prior to his arrival in France.[14] He was a member of the Grupo Minorista, and contributed to their *Revista de Avance*, the first of a number of avant-garde journals to emerge from Havana (Kapcia 78).[15] In 1927, when he was just twenty-three, Carpentier signed the "Declaración del Grupo Minorista," an avant-garde manifesto that was also an attack on then-dictator Gerardo Machado, and was briefly imprisoned (García-Carranza 52). When he was freed, Robert Desnos encouraged him to go into exile in France. The young Cuban writer arrived in Paris in 1928, where thanks to his friendship with Desnos he became affiliated with the Surrealist movement just as it was beginning to fracture (Birkenmaier, *Alejo Carpentier*, 25). When André Breton publicly expelled Desnos from the Surrealist group in 1929, Carpentier was one of the signers of the public "letter" *Un corps* (*A Body*), written by dissenting members of the Surrealist group as an indictment of Breton (Wilson 69). Carpentier was thus never an official member of the Surrealist group, but throughout his eleven years in Paris he contributed to the French Surrealist journals *Bifur* and *Documents*, in addition to his Spanish-language journalism and collaborative ballet and theatre projects.[16]

Lydia Cabrera, daughter of the writer and journalist Raimundo Cabrera, had been writing in an "unofficial" capacity since she was fourteen, when she became the anonymous society columnist—"Nena en sociedad" (Baby in Society)—for her father's newspaper, *Cuba y América* (Castellanos, "Introducción" 18–24). However, she did not go to France explicitly to become a writer; she was also interested in painting, and had had some small success exhibiting her work in Havana (Castellanos, "Introducción" 25). Shortly after her arrival in Paris in 1927, she enrolled in an art history course at the Sorbonne, and her first connections to Surrealism came largely through her friendship with the Cuban painter Amelia Peláez (Hiriart, *Más cerca* 121–22).[17] She began to write her "black Cuban stories" to entertain her companion, the Venezuelan writer Teresa de la Parra, who was suffering from tuberculosis and spent long periods of time in sanatoriums in Switzerland and Spain.[18] Encouraged by de la Parra and then de Miomandre, Cabrera finally began to publish short stories in French literary journals. The success of the French version *Contes negres de Cuba* (*Afro-Cuban Tales*) in 1936 led to the publication of a Spanish-language edition (called *Cuentos negros de Cuba*) in Havana in 1940.

Despite the creative fecundity of this period, Carpentier, in a later reflection on the prevailing mood of the time, highlights the discursive and ideological constraints under which he, like many Latin American intellectuals, found himself in the 1920s: "Había, pues, que ser <<nacionalista>>, tratandose, a la vez, de ser <<vanguardista>>. *That's the question.* Propósito difícil, puesto que todo nacionalismo descansa en el culto a una tradición y el <<vanguardismo>> significaba, por fuerza, una ruptura con la tradición" ("Prólogo a *Écue-Yamba-Ó*" 26). [One had, then, to be "nationalist," trying, at the same time, to be "avant-garde." *That's the question.* A difficult task, given that all nationalism rests on a cult of tradition and the "avant-garde" meant, in essence, a rupture with tradition."] Carpentier is expressing what Carlos Alonso has diagnosed as the "contradictory rhetorical situation" of Spanish American letters: the desire to both affirm Latin American writing as modern while simultaneously confirming Latin America's uniqueness (and thus distance from modernity).[19] Both European and Latin American writers wanted to turn away from the recent past and thus to ally themselves with the modern. Yet while European writers, in the wake of a devastating war, rejected the new conventions of the modern, industrialized society that had led Europe into war in the first place, Latin American writers were anxious to distance their home nations from their colonial past and thus to ally themselves with the modern. Their views on the new trends in literary and artistic creation were conditioned by their particular circumstances as (post) colonial subjects, and by their own national (or colonial) contexts. Carpentier fails to observe here that the tension he identifies was in part due to the fact that "tradition," from a Cuban perspective, was in itself a contemporary fabrication, as he and his fellow writers were at that moment engaged in trying to create a narrative of Cuban "tradition," in deciding what that narrative would be. If European writers, in reaching for the "primitive," were turning away from nineteenth-century constructions of the "folk" (in its German Romantic construction), Latin American writers were in search of their own versions of the "folk"—elements of popular culture that could both be identified as "authentic" (tied to some construction of national "origins") and assimilated into more elite cultural artistic forms.

In this meeting of national interests and avant-garde aesthetics, race—in particular, the use and presentation of blackness—was, in fact, a notable area of tension. Latin American writers in Paris thus found themselves caught between the French fascination for things African (which included the African Diaspora in the Americas) and a need to mediate this desire with regard to their national contexts and national publics. Most Latin American nations had mixed-race populations, which—depending on the country—included both indigenous populations and people of African origin; blackness was therefore not foreign but part of the national panorama and the national history. If Afro–Latin Americans were viewed as other, they were not exotically distant others but rather others within the boundaries of the nation. The characterization of blackness as "primitive" was thus highly problematic from a Latin American perspective. Africa offered European writers an escape from bourgeois convention; in identifying African culture in Latin America with "barbarism," Latin American writers risked identifying Latin American nations themselves as uncivilized or pre-modern.

For the young Carpentier, Afro-Cuban culture seemed to offer a way to navigate between "tradition" and "innovation," between the desire to make it new and the need to not ignore (or obliterate) Cuba's history or contemporary situation. Both he and Cabrera made strong use of Afro-Cuban elements in the texts they wrote and published while in France. Yet in their portrayal of Afro-Cuban characters and the incorporation of elements of Afro-Cuban religion and popular culture in their texts, Cabrera and Carpentier found themselves in the challenging position of writing for two different reading publics; despite some similarities in taste, the cultural demands of the educated Cuban public were in some ways strikingly different from the interests of their Parisian (Francophone, European) counterparts.

As Desnos's vignette and Cassou's response to Cabrera's stories reveal, French audiences tended to conflate Cuban and African representations into one exotic panorama. Blake observes that Europeans were often unconscious of the ways in which musical performances by African American or Caribbean artists were mediated by modern, transnational circumstances: "The French were more than ready to believe that these modern idioms were not only the next best thing to the 'jungle tam-tam,' they were also equivalent to 'savage fetishes'" (5). As Carpentier's article for *Carteles* illustrates, Cuban music was in fashion in the French capital, and music and movement were two of the principal elements through which avant-garde artists recognized and celebrated the primitive aspects of blackness.[20] For French readers, accustomed to viewing Cuban culture through this lens, stories and plays about black Cubans seemed exotic, in line with the general vogue of things African.

Cuban readers, even upper-class white Cuban readers (as many were), held different ideas; while they may have been unfamiliar with the specifics of Afro-Cuban religious practice, they knew black Cubans, as they shared both public and domestic space with them. Cuban elites and the middle class (both white *and* black) tended to distrust any cultural practice seen as being "too" African, precisely because the prevailing view was that African-derived practices were savage and barbaric.[21] As Robin Moore has shown, Afro-Cuban musical forms and rhythms—once deemed lewd, dangerous, or socially unacceptable—were only gradually being incorporated into popular, mainstream Cuban music. Afro-Cuban carnival bands, or *comparsas*, were prohibited from public performance in 1913, a ban that was not officially lifted until 1937.[22] Afro-Cuban *son* music fared better; it eventually became an acceptable form of popular music, mediating "stylistically and ideologically between the cultural practices of working-class Afrocubans and the white and black middle classes" (Moore, *Nationalizing*

Blackness 88). Yet many Afro-Cuban religious practices were in fact not legalized until well into the 1930s.[23] The suppression of these practices by Cuban authorities and the negative associations they often produced in their middle- and upper-class readers meant that tying blackness so directly to Cubanness was potentially problematic for a Cuban readership.

The texts by Carpentier and Cabrera that I explore in this chapter resolve this conflict between the European taste for blackness as exotica and the Cuban ambivalence of identifying blackness as Cuban by making blackness function as something more than simply a demarcation of phenotypical—or even cultural—difference. Stuart Hall and Michelle Stephens have both referred to "black" as a "floating signifier," in that blackness comes/has come to mean something in different cultural contexts. Hall has argued that black popular culture is a "contradictory space," and a "site of strategic contestation" ("What Is This Black" 107). I argue that Cabrera and (in particular) Carpentier take the function of blackness further, employing it as a figure of symbolic oppositionality, symptomatic simultaneously of "otherness" and of "authentic" Cubanness. This use of "black" is more akin to what Erin Graff Zivin, in her study of the figure of the Jew in Latin American literature, has identified as a "wandering signifier." Not only do Carpentier and Cabrera use race in these texts to gesture to other kinds of issues, but like the figure of the Jew that Graff Zivin analyzes, blackness as signifier "exhibits the particular ability to embody contradiction" (4). The strategic use of blackness in their texts can simultaneously communicate primitive transgression and trace the contours of a national sense of belonging.

In Carpentier's work, blackness comes to be synonymous with ideas of the primitive in both its positive and negative connotations. His early texts—in particular, his novel *Écue-Yamba-Ó*, on which I focus my analysis—use an ethnographic perspective to characterize Cuba as "primitive" in an avant-garde sense; that is, primitivism (expressed through blackness) stands in as symbolic of both exotic otherness and a rejection of Western social norms, even as it also identifies as authentic certain Cuban elements that counter foreign threats to the national space. Ethnographic narrative distance, the use of allegorical metaphors connecting blackness with nation, and an emphasis on performative elements associated with Afro-Cuban culture all become means to construct blackness as symbolic. I argue that a similar (racialized) national anxiety is present but displaced in Carpentier's later novel *El reino de este mundo* (*The Kingdom of This World*, 1949). In this novel, blackness becomes an aestheticized marker for the exotic other through the displacement of these anxieties onto the landscape of the Haitian Revolution.

While in Carpentier's texts blackness is symbolic of radical difference (even as this otherness is also paradoxically read as Cuban), Cabrera situates her narrative voice firmly within an Afro-Cuban community, making blackness a marker not of difference but of inclusion and belonging. In Cabrera's tales, blackness is implicitly designated as the site from which enunciation takes place. In this way, Afro-Cuban culture—while still potentially "exotic" from the perspective of her white readers—is rendered neither exceptional nor transgressive; instead, it is contained within a specifically bounded cultural space and limited by other kinds of social hierarchies. While Cabrera locates blackness in the realm of the "folk," her emphasis on class structures—and other kinds of social boundaries—ensure that this racialized stratum of the popular is never confused with Cuban society as a whole.

Afro-Cuban Pastoral: *Écue-Yamba-Ó*

Carpentier's first novel, *Écue-Yamba-Ó* (an Afro-Cuban phrase meaning *Hallelujah*), was begun in Havana in 1927 while Carpentier was in prison and completed in Paris in 1933 (Barreda-Tomás 34, Carpentier, "Prólogo a *Écue-Yamba-Ó*" 24–25). Carpentier in later years largely disavowed his first novel, deriding it as a "cosa novata, pintoresca, sin profundidad—escalas y arpegios de estudiante" (26) [a novice thing, picturesque, without depth—a student's scales and arpeggios]. Caught between the desire to portray (and define) an essential "Cubanness" while still proving himself to be avant-garde, Carpentier identifies his early novel as a "hybrid" product: a text set in Cuba, dealing with a particularly Cuban subject matter, yet written in a language whose style and treatment of race owe a great deal to European Surrealism (26). This stylistic tension, according to Roberto González Echevarría, was to remain unresolved for Carpentier, as similar questions (reformulated differently) surface in later works such as *El reino de este mundo* (Alejandro Carpentier, 67). Yet as Elzbieta Sklodowska notes, *Écue-Yamba-Ó* is more than a failed experiment (*Espectros* 91); in it, Carpentier lays out, rather than resolves, the problematics of his interest in the relationship between the local and the transnational (and the role of race in connecting these spheres). While his text reveals its "hybridity" in its structural elements and choice of setting, this is also equally—if not more—apparent in the novel's ambivalent treatment of race, which celebrates blackness as primitive, particularly the primitive understood as oppositional and transgressive. In this capacity, blackness becomes a tool that allows Carpentier to wed the demands of reimagining national culture to his avant-garde project.

Constructed as a kind of bildungsroman, *Écue-Yamba-Ó* recounts the life of Menegildo Cué, a young Afro-Cuban man who is born and reared on the outskirts of a North American–owned sugar plantation. The novel chronicles his coming of age (both spiritual and physical), his forays into love and violent competition over a woman, his eventual migration to the city, his initiation into the *ñáñigo* (Abakuá) religion, and finally his death in Havana at the hands of a rival *ñáñigo* group.[24] Despite the very Cuban (and, in fact, Afro-Cuban) locus of the story, Carpentier sets his story within a broader frame, showing the ways in which Menegildo—and through him, Cuba—is affected by social and political changes occurring not only in the nation but also internationally. The novel is conceived as a series of vignettes that, while they loosely follow Menegildo's development, continue to mark Cuban blackness as a site of authenticity, particularly in its connection to the land and through manifestations of Afro-Cuban popular culture.

The Sugar Mill: Blackness as Commodity

Menegildo is born to Usebio and Salomé Cué, a poor black couple who have a small farm just outside the grounds of the sugar mill "Central San Lucío." Usebio's grandfather Juan Mandinga was a "negro de nación," an African-born slave (as indicated by his last name, a Cuban term for Africans from the Calabar region), and Usebio's father Luis still vividly remembers his experiences under slavery. Usebio is portrayed as intimately connected to the land; there is nothing he does not know about sugar cane, as he has spent his whole life farming these fields. Yet both his livelihood and his way of life are threatened—not by changes brought about by other Cubans but by foreign outsiders, for a North American company now owns the sugar mill. When the novel begins, Usebio is just managing to scrape by, harvesting his own cane and selling it to the large company. As the "Yankees" begin to push out all other competition, he is forced to sell his land, and becomes a driver, using his cart and oxen to transport sugar cane that is not his.

From its first chapters, the novel identifies the sugar mill as the enemy, a symbol of North American economic domination. Cuban sugar, described at one point as the "blood" of the sugar cane, will ultimately be exported, and "engordará vacas americanas" (36) [will make American cows fat]. Mill life is governed by the demands of the market, and operates according to the rhythm of machines, not men. The text's hyperbolic language personifies the mill as a monster, into whose metallic innards innumerable tons of sugar cane are poured: "La fábrica ronca, fuma, estertora, chifla. La vida se organiza de acuerdo con sus voluntades" (21). [The factory snores, smokes, sighs, whistles. Life organizes itself according to its wishes.] The demands of this "diabetic giant" have engendered brutal working conditions, but they have also created a truly international community, bringing together Spanish, Chinese, Jamaican, and Haitian workers. While the Central San Lucío is not precisely an urban environment, the patterns of transnational labor have created a raucous polyphony of cultural encounters in the midst of the exploitation of the sugar mill.

Carpentier places the rural life of the Cués in contrast to the crude cosmopolitanism of the North American company compound. Engaged in a way of life strikingly similar to that of their grandparents (even in this postslavery era), the Cués are separated from the space of modern industry; they are black, rural, and poor, outsiders with respect to the multi-cultural environment of the North American sugar mill, and to both the local and international economies to which it is connected. Yet while the Cués may be marginalized, they are Cuban. Carpentier does not glorify the Cués' poverty nor their lack of access to the modern economy of the mill, but he implies that their very marginalization has paradoxically prevented them being swept up in the system of foreign neocolonial domination, allowing them to retain a cultural integrity: "Sólo los negros, Menegildo, Longina, Salomé y su prole conservaban celosamente un carácter y una tradición antillana. ¡El bongó, antídoto de Wall Street!" (115). [Only the blacks, Menegildo, Longina, Salomé and their children jealously preserved an Antillean tradition and character. The bongo, antidote to Wall Street!] Much as avant-garde movements looked to primitivism's anti-bourgeois sensibilities as a way to counteract what they saw as the rigidity of the European social order, the bongo drum, symbol par excellence of African music, is shown as antithetical to the capitalist drive for economic profit represented by Wall Street. By identifying Menegildo and his family as black at the beginning of this declaration, the text traces a direct connection between blackness and the primitive drum rhythms. Positioning the Cués' blackness as antimodern, Carpentier gives it an oppositional quality similar to the role that blackness played for the European avant-gardes. Jossianna Arroyo observes that even Cué's name—a derivation of the Efik term *ecué* (sacred son of the palm)—suggests a kind of African authenticity, connecting the family origins to one of the Santería religion's sacred trees (109). In this symbolic placement, blackness also functions as a commodity—an antidote to threats of foreignness in its position as nonmodern.

Afro-Cuban music (and, through it, blackness) is shown as not just (nationally) authentic, but is revealed as the particular cultural capital that counteracts North American capitalist degradation. One early chapter, "Ritmos" (Rhythms), describes in detail an exaggeratedly polyphonic party at the sugar mill, where the music is explicitly racialized: "A media legua de las chimineas azucareras, esa música emergía de edades remotas, preñadas de intuiciones y de misterio. Los instrumentos casi animales y las letanías negras se acoplaban bajo el signo de una selva invisible" (47–8). [Half a league from the mill's chimneys, that music emerged from remote ages, pregnant with intuition and mystery. The almost animal instruments and the black litanies came together under the sign of an invisible forest.] In this description sound defines space; the music conjures up a kind of temporary "invisible forest," which ties blackness again to the Cuban landscape and to a mythic sense of time, placing this arcadian vision as a counterweight to the sugar mill's threatening background presence.

Initiations: Religious Ritual

Thus Carpentier locates the source of the Cués' authenticity in music and religion. As Arroyo and González Echevarría both have noted, the novel not only carries a title with religious connotations, but is also structured along religious lines.[25] Menegildo's coming into maturity, in particular, is marked by religious events: an initiation into Santería (*Regla de Ochá*), a later initiation into the Abakuá (*ñáñigo*) tradition. Even his first foray into love is marked by its religious connection, as he seeks a love spell from the Afro-Cuban priestess. (The chapters are helpfully titled "Initiation(s)" I, II, and III.) The Cués are practitioners of Santería, and although it is never named as such, the religious instruction Menegildo receives during his childhood and adolescence gives Carpentier the opportunity to describe this religious worldview to the reader: "Las criaturas vivían engañadas por un cúmulo de apariencias groseras, bajo la mirada compasiva de entidades superiores. ¡O Yemayá, Shangó y Obatalá, espíritus de infinita perfección!" (66). [People lived in a constant state of being deceived by gross appearances, under the compassionate gaze of superior beings. Oh, Yemayá, Shangó and Obatalá, spirits of infinite perfection!] The scenes in which Menegildo or other family members participate in ritual offerings to the *orichas* represent these ceremonies typographically in the text in a poetic structure, replicating the call and response of the priest and the other participants.

Birkenmaier argues that Carpentier's main intention in *Écue-Yamba-Ó* is to produce an ethnographic study of Afro-Cuban culture in narrative form (*Alejo Carpentier* 59). Certainly, the text does provide evocative descriptions of the spectacles of Afro-Cuban culture—both social gatherings and religious ceremonies. Yet *Écue-Yamba-Ó* is an ethnographic study only if we understand ethnography as operating as something more than a methodology that aims to describe and explain cultural practices, rendering the unknown comprehensible. Carpentier employs ethnographic description in his text in a Surrealist sense—not as a process of documenting to understand, but rather as a means for emphasizing the strange and the disquieting. While the novel provides detailed descriptions of the Cués' altar and of certain rituals, it refrains from explicating these religious practices. By contrasting the Cués' activities with the modern secular economy of the sugar mill and the behavior of the Yankee mill employees and other mill workers, these Afro-Cuban religious performances seem exotic and mysterious.

The Photographs: *Documents* in novel form

Contrasting with the descriptions of these religious beliefs and practices are the unusual photographs that accompany the text. Most of these photos appear to be ethnographic in nature, as they feature religious altars or groupings of statues. Someone familiar with Santería and other

Afro-Cuban religions will recognize many of these figures as *orichas*: Babalú-Ayé (Menegildo's guardian *oricha*, and Saint Lazarus in the Catholic pantheon); La Virgen de la Caridad del Cobre (Our Lady of Charity El Cobre, the Catholic representation of the *oricha* Ochún), and would also recognize the accompanying artifacts—bracelets, hatchets, etc.—as symbols connected to these deities. Yet there is no written description to accompany the images, nor do they seem to correspond in any direct way to the Cués' religious rituals described at the point of their inclusion in the text. As such, as Birkenmaier observes, the photographs "exhiben características surrealistas difíciles de pasar por alto" (*Alejo Carpentier* 65) [exhibit surreal characteristics that are difficult to ignore]. In fact, despite the confusing nature of these images for someone not familiar with Afro-Cuban religious traditions, their presence seems to pull the reader back from the fictional environment that Carpentier's written text constructs.

Carpentier's use of ethnographic elements is reminiscent of the techniques employed in the journal *Documents*: his juxtaposition of (seemingly) unrelated visual and textual elements and his emphasis on the performative often renders his descriptions of rituals or practices more surreal or mysterious than culturally comprehensible. When Menegildo receives his religious education from the priest Beruá, the text gives us a list of the priest's religious "talents" (practices): "El gallo negro que picotea una mazorca de maíz ignora que su cabeza, cortada por noche de luna y colocada sobre determinado número de granos sacados de su buche, puede reorganizar las realidades del universo. Un muñeco de madera, bautizado con el nombre de Menegildo, se vuelve el *amo* de su doble viviente" (66). [The black cock pecking at a grain of corn is unaware that his head, cut off by moonlight and placed upon a determined number of grains plucked from his beak, can reorganize the realities of the universe. A wooden doll, baptized with Menegildo's name, becomes the master of its living double.] While this description intimates the method of the ritual—the black cock will be killed—it does not explain *how* the cock's death can alter reality, nor does it fit this sacrifice into the broader context. This lack of explanation preserves the Cués' experience of the world as governed by powerful and unknowable forces. The ritual is thus portrayed as a brief, violent, and ultimately mysterious textual snapshot; but it is not connected with any of the photographs accompanying the text.

Boundaries of Blackness: The Haitians

In the case of the Cués, a gift for rhythm, physical sensuality, and a sense of the religious as spectacle are characteristics which, while referencing the primitive, also serve to demarcate their blackness as authenticity. Placed in this national context, blackness serves as a counterweight against the forces of foreign domination, but it is only identified as positive in the novel's black *Cuban* characters. Carpentier's text establishes a particularly striking contrast between its portrayal of the Afro-Cuban Cués and the Haitians who appear in the novel, in whom similar behaviors and practices are presented as excessive, extreme, and dangerous. In the first significant mention of Haitian workers in the text, they are described as "a new plague": "[E]scuadrones de haitianos harapientos, que surgían del horizonte lejano trayendo sus hembras y gallos de pelea, dirigidos por algún condotiero negro con sombrero de guano y machete al cinto" (34). [Squadrons of ragged Haitians, who appeared over the far horizon, bringing with them their females and their fighting cocks, directed by some black conductor with a guano hat and a machete at his waist.] This first description emphasizes the extreme poverty of these workers, and significantly uses the slightly more animalistic "hembras" (females) to refer to Haitian women, rather than the customary "mujeres" (women).[26] A negative opinion of Haitians is also expressed by the novel's characters: when Menegildo falls in love with Longina, a woman from Guantánamo, the text is quick to clarify that "Él nunca habría sido capaz de enamorarse de una haitiana" (82) [He would never have been capable of falling in love with a Haitian woman], although neither Menegildo nor the narrative voice clarify precisely why this is so.

While the novel's Cuban and Haitian characters share similar cultural practices with regard to music and religion, the text codes the Haitian variants as more dangerous or inexplicable. In one particularly notable scene, Usebio, searching for a place to shelter his family after a hurricane has wrecked the area, stumbles upon a group of Haitians who are clearly in the middle of a religious ceremony. Rather than experiencing a sense of recognition, what he sees shocks and horrifies him: "En el fondo del barracón había una suerte de altar, alumbrado con velas, que sostenía un cráneo en cuya boca relucían tres dientes de oro ... En el centro, una estatuilla con cabellera de clavos, que sostenía una larga vara de metal. Un rosario de muelas... Tambores y botellas... Y un grupo de haitianos con ojos malos" (54–55). [At the back of the *barracón* was a kind of altar, lit by candles, on which rested a skull in whose mouth shone three golden teeth... In the center, a small statue with a headdress of nails, holding a long metal bar. A rosary of molars... Drums and bottles... And a group of Haitians with evil eyes.] The altar is crowded with human bones and teeth, symbols of cannibalesque violence, and the text's gaze draws the reader from these suggestive remains to the Haitians' malevolent stares. If the Cués' religious spectacles emphasize Afro-Antillean mythic rhythms, the Haitian altar is an incarnation of the dangers of primitive excess, the European nightmare vision of Africa, the dark side of instinct and the irrational. Usebio runs from the scene, screaming "¡Lo' muelto! ¡Lo' muelto!" (27) [The dead! The dead!]. Menegildo's family may practice Santería, may consult healers who cast spells, but they do not call on the spirits of the dead or use human bones in their rituals.

Birkenmaier, citing an article that Carpentier wrote for the French journal *Bifur* ("Lettre des Antilles," 1929), notes that the texts' anti-Haitian sentiments reflect Carpentier's own opinions at the time. She argues that his negative portrayals of non-Cuban blacks had to do with the fierce competition for jobs in Cuba, thanks (as *Écue-Yamba-Ó* shows) to the importation of Haitian and Jamaican workers by U.S. companies (*Alejo Carpentier* 64). Yet as we have seen, the Haitians in the text are more than mere threats to Cuban labor; the concrete material circumstances that might lead to discord between Haitian and Cuban workers are masked in questions of national and cultural identity. Exploring this connection, Sklodowska argues that Haitians in the novel are perceived as dangerous to Cuban society both because of their blackness and because of their history (the slave uprising that became the Haitian Revolution) (*Espectros*, 93). Certainly, Haitians in *Écue-Yamba-Ó* represent the primitive incarnated as the total other, in which blackness comes to be associated with the animalistic, the unknowable, the dangerous, the out of control. In the meeting of violent history and racialized otherness, they thus provide a perfect negative pole against which to position Cuban blackness. By identifying these elements of Haitian blackness as "the dangerous primitive," Carpentier can situate Cuban blackness as moderate—"less" primitive, "less" exotic.

The Dangers of Blackness: Menegildo

The tensions and contradictions in *Écue-Yamba-Ó*'s contrasting portrayals of blackness are particularly visible in Carpentier's treatment of his protagonist. Menegildo, born into a space already identified as "not-modern," is presented as a kind of exemplary "primitive" individual, in that his actions are motivated almost exclusively by innate desires and drives. As a toddler, he is left largely unsupervised, free to explore his family's hut through his own five senses. Denied a formal education, he is kept out of school to help Usebio haul sugar cane. By the time he reaches adolescence, he has thus become a being operating primarily on instinct rather than intellect, uneducated, yet physically and musically dexterous: "Era cierto que Menegildo no sabía leer, ignorando hasta el arte de firmar con una cruz. Pero en cambio era ya doctor en gestos y cadencias. El sentido del ritmo latía con la sangre" (36). [It was true that Menegildo didn't know how to read, ignorant as he was even of the art of signing with an 'x.' But he was already an expert at gestures and cadences. A sense of rhythm beat in his blood.] Menegildo reveals a similarly innate connection to the elements of Afro-Cuban religion. When as a crawling toddler he first encounters his mother's altar, he is instinctively drawn to what he sees as a "teatro mágico" (magical theatre). The description indicates that even as a small child, Menegildo understands something of religious ritual as a kind of performance, for he recognizes the altar as a place where this symbolic drama occurs. He is both drawn to the altar's marvelousness, and instinctively respectful of its power. In this way, spirituality and religious practice are tied to the realm of the instinctual, rather than the intellectual or rational arena.

Carpentier's text seems torn between presenting Menegildo as a representative of primitive blackness and bringing us into Menegildo's individual mind, between using Menegildo as an archetype and creating a unique human subject. The text occasionally describes his emotions at a certain moment, allowing for a glimpse of Menegildo's complex understanding of his situation. When as an adolescent Menegildo first approaches the sugar mill on New Year's Eve, he exhibits the anxiety of a young man who has little knowledge of the world, who is conscious of his own innocence and lack of experience and sophistication. In contrast, many of Menegildo's actions are presented as animalistic behaviors in which he displays little awareness or restraint.

Menegildo's conflict with the Haitian Napolión points explicitly to the novel's difficulty in controlling the border separating novel's two versions of blackness (Cuban and Haitian) and the intersections of blackness, masculinity, and paternity. Described as malicious and abusive, Napolión is married to Longina, a Cuban woman with whom Menegildo falls in love. The two men become rivals for Longina's affections, and Menegildo's dangerously unbridled passion for Longina almost gets him killed. Suspecting (rightly) that Menegildo is romancing his wife, Napolión attacks Menegildo from behind one night, beating him badly. Menegildo, feeling that he must retaliate, kills Napolión, an action that lands him in jail in Havana. While Menegildo's own passions are largely shown in a positive light throughout the text, particularly where music and spirituality are concerned, when he attacks Napolión, the division the text has carefully established between Afro-Cubans and other blacks begins to unravel. Menegildo's attack might be understood as both a preemptive strike in self-defense and an attempt to recover his honor or save face. Certainly, the encounter adds substance to his declaration, "Macho 'e sido siempre" (111). [I've always been macho.] Yet his stabbing of the Haitian is in fact more violent than Napolión's initial attack, and Menegildo also clearly derives pleasure from the violence itself: "Ahora iba dando saltos, sin sentir cansancio . . . Estaba furioso, estaba alegre" (122). [Now he was jumping, without feeling tired . . . He was furious, he was happy.] While Menegildo's violent act could be seen as an attempt to "control" Haitian violence, in the end it goes far beyond Napolión's in intensity and execution, revealing a side of Menegildo that neither he nor we have previously seen.

Criminality and Social Control

If Menegildo's violence (and his own reaction to it) resemble that of his Haitian nemesis, what most significantly differentiates his stabbing of Napolión from Napolión's own attack is the swift way in which the law steps in to control this violence. For Menegildo does not get away with Napolión's murder; he is arrested and sent to prison in Havana. The law thus steps in to control this transgression, making Menegildo visible in the eyes of the state. Ironically, his violent act allows him to see parts of

Cuba that were previously unavailable to him; his removal to a Havana jail thrusts him into the modern urban environment: "Menegildo estaba maravillado por la cantidad de blancos elegantes, de automóviles, de caballitos con la cola trenzada. . . ."(124). [Menegildo was amazed by the large number of elegant white people, of automobiles, of horses with braided tails.] His crime also makes him visible in the eyes of the law (and implicitly the state) as he was not as a marginalized peasant. The "anthropometric examination" that is made of him when he enters the jail makes his physical body visible (and thus places it under official control) as it had not been previously: "Cada cicatriz, cada matadura de su cuerpo fue localizada sin demora. Su retrato, en pies y pulgadas, capacidad craneana y enumeración de muelas cariadas, quedó trazado con pasmosa exactitud" (126). [Every scar, every mark on his body was located without delay. His portrait, in feet and inches, cranial capacity and the enumeration of decayed molars, was drawn with stunning exactitude.] In this "portrait" of Menegildo, Carpentier documents anthropology operating on its most reductive levels. While the description may have been (and probably was) based on actual criminological practices in use during the first decades of the Cuban Republic, it also harkens back to anthropological documentation of "primitive" peoples, connecting Menegildo to other images of native peoples as colonized subjects, and further identifying him as a transgressive element to be controlled.[27] This use of ethnography runs counter to the ways in which Carpentier displays a mixing of the ethnographic and the surreal earlier in the novel with the photographs and descriptions of religious rituals. Those earlier juxtapositions render Afro-Cuban religion strange and exotic, but they open up the space of the text. As Menegildo's anatomy is documented, both Menegildo as subject and the reader (as voyeur) are controlled.

The Closing of the Circle

The novel's cyclical structure further problematizes the text's ambivalent treatment of Menegildo. *Écue-Yamba-Ó* might be read as a chronicle of Menegildo's "modernization" (and maturation), accomplished in successive steps: he attains physical maturity, religious understanding, and finally a knowledge of the world outside his rural home as he journeys to the city (and is finally released into the city after just a short time in jail). Yet his contact with the urban world of Havana also marks his further encounter with Afro-Cuban religion, in an ambivalent manner, when Menegildo is initiated into the *ñáñigo* religion. On the one hand, this religious initiation marks a further stage in his maturation; he is formally accepted into a community and given greater responsibility. This could be seen as an intimate encounter with the "essence" of Afro-Cuban culture, his last phase of coming into manhood; but it also sets in motion the cycle of violent rivalry that will end with his death at the hands of a rival *ñáñigo* group. By this point, the chaos reflected in the novel is only visible at the level of the lumpen proletariat represented by the *solar* that Menegildo and Longina inhabit, and in the violent battles between the rival *ñáñigo* sects.[28]

Following Menegildo's death, Longina returns to the country and joins the Cué family in their compound, where she gives birth to Menegildo's son. Arroyo suggests that the crisis in which Menegildo's family finds itself is meant to reflect Cuba's own state of crisis under the Machado dictatorship (107). Yet by condemning Menegildo's wife and child to return to the country, Carpentier denies his black characters (and, by implication, their culture) the possibility of positive change. Menegildo's son (who bears his father's name) will be raised in the Cués' home, the site of authenticity, but this authenticity comes at the price of a certain stasis. González Echevarría rightly observes that this emphasis of the borderline between city and country (and the relegation of Menegildo Jr. to the rural space) "keeps black culture outside of history" (*Alejo Carpentier* 84). This is not a casual fact but a strategic gesture on Carpentier's part. As anthropologist Johannes Fabian has argued, a denial of coevalness is one of the principal strategies that anthropological discourse (particularly when used as a tool of empire) employs in order to both characterize its subjects as primitive, and in fact to locate them as subjects at all.[29] Only by placing the Cué family outside of history can Carpentier promote their Afro-Cuban cultural practices as representative of Cuban autochthony without having to let blackness itself into the space of the nation.

Blackness and the Marvelous Real: *The Kingdom of This World*

In *Écue-Yamba-Ó*, blackness—in its Cuban incarnation—provides the young Carpentier with the cultural material for countering foreign (and principally North American) domination, yet the text itself must find a way to set boundaries around this same blackness before its identification with the primitive overwhelms both its designated symbolic function and its implications for Cubanness. By 1949, when Carpentier published *El reino de este mundo* (*The Kingdom of This World*), he chose to displace many of these issues safely far away from Cuba. Perhaps his best-known novel, *El reino de este mundo* takes place during the Haitian Revolution (1791–1804), and features a slave protagonist, Ti Noel, who witnesses (and participates in) some of the Revolution's significant events. Like Carpentier's first novel, *El reino de este mundo* is concerned with discourses of modernity, and the arrival of modernity in the Caribbean: while *Écue-Yamba-Ó* deals with Cuba's incorporation into a world organized by North American capitalism, *El reino de este mundo* focuses on the end of the colonial era in Haiti, which was also the moment in which the French ideals of Enlightenment ushered in a new "modern" era, and in which the first successful slave rebellion in the Americas reframed those Enlightenment ideals.[30] Yet in contrast to Carpentier's early Afro-Cuban texts, which were set in the period in which Carpentier wrote them, *El reino de este mundo* is a historical novel set in a time and place clearly separate from Cuba, even if the Revolution itself had wide-reaching consequences for both the Caribbean and the world.

Carpentier clarifies some of his reasons for choosing Haiti as *El reino de este mundo*'s setting in his prologue to the novel, an essay that was later published (in an expanded form) as "De lo real maravilloso americano" (On the American Marvelous Real). Indeed, as Javier Muñoz-Basols has noted, it is often difficult not to see the prologue as a fundamental part of the novel itself (44). In this text, Carpentier introduces what he calls "lo real maravilloso" (the marvelous real), the idea that Latin America's history and environment go beyond the boundaries of what is normally considered as "real." Carpentier's prologue, while laying out his fusion of the "real" and the "marvelous" (and the resolution of the implicit dialectic contained in these two terms) is thus structured, intentionally, as a discovery narrative. His visit to historic places in Haiti—the palace of Sans-Souci, the Citadelle de La Ferrière—allows him to gain a firsthand understanding of the marvelous real. In the later version of the essay, this journey of discovery has been expanded, so that only after recording his travels in other parts of the globe—China, Iran, Russia—does his essay turn to Latin America, and eventually to Haiti: "Vuelve el latinoamericano a lo suyo y empieza a entender muchas cosas" ("De lo real maravilloso" 20). [The Latin American returns to his own and begins to understand many things.] Compared with foreign places of wonder, Latin America can offer the world its "marvelous real": a history so outrageous as to go beyond fictional narrative, a landscape beyond the artistic imaginings of the world's greatest civilizations.

Carpentier's celebration of Latin America's natural gifts is intended to contrast with the European artistic search for just such natural inspiration. In a disavowal of his own early involvement in the Surrealist movement, Carpentier sustains that European Surrealism is an inauthentic and forced attempt to produce the kind of expansion of reality that Latin America has naturally: "[C]uando André Masson quiso dibujar la selva de la isla de Martinica, con el increíble entrelazamiento de sus plantas y la obscena promiscuidad de ciertos frutos, la maravillosa verdad del asunto devoró al pintor, dejándolo poco menos que impotente frente al papel en blanco"("Prólogo a *El Reino*" 53). [When André Masson tried to draw the jungle of Martinique, with its incredible growth of plants and the obscene promiscuity of certain fruits, the marvelous truth of the subject devoured the painter, leaving him virtually impotent before the blank page.] In this description, even the plant life is violently, sexually dangerous—exotic and transgressive. The Cuban primitive from *Écue-Yamba-Ó* has been transformed into the "marvelous real"; European achievement is no longer countered with a nebulous (and dangerously polymorphic) cultural "authenticity" but with natural phenomena.

As Carpentier tells it in his prologue, he too was overwhelmed by Haiti's sense of the marvelous during a visit to Haiti in 1943. This trip, and his subsequent investigations into Haitian history, became both the inspiration for his elaboration of the marvelous real and one of his primary examples. Despite the essay's staging of Carpentier's moment of epiphany at the fortress of Sans-Souci, this genesis of his interest in Haiti is a carefully constructed fiction; as Birkenmaier shows, Carpentier had been interested in Haiti long before the visit he describes in the prologue (*Alejo Carpentier* 100–101). Indeed, Carpentier's choice of setting was anything but spontaneous; it was a highly strategic choice. Haiti, in the 1920s and 1930s, was seen as the site of the exotic primitive in the Americas par excellence. Its history as the first independent black nation in the Americas and its Afro-Caribbean culture (in particular the Vodou religion) made it the focus of numerous ethnographies and travel narratives in the 1920s and '30s.[31] Carpentier was familiar with this literature; in fact, he had given William Seabrook's sensationalist travel narrative *The Magic Island* (1929) a favorable review in *Carteles*.[32] His trip to Haiti in 1943, rather than being the beginning of an interest in the country, could in fact be seen as the culmination of a growing interest (ethnographic, musical) in Haitian culture, particularly in Vodou. As Lizabeth Paravisini-Gebert puts it, "[T]o Carpentier, Haiti is as exotic as his native Cuba would be to a European" (118). Given its *a priori* status as hemispheric other, Haiti thus serves Carpentier as a perfect site to explore the intersection of (and the contrasts and conflicts between) Western (Enlightenment) rationality and the "primitive" mindset of African slaves. Setting his novel in the time of the Haitian Revolution separates these two mentalities by race and class (the plantation colonist aristocracy versus the African slaves). In this stark environment of colonial oppression, blackness emerges as a transgressive, contestatory element. Eighteenth-century Haiti is significantly not Cuba; by focusing on this historically bounded environment, Carpentier can connect blackness to Caribbean history (and "the marvelous real") without needing to define the present relationship of Afro-Cuban culture to Cubanness.

Racial difference itself thus becomes the vehicle through which Carpentier stages this conflict between the "old worldview" and the New World's marvelous real. His understanding of Haitian culture and history, including his knowledge of Vodou, becomes a means for elaborating his concept of the "marvelous real" in the Haitian context. In the rigidly segregated society of colonial Haiti, racial and class differences are clearly delineated (and carefully policed). Just as the "primitive" reality of the Cué family is set against the foreign threats in *Écue-Yamba-Ó*, in *El reino de este mundo* Carpentier contrasts the worldview of the African slaves, which is one ruled by the supernatural, with the Enlightenment rationality followed by the French Creoles.

The true hero of Carpentier's story, from the point of view of the slaves (and the Revolution), is Mackandal, a runaway African slave (and a real historical figure) who was responsible for inciting some of the earliest incidents of slave rebellion leading to the Revolution. After losing an arm in an accident with a cane press, Mackandal runs away from the plantation and begins organizing the rebellion from his hideaway in the hills. As a *cimarrón* (runaway slave), Mackandal occupies a symbolic position for both white elites and black slaves. For the whites, he is the monstrous, the unspeakable, the unsubjugable other. Even his particular African regional identity carries with it the threat of social upheaval: "Además, todo mandinga—era cosa sabida—ocultaba un cimarrón en potencia.

Decir mandinga, era decir díscolo, revoltoso, demonio" (22). [Besides, it was common knowledge that every Mandingue was a potential fugitive. Mandingue was a synonym for intractable, rebellious, a devil (21).] For the slaves, on the other hand, Mackandal both represents resistance and also acts as the site of a certain authenticity of cultural origins. As someone from Africa, he carries with him a knowledge of the "homeland" that allows him to function as a living connection between Africa and the Haitian slaves, who are ignorant of this culture and history. For Ti Noel, Mackandal's escape marks the disappearance of "todo el mundo evocado por sus relatos"(23) [the whole world evoked by his stories (22)]. Yet after he escapes, Mackandal also gains a knowledge of local plants (and particularly of poisons), proving that his skills are not simply limited to Africa. As he expands his magic powers, he learns to transform himself into insects and animals, literally becoming part of the "marvelous" excess of Haiti's physical environment.

The connection between blackness (and the racial difference it implies) and the marvelous real is most clearly established in the scene of Mackandal's execution. Because of his leadership role in the rebellion, Mackandal is to be publicly burned alive in the main square of Cap Français. Carpentier describes the execution as if it were a performance. The slaveowners have set the scene; they have built the bonfire, taken up their positions as spectators in the plaza below, and most importantly, have gathered all the slaves in the square to witness the event. It is clear that the whites view the event as a spectacle. By forcing the slaves to watch Mackandal burned at the stake, they hope to teach them a lesson—"esa letra entraría con fuego y no con sangre" (40) [the lesson was to be driven home by fire, not by blood (44)]. Slaves who defy the social authority of the plantation owners must be shown that their actions will bring reprisal, that there is a price to be paid for trying to disrupt the social order.

The dominance of this social system (and its accompanying worldview) seems impossible to contest, and yet as the execution plays out, Carpentier shows the way in which the slaves subvert (reject) the whites' version of reality (and thus, their power). Mackandal is tied to the stake and the bonfire is lit according to plan, but at the last minute he slips his bonds, and for a second it looks as though he will successfully escape. It is here that Carpentier splits the narrative perspective: while the whites are able to recapture Mackandal and thrust him back into the bonfire, the slaves witness not his death but his full escape, as he *flies* upward and soars away over the crowd. The slaves cry out, "Mackandal sauvé!" (41) [Mackandal saved! (46)], an assertion that becomes a triumphant rallying cry; their leader has not been killed but has instead been transformed. What should have thus become a harsh lesson in plantation discipline becomes a model story of liberation.

Yet Mackandal's execution only enacts a fantasy of liberation, not a true or real escape. In relaying the conflicting perceptions (interpretations) of Mackandal's execution, Carpentier privileges the perspective of the white landowners, as the reader is led to conclude that what "really" happened was that Mackandal was executed. In presenting this as "reality," Carpentier does not necessarily invalidate the slaves' version of events, but neither does he give the reader access to anything beyond the performance of the slaves' worldview. The slaves' version thus emerges as an "alternative" version, but not the "real" version, since the text ultimately affirms that Mackandal was indeed executed. González Echevarría has shown that Carpentier borrowed extensively from eyewitness accounts of the period in composing his text (*Alejo Carpentier*, 133–37). The slaves' version—which we might call the "marvelous real" version, thus seems to function as a transgressive counterpoint to the dominant rationality of the white aristocracy, when in actuality, as James Pancrazio observes, the text "is configured . . . so that readers will 'see through' the deception of myth" (*Logic of Fetishism* 169). Rather than legitimating a sustained counternarrative, it serves mainly to question and provoke.

Ti Noel, the protagonist of *El reino de este mundo*, is a slave coachman on the plantation of M. Lenormand de Mezy. As such, he occupies a relatively privileged position in the slave hierarchy, in that he has a significant amount of freedom and a vantage point from which to observe both the world of the slaves and that of the plantation owners, often serving as a window onto scenes of conflict between the two worldviews. González Echevarría argues that he is "a positive presence, a witness to a series of events beyond his comprehension" (*Alejo Carpentier* 157). While Ti Noel is primarily an observer, I disagree with the assertion that he does so uncomprehendingly. In the novel's very first scene, in which Ti Noel visits the town of Cap Français with his master, the sly way in which his vision juxtaposes the calf heads in the butcher shop and the powdered wigs in the dress shop next door reveals that he knows what is at stake. The problem, as Barbara Webb points out, is that as he mediates between these two worldviews, Ti Noel functions as a "literary trick" that allows

Carpentier to portray the slaves' worldview without necessarily subscribing to it himself.[33] As a black slave, Ti Noel is privy to the slaves' perspective, but through the third-person narrative voice, the reader is kept separate from many of the fundamental aspects of his worldview. The lack of comprehension is not Ti Noel's but the reader's. While Carpentier allows the reader access to Ti Noel's emotions, his actions are often inexplicable and occasionally shocking. We think we have come to know him, until one of his actions reminds us of this distance, such as when, during the slaves' first revolt, he rapes Mme. de Mezy, the plantation owner's wife. The violence of this action—described as the realization of Ti Noel's fantasies—turns him again into the "primitive other," on the brink of inexplicable violence.

By choosing to view the Haitian Revolution through Ti Noel, Carpentier's novel, more than portraying the events of the Revolution from the slaves' perspective, strangely sidelines the events of the Revolution itself. Ti Noel, present for some of the Revolution's initial events, is then taken by his master to Santiago, Cuba, as M. de Mezy attempts to wait out the violence. The central conflicts of the Revolution, as well as historical protagonists of the conflict such as Jean-Jacques Dessalines and Toussaint L'Ouverture, thus never appear. In this way, while it tells a radically different story, the circularity of *El reino de este mundo*'s plot strangely echoes that of *Écue-Yamba-Ó*. As depicted in the later novel, the Haitian Revolution, rather than liberating black Haitians, initiates a new cycle of exploitation, as King Henry Christophe turns away from his country's needs in an attempt to re-create the customs of the French court. After escaping from virtual enslavement as a forced laborer building the fortress of Sans-Souci, Ti Noel eventually finds himself with nowhere to go but back to the plantation where he had lived as a slave. The novel's last scenes show him turning himself into animals and insects, practicing the techniques of physical transformation that Mackandal has taught him. Yet these techniques are, in fact, strategies of disappearance, of blending in to the point of invisibility, what James Pancrazio has identified as the construction of identity "through erasure" (*Logic of Fetishism* 152). As such, Ti Noel's transformations enact a kind of return to maroonage, to the figure of the escaped slave, but in a defensive, rather than a revolutionary way.[34] In becoming one with the landscape, Ti Noel thus chooses a kind of invisibility for his worldview—and implicitly for blackness. He—and by implication, his perspective, the "marvelous real"—will thus continue to remain outside history.

Black Like Us? Lydia Cabrera's Cuban Stories

In contrast to Carpentier's restless comparativism, which locates blackness in a position of symbolic oppositionality, there is nothing in Lydia Cabrera's *Cuentos negros de Cuba* to indicate that Cabrera wrote the stories while residing in France (despite the fact that she wrote them there). Certainly the book's foreword, written by Fernando Ortiz, makes no attempt to connect Cabrera's stories to anything beyond the local Afro-Cuban community from which he indicates she had gathered them. Beyond Ortiz's preface (which erroneously characterizes the stories as "translations," something I will return to in a later chapter), Cabrera herself gives the stories no further introduction, nor indicates by anything in their presentation how they should be read within an international or (African) Diasporic context. If, as the title asserts or insists, these are *black* Cuban stories, there is nothing within the texts themselves that attempts to specifically code (or decode) blackness for the reader. This highlights a principal difference between Cabrera and Carpentier: while Carpentier uses blackness to explore Cuba's unique place in an international context, Cabrera uses blackness as a more localized category of belonging. Blackness in her work alludes to structures of meaning (from an ethnographic standpoint), but does not necessarily fulfill any weightier symbolic or allegorical function.

Although, as I discuss elsewhere in this study, Cabrera's texts in many ways play with or even defy the structure of typical folktales, the stories in *Cuentos negros* fall into two general categories. In the first are texts—such as "Bregantino Bregantín," "Cheggue," "Eya," and "Walo-Wila," the first stories in the collection—that could most easily be considered folktales. The time in which they occur is unspecified, and their setting is unnamed, or is identified by a name that a geographer would be hard-pressed to locate on a real map. Some of these places, such as the kingdom of Cocozumba in "Bregantino Bregantín," might just as easily be African as Cuban. These stories contain what might be viewed as archetypal characters or storylines: the suitor who must pass the test to win his beloved ("Walo-Wila"), or a king's outcast son who grows up to defy his tyrant father and restore order to the kingdom ("Bregantino Bregantín"). Some, like "Cheggue," in which a boy is warned not to enter the forest after a stray arrow, yet does so anyway (and pays the price), contain a kind of moral or message. They do not attempt to represent things with a total degree of verisimilitude, yet while the characters and actions almost always contain deeper levels of meaning, these significations are not (necessarily) tied to ideas of race. Some of these stories depict human beings, while the protagonists of others are anthropomorphized animals. These tales distinctively construct blackness not as other (something to be spoken about) but as the place from which enunciation takes place.[35] Indeed, a significant number of stories in the collection—for example, "Bregantino Bregantín," "Walo-Wila," and "La Loma de Mambiala"—contain few or no references to the racial identity of their characters at all.

Blackness may operate inclusively from within Cabrera's texts, but this does not necessarily mean that the reader is implicated (included) in this race-identified community. It should be remembered that these stories were read by (and implicitly written for) largely white audiences, and that these audiences were both European and Cuban. While race both implicitly and explicitly serves as a marker of belonging within the narrative confines of the stories themselves, the different cultural references (tied to race) in the stories allow for multiple readings, based on one's level of familiarity with Cuban culture. This means that "blackness" functions as a signifier in Cabrera's stories in ways that are simultaneously more clearly defined (tied to local racial and class systems) and slipperier, more open to alternate and contradictory readings. In what follows, I offer close readings of three stories from *Cuentos negros* to show the ways in which Cabrera both anchors and frees a reading of blackness in her texts.

Like Carpentier, Cabrera's texts emphasize the religious and musical aspects of Afro-Cuban culture. Carpentier is interested in representing the material and performative elements of these cultural practices. Cabrera, however, incorporates these elements into the text allegorically, using them to expand the dynamics of meaning. Thus while blackness itself may not fulfill the same symbolic function that it does in Carpentier's work, these cultural elements act to expand the realms of meaning of Cabrera's texts.

"Los compadres" ("The Pals"), one of Cabrera's most iconic tales, operates on two levels, the mythic and the mundane, and each level both echoes and illuminates the other. The story's first sentence links these two narrative planes: "Todos somos hijos de los Santos, y lo de la malicia y el gusto de pecar ya le viene al hombre de los santos" (67). [We are all sons and daughters of the Saints, and the idea of malice and the pleasure in sinning comes to man from the saints.] This first statement sets the scene, connecting through the first-person plural "we," the story's characters, the story's narrator and, implicitly, the reader to the cosmology of Afro-Cuban Santería. As it does so, it includes the reader in the cultural listening; there is no explanation of what it means to be the "son or daughter of a saint," as if that practice does not need clarification. This will be a story that deals in moral territory—the temptation to sin—although the phrase "el gusto de pecar" [the joy of sinning] identifies sin as simultaneously negative and pleasurable. The story that follows is composed of two parts: it begins with what is essentially a series of *patakíes*, or legends about the *orichas*, before moving on to a story of human conflict. In the first *patakí*, Ochún, the *oricha* of fresh water and romantic love, falls in love with her nephew Changó, the god of Thunder, only to learn he is her nephew when Yemayá, *oricha* of the ocean and Ochún's sister, recognizes Changó as her son. In the second, Aphrodite-like Ochún leads Orula, Yemayá's husband, to be unfaithful to his wife.[36] Both of these brief narratives deal with sins that are sexual in nature, and this same sexual temptation drives the narrative in the earthly realm. Dolé, the story's female (human) protagonist, "was a daughter of Ochún," and like Ochún, she is driven by a sexual desire for men whom she should not have. After Dolé is caught deceiving her loyal husband, Evaristo, she swears to never again be unfaithful. Yet her inability to resist her sexual desire proves to be her undoing. When Evaristo dies, Dolé's affection turns to Evaristo's best friend Capinche. Evaristo, however, is determined even from beyond the grave to make sure that Dolé honors her promise to him, and his spirit returns to torment his wife, who eventually also sickens and dies. The final victim of forbidden sexual desire is Capinche, who, upon seeing Dolé's body laid out, is so overcome with longing that he has to be prevented from making love to her corpse.

Cabrera utilizes the shifts in the text between the mythic timelessness of the *orichas* and the temporal specificity of an urban Havana neighborhood at the turn of the twentieth century to communicate the close relationship of the physical and spiritual worlds in Afro-Cuban cosmology. While the morality play of the story is something that might occur in many cultural contexts, the cultural milieu of the story is profoundly Afro-Cuban. The "compadres" of the title, Evaristo and Capinche, are former slaves: "En otros tiempos—siendo de la misma dotación—juntos habían tumbado mucha caña y ahora, libres los dos, Evaristo torcía tabaco en la fábrica, Capinche cargaba en los muelles y se estaba volviendo zambo" (71). [In other days—being from the same crew—they had cut cane together and now, both free, Evaristo rolled tobacco in a factory, Capinche worked on the docks and was becoming knock-kneed.] In this brief sentence, Cabrera lays out a whole historical trajectory for her characters—their first experiences under slavery on a rural sugar plantation, their transition to an urban lifestyle—and simultaneously provides a temporal location for the action of the story (after slavery, but soon enough after for former slaves to be a vital part of the work force).

The clearest expression of the Afro-Cuban environment of the story can be found in the language. As with other stories in the volume, the text is full of African words that have been incorporated into Spanish. For example, Capinche is described as being "en *querindango* con una lavandera de buenas prendas, que era santera" (70, emphasis mine) [mooning after a well-dressed washerwoman, who was a santera]. The use of Afro-Cuban words such as "querindango"—along with others such as "gandinga," "chévere," "chunga"—alters the sound and texture of the description. Only occasionally is the meaning of a word explained by a brief footnote; in most instances, readers are left to glean the meaning of a word through its use. The same is true of the sections of Afro-Cuban song that are inserted. When Dolé, seeking to distract Evaristo from her infidelities, sends him to hunt alligator eggs, a short song appears in the text: "Saúla bómbo, saúla bómbodil,/ Saúla bómbo, saúla, ¡bobo se va!" A speaker not familiar with *Lucumí* (the Yoruba dialect spoken in Cuba) will have no idea of what this says, although it can be inferred from the use of the Spanish "bobo" and the statement prior to the appearance of the song, that Dolé and her lover are laughing at Evaristo, that the song is about someone stupid. Rather than constructing blackness as a marker for otherness within the text (as Carpentier does when he contrasts the Cués' religious practice with life at the mill), Cabrera's text uses these markers of cultural knowledge to create a community of belonging, one that includes the narrative voice (who uses this language). The only potential other would be the reader (who may or may not know the meaning of these *Lucumí* phrases), yet this "otherness" can only be defined by the reader's knowledge or lack thereof; the text itself does nothing to establish or emphasize it. "Los compadres" can be described as a story about the danger of acting upon inappropriate desire, but it is not clear that the story intends merely to present this rather simplistic moral. Both for the *orichas* and for Dolé and Capinche, there are consequences (sometimes negative) of experiencing "the pleasure of sinning" and acting on desire, but these are not necessarily related to the moral behavior of the characters. After all, was it wrong for Dolé to break her promise to Evaristo and desire Capinche once Evaristo was already dead? The human characters' dilemmas expose a moral ambivalence already present in the *patakíes*; should Ochún be held at fault for sleeping with her nephew Changó if she did not know he was her nephew? In both of these situations, however, there is a price to be paid for sinning, even if it does not necessarily negate the pleasure of the action. By linking the earthly and the heavenly, Cabrera demonstrates (without needing to narrate or explain) the way that Afro-Cuban cosmology intersects with and relates to life in an Afro-Cuban community. Juxtaposing Dolé's story with that of Ochún and Yemayá reveals the human desires and weaknesses of the *orichas*, the ways in which their stories reflect human interactions. But as Cabrera indicates when she mentions that Dolé is "a daughter of Ochún," human beings also have a relationship to the *orichas* that extends beyond the metaphoric. As illustrated by the man in the story who is run over by a truck of mangos after he fails to build an altar to San Lázaro as he had promised (79), while people suffer for betraying their fellow human beings, this is nothing compared to what happens when they fail to honor their agreements with the *orichas*.

"Bregantino Bregantín," the first story in the collection, is another narrative in which multiple levels of meaning operate through religious imagery. The tale is set in the kingdom of Cocozumba, making the story one of the few in the collection that seems to possibly be set somewhere in Africa, rather than in Cuba. As a number of critics (including Ortiz in his introduction) have noted, "Bregantino Bregantín" is a story with notable Freudian overtones. The princess Dingadingá, desiring to get married, is married off by her parents to the Glowworm. The Glowworm dies, and bequeaths his job and his kingdom to Toro (the Bull). Assuming the throne, the Bull becomes a kind of dictator. To guarantee his power over the kingdom, he decrees that he will be the only male in it, and that all the women in the kingdom are to be his concubines. All men are slaughtered, as is any male child born thereafter. Yet one woman, Sanune, dares to defy the king. She takes the body of her little son into the forest and offers him to the *orichas*, who bring him back to life and hide him from the Bull. The young Bull (Sanune's son) grows to maturity, and finally kills his father in a duel.

On one level, "Bregantino Bregantín" can be read as the realization of a classic Oedipal conflict; the son, desirous of his father's position, eventually kills his father, and takes his place. Cocozumba under the Bull's reign is the perfect patriarchy; one man reigns supreme, maintaining absolute political and reproductive power. On another level, however, this is a story about balance, both social and religious. Bregantino Bregantín, the son, kills his father, but rather than installing himself as a new tyrant, he restores the kingdom to its earlier harmonic state: "busca hombres—uno para cada mujer" (28) [he searches for men, one for each woman]. While it is a "happy" ending, it is also a conservative one. The father Bull has been a tyrannical radical, wanting to install a new (and disastrous) system; the son restores balance by returning the society of Cocozumba to its (timeless) status quo.

It is also possible to read the story in a more directly symbolic light, as it allegorically portrays the conditions of slavery (albeit a system of slavery operated along rigidly gendered lines). When Sanune saves her son, she flees to the woods much as runaway slaves fled to the bush. Given the symbolic role of the wilderness (and its flora and fauna) in Afro-Cuban religion, Sanune's flight is a search for both physical and spiritual protection, and her plea for help is heard. "La selva . . . abrió los brazos acogedora" (22) [The forest . . . welcoming, opened its arms]. Indeed, it is due to the intervention of the *orichas* that Bregantino Bregantín is rescued from the dead and raised in safety and the balance restored. The *orichas'* decision to intervene connects the idea of balance with the concept of destiny; balance is restored because the gods will it so. Seen this way, the story offers a critique of slavery and a projection of its demise.

In this reading, however, the de facto slavery in which Cocozumba's women are forced to exist during the Bull's reign is a slavery defined by gender rather than race. While it could be argued that the slippage between the two categories is precisely what allows the story to comment on slavery along racial lines, reading this way also presents the possibility for a less liberating understanding of the text. If the Bull's enslavement of women is truly along gender lines, Bregantino Bregantín's appearance merely corrects the most egregious abuses of patriarchy without questioning the general operation of Cocozumba's society as patriarchal. The problem is the Bull's excess desire for power (exercised through masculine dominance), and his son's reestablishment of the previous system (in accordance with the *orichas*, no less) does not appear to challenge male superiority. After all, Sanune's rebellion is not revolution; it is a flight. The story argues for a restoration of social balance but does not, in the end, question the organization of society. On the contrary, it suggests that balance is lost when those boundaries are questioned.

A paradigmatic story for understanding how Cabrera's narrative positioning operates with regard to race is "El limo del Almendares," which comes towards the end of *Cuentos negros*. On one level, the story is a narrative of origins, a folktale that explains "why" or "how" something came about; in this case, it explains the presence of the mud on the bottom of the Almendares, the river that runs through western Havana. The story centers on a beautiful *mulata* (mulatta), Soyán Dekín, and Billillo, a black *calesero* (or coachman-slave) who loves her in secret. The mayor (of Havana) proclaims Soyán Dekín the most beautiful *mulata* in the world, and the community organizes a party in her honor, where she spends the night dancing with the mayor himself. Billillo, eaten up with jealousy, goes to see a sorcerer who puts a dark spell on him. Instead of attacking the mayor, an enchanted Billillo attacks Soyán Dekín as she is washing clothes by the river. When he finally comes to his senses, it is too late; Soyán Dekín drowns, and her hair becomes the mud at the bottom of the Almendares.

Faithful to the prerequisites of a tale of origins, Cabrera does not explicitly date when this story takes place. Yet she includes certain descriptive elements in the story that in addition to locating it an urban, largely Afro-Cuban environment give us an approximate time frame for the setting. The clearest temporal marker is Billillo's role as a coachman-slave; as William Luis notes, coachman-slaves were "common figures" in Havana in the eighteenth and nineteenth centuries (44). The dance in Soyán Dekín's honor also significantly takes place in the local *cabildo*. Organizations established by slaves who arrived in Cuba from the same location in Africa, *cabildos* were designated originally as meeting places by the Spanish authorities; they later grew into mutual aid societies and centers for Afro-Cuban religious practice (Brown 27). Designating the *cabildo* as the center of the community makes it clear that the story takes place in an Afro-Cuban neighborhood, and further references the colonial era, since after Independence other kinds of religious centers and clubs (particularly social organizations such as *Club Atenas*, which catered to middle-class Cubans of color), began to provide some of the services originally provided by *cabildos*.

The juxtaposition of these two time frames—the "immemorial" time of origins and the concrete (linear), historical time of Cuba's experience as a colony—problematizes the idea of "origins" as a structuring device for Cabrera's tale, and gestures towards the relationship between race and history in Cuban identity. Since black Cubans are not indigenous to Cuba, any discussion of blackness necessarily connects back to Cuba's plantation economy and the slave trade. By thus contextualizing her story, Cabrera seems to imply that an Afro-Cuban "origin" tale is thus never *not* connected to a sense of historical time.

Through this historical contextualization, race can thus be seen as an essential, if subtle element of Cabrera's tale. While the basic plot of "El limo"—a rivalry for the attentions of a beautiful woman, a man ensnared by his own spell, a wrongful death—could occur in a variety of contexts, Cabrera adds cultural details that anchor the story not only to Havana but also to Cuban race relations. Soyán Dekín is *mulata*, raised in an Afro-Cuban environment, but with more opportunities for social mobility than even a free black. Billillo is black and a slave (although a slave with certain privileges), while the mayor is a powerful member of the white elite. Part of Billillo's jealousy seems to come precisely from the fact that his rival is white, his sensation that Soyán Dekín may be flirting with the mayor precisely for the possibilities he offers for improving her social standing: " . . . [B]uena estaba Soyán Dekín en su apogeo, para querida de un Don!" (127) [Soyán Dekín was at her peak, lovely enough to be a lord's beloved!], and his assumption that she will naturally prefer the mayor because of both his race and position. While Soyán Dekín states as she is dying that it was Billillo she truly cared for, "El limo" can be read as illustrating the devastating effect that impressions of racial and class hierarchy have on the pair's potential romance. The tragic aspect of the story (in racial terms) is given an added edge of irony by the fact that the spell that turns Billillo into a zombie who attempts to kill Soyán Dekín is given to him by the Afro-Cuban "brujo de la Ceiba" [witch doctor by the Ceiba tree], to whom he goes for aid with the situation.

As a story of origins, "El limo" presents itself in the guise of an Afro-Cuban folktale. Yet through both its plot and its characters, it makes a number of significant gestures toward foundational texts of Cuban literature. As Luis notes, coachmen-slaves were the frequent subjects of nineteenth century Cuban novels; a coachman-slave is the protagonist of Anselmo Suárez y Romero's *Francisco* (1839), and coachmen-slaves are featured in the novels of Cirilo Villaverde and Martín Morúa Delgado and in the autobiography of Juan Francisco Manzano (Luis 44). Coachmen-slaves were often characterized as dandies; they were well dressed, enjoyed a more privileged status with their masters, and could sometimes earn enough money to be able to buy their freedom.[37] Yet perhaps because of this elevated status, as Luis notes, the coachman-slave was often seen as a tragic figure, someone with elevated expectations, whose hopes for the future could be easily dashed. In this respect, Billillo's unrealized desire for Soyán Dekín—someone socially and racially above him—fits the general profile assigned to the coachman-slave by these more canonical texts. While the love between Soyán and Billillo is most clearly done in by his jealousy, given their differences in race and class, their relationship was always at risk.

More than the coachman-slave, the figure of the *mulata* was used as both a visual and literary symbol of Cuba and Cuban society from the nineteenth century onwards. As scholars such as Vera Kutzinski have shown, the *mulata*, by virtue of her mixed-race background, also functions as "a symbolic container for all the tricky questions about how race, gender, and sexuality inflect the power relations that obtain in colonial and post-colonial Cuba" (*Sugar's Secrets* 7). By making Soyán Dekín's hair become part of the Almendares, Cabrera creates a physical connection between the woman and the city, literally making the *mulata* part of Havana. Soyán Dekín is a paradigmatic Cuban *mulata* figure: beautiful, sensuous, and ultimately tragic. The tragic nature of Cabrera's tale is reminiscent of nineteenth-century Cuban antislavery novels such as Cirilo Villaverde's *Cecilia Valdés* and Gertrudis Gómez de Avellaneda's *Sab*, both of which contain *mulato* or *mulata* protagonists who are fated to love someone socially (and racially) inaccessible to them. "El limo" both gestures towards these popular texts (which would have been well-known to Cuban readers) and turns the tables on them. Both Sab and Cecilia Valdés fall in love with inaccessible white superiors, and their tragic ends can in part be explained as a result of this impossible pairing. Soyán Dekín, on the other hand, is not done in by her own unrequited love for someone above her in terms of both race and class, but by Billillo's misreading of her association with the mayor along the lines of these previous narratives.

While the story's connections to nineteenth-century novels emphasize the tragic elements of its ending, Cuban readers with some knowledge of Cuba's *teatro vernáculo* (Cuba's comic theatre, something akin to vaudeville) might have gone on to read "El limo" somewhat differently. As Robin Moore and Jill Lane have shown, Cuban comic theatre was organized around racially identified stock characters, among them the *calesero* (coachman-slave) and the *mulata*.[38] In the context of the *teatro vernáculo*, the *mulata* figure is frequently the temptress, a symbol of hypersexualized feminine desire who drives men to ruin (Moore 49–53, Lane 197–208). "El limo" at the outset presents a similar setup: whatever Soyán Dekín feels for the mayor, it is clear that he has succumbed to her beauty and charm, and that she has benefited socially (and stands to benefit more) from his admiration. While it may be something of a stretch to interpret Cabrera's tale as straight farce, when read against the backdrop of comic theatre it is a narrative in which the boundary-flouting temptress *mulata* gets her comeuppance. Soyán Dekín, despite initial appearances (and her possible aspirations), is not destined for greatness and a place at the mayor's side. In the end, she will get no further than the banks of the river.

Despite Soyán Dekín's tragic end, both "El limo" and the stock tales of the *teatro vernáculo* operate according to the idea of balance. In both models, the social structure that is initially threatened—whether comically or tragically—is, in the end, restored. Social stability—a balance created and maintained by both class and racial structures—is maintained. In the case of Cabrera's story, the significance of the restoration of this balance is ambiguous. An (Afro-Cuban) reader could interpret this very restoration as tragic; both Soyán Dekín and Billillo are ultimately unable to escape the racial and class hierarchies by which they are bound. Yet a reader could also see this rebalancing in a positive light; the threats to this social order have been eradicated.

In reinforcing existing social structures within narratives that present Afro-Cuban culture as the narrative center, Cabrera's texts pull a sleight of hand. They disrupt the expected site of enunciation (at least for a majority white readership), yet this disruption does not necessarily serve to question racial or class hierarchies. This discursive situation, first evident in the stories in *Cuentos negros*, is continued in Cabrera's second book of stories, *Por qué... Cuentos negros de Cuba* (1948). In contrast to Cabrera's first collection, all of the stories in *Por qué* share the characteristic of being tales that attempt to "explain" the existence of an animal, a custom, or a situation. Yet even these "origin" stories reference the history and social and racial organization of contemporary Cuba.

"[¿Por que?] Hay hombres blancos, pardos y negros" [Why There Are White, Brown and Black Men], the first story in the collection, is iconic in its demonstration of speaking of "origins" while referencing history, and sets the tone for the other stories in the collection. As its title suggests, this tale offers an explanation for the origins of different races. In this version, all men are originally black, in the image of the creator: "Quien fabricó el mundo, hizo a los hombres de un mismo color" (11) [He who made the world, made all men the same color]. When one man decides that he doesn't want to be dark but "blanco como el día" (11) [white like the day], Olofi (the creator) shows him and his two brothers to a well whose water will whiten his skin if he bathes in it. The first brother, upon bathing in the well, becomes entirely white. The second brother, bathing in water already muddied by the first, becomes only slightly paler, and by the time it is the third brother's turn, he is only able to lighten the palms of his hands and the soles of his feet.

Had the tale ended there, it would resemble other such stories that circulate in both folklore and popular mythology. But Cabrera's story does not end here. The white man, upon seeing his brothers, declares, "Ya no somos hermanos, sois mis esclavos" (13) [We are no longer brothers; you are my slaves], and enslaves both the black and the brown man seemingly without resistance. As in Cuban colonial society, the "brown" (or *mulato*) man is taken to the city, where he becomes a house servant, while the black man is sent to the country, where he is made to do menial and difficult labor. When the black man bemoans his fate, it is the Devil who appears to comfort him: "'¡Pobre negro!'—exclamó el Diablo—'nadie te quiere, pero yo que soy tan negro e indeseable como tú, te querré un poco'" (13) ["Poor black man!" exclaimed the Devil. "No one loves you. But I, who am as black and unwanted as you, will love you a little"]. He caresses the black man's head, burning it and causing his hair to curl. Running away from the Devil, the man runs into a tree (flattening his nose) and is stung by a scorpion (swelling his lips). Olofi, who has been watching all of this, "comprendió que había cometido una ligereza"(14) [understood that he had been thoughtless], and absents himself from the world without attempting to rectify his mistake, implicitly leaving human beings to their own devices.

Cabrera's story is problematic on a number of levels. As with the stories in *Cuentos negros*, this tale identifies blackness as the central—or original—race, the color not only of all people in the beginning but also the color of the creator. Yet when the brothers bathe in the pool and people of different colors are created, the story creates an immediate hierarchy from which it does not deviate and which it does not question. The black brother, while bemoaning his lot, accepts it, and Olofi sees the enslavement of both brothers, but does not act on it. By inserting slavery into this narrative—a slavery, furthermore, that recalls the Caribbean system of slavery in its construction of social and racial hierarchies—the story suggests a direct correlation between race and social position, and also implicitly legitimates the system of slavery as something that has been there since different races emerged.

As the first tale in the collection, by seemingly affirming (or at least not questioning) a racial hierarchy, "Hay hombres blancos, pardos y negros" also establishes an important ideological framework for the rest of the collection. It locates the narrative center of these stories not just within Afro-Cuban culture (or Afro-Cuban communities) but more specifically within Afro-Cuban culture in the colonial era. In doing so, it seems to identify colonialism as a moment of origins and slavery as understandable, even if the story's last sentences suggest that we are no longer in that moment. This gesture also identifies the Afro-Cuban narrative voice as carefully contained within these hierarchies, regardless of what may happen in subsequent stories.

Leaving Montmartre: Blackness at Home and Abroad

That *Écue-Yamba-Ó* was partially written in Paris is not at all surprising; what is surprising is the fact that Carpentier wrote most of it before leaving Cuba. For Carpentier, to understand the Caribbean, one must travel to China and Russia and Europe, and only then can one return home. In Carpentier's worldview, Cuba (or the Caribbean, as the case may be) is always understood in relation to other cultures, other nations, and other worldviews. To borrow a phrase from Édouard Glissant, the nation comes into being only through a poetics of relation. Because Carpentier is interested in Cuba as it is positioned in the broader (Western) context, he views blackness in a comparative context; it is always already constructed as other *in opposition to* something. Thus even when his texts celebrate the primitive (and through it, blackness), they do so in a way that locates blackness in a position of otherness. This otherness can be positively oppositional (as it counteracts the threat of foreign domination) or it can simply stand in for the unknown (in a Surrealist sense), for forces or practices that are not understood, that are beyond our understanding. In Carpentier's texts, blackness responds to an anxiety about lack, replacing it with transgressive excess. Despite the detailed cataloguing of Menegildo's body, blackness in these works functions as a kind of cipher, an absent presence.

Despite having begun her writing career in the turbulent avant-garde environment of Paris in the 1920s, Cabrera keeps her stories close to home. While Parisian readers could (and did) read them as illustrations of an exotic worldview, her texts signal multiple readings for her Cuban readers. The use of separate spaces—and separate narrative points of view in these stories—anticipates the use of space in Cabrera's later ethnographic work. Cabrera does not name blackness as "exotic" in her stories, but it could be argued that she constructs it as other through locating the reader outside the perimeter of the communities of racialized cultural belonging she identifies. A significant number of the *Cuentos negros* can be read as narratives about balance, whether that balance is achieved through spiritual, political, or social means. One way to read this emphasis would be to see it as a characteristic of the Afro-Cuban worldview, or of the Afro-Cuban narrative context. (After all, many Western folktales are about wrongs put right.) The way in which race structures these narratives of balance, however, suggests that while race can serve as a marker for belonging, it is also a way of reaffirming other kinds of social difference. If Carpentier sets limits around blackness by (positionally) sailing for other shores, Cabrera does so by retracing the social landscape of home.

3

THE NATIONAL ART OF SIGNIFYIN(G)

Nicolás Guillén and Lydia Cabrera

In his 1928 essay *Indagación del choteo* (*Investigation of the Choteo*), Cuban scholar Jorge Mañach analyzes a form of humorous wordplay known in Cuba as *choteo*. A kind of spontaneous *burla* (joking or poking fun), the *choteo* is fundamentally performative in nature, improvised wordplay that makes fun of something or someone. Yet the *choteo* goes beyond simple humor; "ataca o esquiva por medio de la burla lo demasiado serio" (73) [it attacks or avoids by way of poking fun at what is too serious], serving either as a way to express solidarity and respect, or as a means of destabilizing power relations (enacted by those at the bottom).[1] In his study, Mañach identifies the *choteo* as a peculiarly Cuban form of linguistic expression, with strong connections to Afro-Cuban culture.[2]

In both its performative and functional characteristics, as well as its identity as an African-derived form of expression, the *choteo* closely resembles Signifyin(g), a term that according to Henry Louis Gates Jr. can be used to refer to a body of culturally performative elements that function in an African American linguistic context. In fact, Gates chooses to spell the term "Signifyin(g)" to identify it as a black signifier and to set it apart from the white "signifying"(46). Although frequently associated with verbal riffs and ripostes, "doing the dozens," and "yo' mama" jokes, Signifyin(g) covers a variety of linguistic practices. Like the *choteo*, it is more than a joke or a verbal exchange; it functions as "a pervasive mode of language use" (Gates 80), a practice of wordplay of both a humorous and/or critical nature. Despite the humor that it may produce, it maintains a serious intention. Indeed, just as the destabilizing of the established order implied by the *choteo* produces a desired shift in social hierarchy, the improvisational character of Signifyin(g) also temporarily creates and opens linguistic space, resulting in a potential multiplicity of meanings.

In *The Signifying Monkey: A Theory of African-American Literary Criticism*, Gates presents an epistemological examination of the concept of Signifyin(g), tracing how these rhetorical language strategies, African in origin but embedded in black culture in the United States, are transformed into textual strategies at work in African American literature. He investigates what happens when a rhetorical strategy tied to the temporal moment of the performance is transferred to a very different written form. In this transition from the oral to the written, Signifyin(g)—in this case the practice of expanding, amplifying, altering, or changing a literary piece—also becomes a means of identifying a text's location within that genre. According to Gates, African American writers have created a canon of African American literature precisely through intertextual Signifyin(g) on each other's work. In addition to highlighting social bonds, Signifyin(g) is thus a strategy that fashions a literary community of texts through an appeal to cultural commonalities and shared modes of both oral and written communication.

Signifyin(g) and the *choteo* are both examples of what the Martinican theorist Édouard Glissant would call "practice[s] of diversion" (*Caribbean Discourse* 18). Diversion (*détour*), for Glissant, is the way in which a colonized population (or one emerging from the experience of colonization) attempts to deal with the experience of domination when that power structure is not present in a way that allows it to be openly contested. Practices of diversion subvert the sociopolitical status quo, often through trickery or humor, as is the case with Signifyin(g) and the *choteo*. Glissant observes that "[d]iversion is not possible when a nation is already formed" (18), since strategies of diversion are precisely the way in which a people moves (indirectly) to take control of their cultural production. In addition to attacking situations of unequal power, strategies of cultural diversion thus also result in—and allow for—the production of local cultural practices. While diversion can be an oral strategy (Signifyin(g) and *choteo* in their simplest versions), Glissant recognizes the creative force present in diversion when he argues that it also becomes a way in which Caribbean writers produce national literatures that are not imitations of European models.

Mañach recognizes the *choteo*'s power for positive social protest in language that strongly echoes Glissant's description of diversion: "No todas las autoridades son lícitas o deseables, y por eso siempre fue la burla un recurso de los oprimidos" (85). [Not all authorities are licit or desirable, which is why humor has always been a resource for the oppressed.] However, for Mañach, the *choteo* is at best an ambivalent example of Cuban popular culture. Despite his admission that the *choteo* has sometimes exercised "una función crítica saludable" [a healthy critical function], he sees the Cuban tendency to systematically undermine authority—"tirarlo todo al relajo" (85) [to take nothing seriously]—as a weakness of character, an inability to be serious that ultimately leads to an inability to produce "serious" culture or "real" authorities (such as those in Europe).

For Mañach the *choteo*, rather than something to be celebrated, is evidence that Cuban culture is still at a developmental stage that he hopes will soon be overcome. However, in practice, at least, not all of Mañach's contemporaries shared his views.[3] This chapter examines some of the ways in which Signifyin(g), as *choteo*-like verbal play, as intertextual commentary, and as literary improvisation, operates as Glissantian diversion in Cuban literature of the 1930s and 1940s. I argue that Cuban writers in this period employ Signifyin(g) both rhetorically and structurally, but in new and creative ways. Gates sees structural Signifyin(g) as the way in which African American writers identify their work as African American (by employing and adapting a variety of oral and written forms) and place their work in intertextual dialogue with other African American texts. However, as used by Lydia Cabrera and Nicolás Guillén, Signifyin(g) in the Cuban context becomes *both* a racial and a national strategy. In their short fiction and poetry (respectively), these two Cuban writers Signify across genre, borrowing from—and playing with—musical forms, poetic conventions, and popular and "high literary" genres as a way of creating "authentically" Cuban texts in which the authentic is also (simultaneously) marked as Afro-Cuban.

In their representations of aspects of Afro-Caribbean culture, Guillén and Cabrera avail themselves of the rhetorical strategies of Signifyin(g) as both a reflection of Cuban orality and as intertextual commentary, using these strategies as links between the new "avant-garde" texts and other kinds of texts, oral and written, which had previously existed in these locales. As they do so, their texts subvert, contest, or play with contemporary assumptions of literary and cultural authority, disrupting the cultural norms inherent in traditional reading practices. In his poetry collection *Motivos de son* (1930), Guillén relies specifically on the *choteo*-like aspects of humor and wordplay to create a pointed social commentary, a preoccupation that becomes a more central focus in the later poems that make up his subsequent collections *Sóngoro cosongo* (1931) and *West Indies, Ltd.* (1934). In her short-story collection *Cuentos negros de Cuba* (1936), Cabrera Signifies on the form and content of the traditional African or Afro-Cuban folktale, challenging both narrative traditions and sociocultural hierarchies. In Cabrera's and Guillén's texts play—understood as textual improvisation (both linguistic and structural)—becomes a political tool in their attempt to include Afro-Cuban cultural material, a method of making potentially "unwelcome" racial elements a fundamental part of these writers' uniquely Cuban products.[4]

The Spectacle of Play

On June 15, 1930, the young Afro-Cuban poet and journalist Nicolás Guillén published a brief article in the Havana daily *Diario de la Marina*, addressed to journalist (and fellow Cuban) Ramón Vasconcelos, in defense of his newly published *Motivos de son*, a collection of eight short poems that Vasconcelos had recently attacked (via an article in the Cuban newspaper *El País*) for their Afro-Cuban characteristics. Vasconcelos had taken issue with Guillén's deliberate use of the *son* musical form, an explicitly Afro-Cuban musical genre, and one that was still associated with working-class black Cubans. He took the younger writer to task for structuring his poems as if they were *son* songs, arguing that in spite of the *son*'s folkloric value, Guillén was catering to "la musa callejera, fácil, vulgar, y descoyuntada" (243) [the street muse: easy, vulgar, and disconnected]. What angered Vasconcelos was less the literary representation of a racialized subject than Guillén's portrayal of blackness as tied to working-class, popular culture, in particular Guillén's marriage of this racialized popular form to the "high literary" genre of lyric poetry.[5]

Guillén was certainly not the first Cuban poet to employ Afro-Cuban imagery or themes in his work; indeed, *Motivos de son* debuted in the midst of a national fascination with *Afrocubanismo* (Afro-Cubanism)— as expressed in music, literature, and the visual arts. What sets him apart (both in his response to Vasconcelos and in his poetic production) from other poets of the era—black and white—who chose to portray Afro-Cuban imagery in their poetry is the clearly articulated nationalist perspective driving his work and the fact that this idea manifested itself in his choice of poetic form. In "Sones y soneros," his response to Vasconcelos, he legitimates his use of the *son* form by outlining explicitly ideological goals for his new poetry:

> [C]reo que los "poemas de son," desde el punto de vista literario, y por la significación que en el mundo tiene hoy lo popular, constituyen un modo de estar en la "avanzada," como quiere el gran periodista cubano. Entre nosotros, donde a menudo no pensamos más que con cabezas de importación, precisa cierto heroísmo para aparecerse con unos versos primarios, escritos en la forma en que todavía hablan—piensan—muchos de nuestros negros (y no pocos blancos también) y en los que se retratan tipos que a diario vemos moverse a nuestro lado. (*Prosa de prisa* 1: 20–21)

> [I think that the "*son* poems," from a literary perspective and for the meaning that the popular has in the world today, constitute a way of being "avant-garde," as the great Cuban journalist would have it. Among ourselves, where we often think only with "imported heads," one needs a certain heroism to come out with some first verses written in the way in which many of our blacks (and more than a few whites as well) speak—think—and in which the people we find daily by our side are portrayed.]

Rather than pandering to high literary poetic convention, Guillén intends to reproduce, within the musical framework of the Cuban *son*, the rhythm of popular—and particularly Afro-Cuban—speech. He is seeking a uniquely Cuban literary text, a genuinely Cuban product that can counteract the "imported heads," the vogue of things foreign and especially North American, and the desire to look outside Cuba for sources of cultural production. Guillén's creation of a text that is simultaneously new ("avant-garde") and authentically Cuban rests on his observation (and recreation) of the color and texture of local speech. What bothers Vasconcelos about Guillén's poetry—its contemporary, local, urban, working-class representation of blackness—is precisely what Guillén holds up as the key to the production of a truly national text.

Both the philosophy and the underlying techniques that Guillén develops in *Motivos de son* are revealed in his further defense of his poetry in "Sones y soneros." Rather than continuing to elaborate his reasons for his choice of a poetic style, he ends his article to Vasconcelos with an anecdote, which could be read as a kind of parable: "El son de los que protestaron contra el son" (The *Son* of Those Who Protested the *Son*). In this story, a group of black men have gathered to protest the *son*. They vote to ban it, only to discover that their "yes" votes have themselves become the chorus for a *son*: "¿Uté ta confomme? / Sí señó" (*Prosa de prisa* 1: 22). [Do you agree? Yes, Sir!] Guillén describes the *son* produced by "los que protestaron contra el son" as the model he used for his own poetry: "verdaderamente sencillo, verdaderamente fácil, verdaderamente popular" (*Prosa de prisa* 1: 21) [truly simple, truly easy, truly popular]. The story of "those who protested the *son*" offers the reader an excellent example of verbal Signifyin(g); the impact of the joke lies in the way that the *son* is re-created and performed in the exact moment in which its rejection is supposed to be taking place. The *son* form thus shows itself to be such a fundamental part of local expression that no one can escape using it.

When Guillén ends with this humorous anecdote, he is "Signifyin(g) *on*" Vasconcelos; according to the story, even those who are against the *son* as a form of expression cannot help falling back into it. His retelling of the story, performed within the context of the reading of the article, defends his use of the vernacular by staging its own defense. This Signifyin(g) at the end of Guillén's text intentionally acts to destabilize Vasconcelos's hierarchical critique, to open a space for other possibilities. Guillén's message to Vasconcelos is twofold: first, these linguistic practices are more deeply ingrained than we might imagine them to be. Secondly, do not condemn or reject that which may be a fundamental part of yourself. It is no coincidence, I think, that Guillén chooses this technique to address Vasconcelos, as the dissenting journalist was himself Afro-Cuban. Through embedded performance of "The *Son* of Those Who Protested the *Son*," Guillén simultaneously critiques Vasconcelos's attitude and includes him as a member of a community; he presents the anecdote knowing that a complete understanding of its humor will only be available to a cultural insider such as Vasconcelos. Guillén's use of Signifyin(g) thus implicitly identifies both poet and journalist as members of not just a Cuban community but an Afro-Cuban community, and appeals to blackness as a common marker.

The debate between Guillén and Vasconcelos highlights a preoccupation with the relationship between cultural production and national identity visible not just in Cuban writing but also in much Latin American literature of the time. Guillén was not the only writer to be concerned with the "imported heads," with the tension between outside (European) models and the need to locate an idea of what was undeniably national. The 1920s and 1930s were decades in which writers throughout the region made use of literature to advance and conceptualize a vision of national identity. In particular, writers such as the Argentine Ricardo Güiraldes, Rómulo Gallegos of Venezuela, and José Eustacio Rivera from Colombia produced a series of regional novels that came to be known as *novelas de la tierra* (novels of the land), texts that make the connection between culture and nation a central feature of both their theme and plot. In the hands of these writers, the search for national culture within the pages of a novel was thus simultaneously a strategy for both literary and cultural empowerment. These novelists saw "culture" as something that could fill a perceived lacuna; a strong, unique national culture could make up for the postcolonial identity of these countries, as well as their uneven economic development and mixed-race populations.[6] To capture (and thus produce) a kind of "authentic culture," these novelists focused on national "types," such as the Argentine gaucho, or on a symbolic appellation of the nation's indigenous culture. In the absence of a historical tradition of the "folk" (as in Europe), they constructed an idea of national culture that was ahistorical in nature, to be found in essence rather than in historical facts or experience. Through their appeal to what was "essentially" Venezuelan, Argentine, or Colombian, these novels seemed to offer a kind of solution to a perceived crisis in the identity of national culture and the relationship of that culture to modernity.

As I have discussed previously, Cuba's particular history with regard to race made calling up an ahistorical, essentialized idea of national folk culture particularly challenging. Both Cuba's history and economy had been connected to the plantation system, and thus to slavery and the significant population of black Cubans. In the absence of any significant indigenous presence on the island, Cuba lacked an "original" population to use, whether in a symbolic or literal way, in a definition of national origins. Any search for an "authentic" cultural production meant addressing race, and addressing blackness—or even referencing "the land" itself—risked referencing the plantation system and its connection to the very historically grounded experience of slavery. Using Afro-Cuban culture without calling into question the ahistorical idea of cultural origins from which the *novelas de la tierra* operated was a difficult balancing act.

Notwithstanding the paradoxes of this discursive situation, race in

Cuban discourse in the 1930s was itself the subject of much public debate. Guillén's poems were published in a section of the newspaper *Diario de la Marina* (*The Marina Daily*) entitled "Ideales de una raza" ("Ideals of a Race") edited by Gustavo Urrutia, who was himself Afro-Cuban. As its name might indicate, Urrutia's newspaper section had become a space for discussing issues connected to race in Cuba, not only in journalistic essays but also through poems and short vignettes featuring Afro-Cuban imagery. *Afrocubanismo*, the adoption of Afro-Cuban musical forms and the use of Afro-Cuban imagery in mainstream Cuban art and literature, was a visible trend in the 1920s and '30s. *Negrista* poetry (texts by white writers that often contained stereotypical or exaggerated images of black Cubans) had been a visible presence in Cuban literary publications for several years prior to the publication of *Motivos de son*, although this earlier poetry by writers such as Emilio Ballagas and Ramón Guirao often merely reproduced a superficial racial difference (Arnedo-Gómez 11–12; Branche 163; Duno Gottberg 89–95; Kutzinski, *Sugar's Secrets* 154–62; Mullen, "Emergence" 442–43).

Just six years after Guillén and Vasconcelos aired their differences, the Paris press Gallimard, which had published a number of Surrealist texts, brought out a slim volume of short stories entitled *Contes negres de Cuba* (*Afro-Cuban Tales*, 1936).[7] The book's author, Lydia Cabrera, was from Havana but was at the time living in France. As I discuss in chapter two of this study, Cabrera's tales were warmly received by a literary scene that had for some time been drawn to African imagery as the expression of a freedom they felt bourgeois European culture had stifled. Yet Cabrera's creations go beyond the retelling of African tales; they are multilayered texts that mix periods and cultural and temporal frameworks. As she herself makes clear in the title, they are not just "black stories" but black Cuban stories.

Given the decade lapse between *Motivos de son* and the Spanish publication of *Cuentos negros* in 1940, critics have tended to connect Guillén's poems and Cabrera's short stories only tangentially. It is my contention, however, that Cabrera's work is more closely related to Guillén's than has previously been understood. In her stories, Cabrera, like Guillén, intentionally articulates a very particular relationship between race and nation, such that blackness becomes the center of the narrative rather than a condition of otherness. In their use of historically relevant detail and their treatment of temporal context, both Guillén and Cabrera posit a very different relationship between culture and history than either previous *negrista* poets or the *novelas de la tierra*. While they may choose to portray the people and situations around them, their writing is nourished by an understanding of Cuba's history (particularly its position as a Spanish colony, and the experience of slavery) and its effect on the situations of their day (the creation of a black working class, the maintenance of Afro-Cuban religious traditions). Their texts propose a cultural specificity that foregrounds blackness through the use of specific elements of Afro-Cuban cultural expression, local linguistic patterns, and the mixing of oral and written traditions.

Vera Kutzinski argues that *Afrocubanismo* was in fact a way in which Cuban high literary culture attempted to co-opt Afro-Cuban culture to create an ahistorical national essence similar to that portrayed in the *novelas de la tierra*: "Anthropology and literature collaborated in amalgamating nationalism and culture into a depoliticized ethnographic discourse whose effect was both to recuperate and to absorb *la gente de color* through their folklore" (*Sugar's Secrets* 145). Kutzinski includes Guillén in her critique, despite the fact that he sets himself apart from earlier *negrista* poets, who focused on the folkloric elements of blackness, by locating his poetry within the social and linguistic parameters of daily urban life. While I do not contest the overall validity of Kutzinski's claim, I contend that the *Motivos de son* poems mark an important shift in the way blackness was represented in Cuba, not simply for their treatment of race but for the literary and cultural strategies they employ in their treatment of it. Guillén himself may have increasingly looked to "recuperate and absorb" black Cuban culture, but his poems, in fact, go beyond his stated intentions in their representations of race. Like Cabrera's *Cuentos negros*, Guillén's poems explore alternate visions of Cubanness as much through the form of the text—the presence and practice of Signifyin(g)—as through a new presentation of Afro-Cuban subjectivity.

For both Cabrera and Guillén, play—visible as both linguistic and rhetorical devices and as narrative strategies of inclusion—serves as a way of mediating race in their texts in the name of cultural autochthony. Play is what allows their texts to treat race in a way that moves beyond the superficially folkloric. As texts that mix Afro-Cuban-influenced language structures with elements of avant-garde writing, Guillén's *Motivos de son, Sóngoro cosongo,* and *West Indies, Ltd.,* and Cabrera's *Cuentos negros de Cuba* utilize a hybridization of high-culture literary style with popular linguistic and narrative styles to augment existing elements of wordplay, improvisation, and humor already available in language production in the Caribbean. The radical nature of their work, I argue, lies in the ways in which they use these elements of rhetorical and literary play to foreground Afro-Cuban expression within Cuban cultural production as a whole.

Guillén and the *Choteo*

By the time he published *Motivos de son*, Guillén had already made a name for himself as an outspoken journalist where issues of race were concerned. In a series of articles—"El camino de Harlem" ("Harlem's Road"), "La conquista del blanco" ("The Conquest of the White Man"), and "El blanco: he ahí el problema" ("The White Man: That's the Problem")—all published in 1929, Guillén criticized Cuban society for what he saw as its unacknowledged racist attitudes. "El camino de Harlem," for example, holds up the segregated neighborhoods of New York City as an example of a failed racial democracy and warns of the danger of creating similar racially divided social spaces within Cuba. Guillén urges his readers to apply themselves to "la hermosa tarea de actuar en cubano" [the beautiful work of acting in Cuban], defining work towards mutual respect and a shared understanding as national behaviors (*Prosa de prisa* 1: 5–6).

Motivos de son was Guillén's first experiment in creating a kind of poetry that incorporated explicitly national or racial elements.[8] While his essays make direct, serious observations about the racial conflicts and divisions within Cuban society, *Motivos de son* makes the medium the message, as it uses both plays on the *son* form and the *choteo* and its fusion of the humorous and the playful to enact a social critique. A musical form that has been compared to African American blues, the *son* is composed of an eight-line "exposition," consisting of one or two verses, followed by an *estribillo* (chorus, later called a *montuno*), which features a call and response repetition of two different lines.[9] Each of the eight poems in Guillén's collection faithfully reproduces the structure of the musical form, a form that given the popularity of *son* songs in the late 1920s and early 1930s would have been recognizable to Cuban readers from a variety of backgrounds.

The first poem of the collection, "Negro bembón" ("Big Lipped Nigga") utilizes interplay between the *son* rhythm, local speech pattern, and *choteo* to interrogate racist physical stereotypes at work in Cuban society.

¿Po qué te pone tan brabo,
cuando te disen negro bembón,
si tiene la boca santa,
negro bembón?

Bembón así como ere
tiene de to;
Caridá te mantiene,
te lo da to.

Te quejaba todabía,
negro bembón;
sin pega y con harina,
negro bembón,
majagua de dri blanco,
negro bembón;
sapato de do tono,
negro bembón . . .

Bembón así como ere,
tiene de to;
Caridá te mantiene,
te lo da to. (*Obra poética* 1: 87)

[Why you get so mad
when they call you big-lipped nigga,
when ya mouth's divine,
negro bembón?

Big-lipped as you iz
you got everythin;
you live off grace,
you got everythin.

An still you bitch,
negro bembón,
in the thick of everythin,
negro bembón,

stiff white drill suit,
negro bembón,
two-tone shoes,
negro bembón ...

Big-lipped as you iz
you got everythin;
you live off grace,
you got everythin.][10]

By manipulating the orthography to reflect spoken dialect, Guillén lends a sense of immediacy to his poem. The written text thus presents itself as a performance, generating its own sense of orality and establishing the verbal space in which the *choteo*-like elements can play themselves out.[11] (This performativity would later be heightened by the fact that these poems were often used as texts to be declaimed by professional actors and were eventually set to music.) The use of local dialect also creates a sense of equality in the narrative tone of the text; it identifies the speaker as coming from a similar environment as the "negro bembón" he addresses. The use of a more sophisticated poetic voice would have created a sense of inequality between the between the speaker and the "negro bembón" on whom he is Signifyin(g). Guillén's poetic voice rejects the literary descriptive conventions of a "literate" speaker, shortening the distance between the speaker and his poetic subject, and inviting his reader to come at least part of that distance as well.

The first stanza of the poem appears to question the man's self-rejection of his own facial characteristics. Why get so angry at the people who call you "negro bembón," asks the speaker, if you have a sweet mouth? The speaker pokes fun at the man for his quickness to anger. At the same time, behind the laughter lies a questioning of the negative context behind the term *bembón*, for the second stanza goes on to confirm rather than deny the original description of the poem's subject. Why should this term be offensive, the speaker seems to suggest? Why reject your own identity? The speaker makes it clear that *bembón* is more than a physical description, carrying with it other connotations of (racial) identity and social class.

These first two stanzas of the poem contain another inner joke in their play on the words *santa* and *Caridá*. *Santa* can mean sweet, but it can also mean saintly, blessed, lucky. *Caridá* could either be the name of a woman, or a reference to the Virgen de la Caridad del Cobre (Our Lady of Charity of El Cobre), Cuba's patron saint, an indication that the man receives some kind of charity. In either case, the implication is that the "negro bembón" does not pay for his upkeep himself. Keith Ellis suggests that *Motivos de son* can be read as a series of love poems in which what is revealed is "love as it is clearly determined by the historical conditions in which it attempts to exist" (66). Yet "Negro bembón" alludes to a potential romantic relationship only indirectly, choosing instead to emphasize the problems and contradictions of the man's self-image and economic status. The speaker, while questioning the injustice that makes the term *bembón* into something offensive, sarcastically observes that the man presents himself as dandy, a man of money and social position, while it is Caridad who makes the material advantages—two-toned shoes and the linen suit—available. The adoption of the persona of the dandy is also the man's attempt at racial whitening.

The *choteo*-like aspects of "Negro bembón" are supported by the musical character of the poem, particularly in the third stanza of the poem, which functions as the *estribillo* (chorus) of the musical form. The rhythm created by the repetition of words and phrases ("negro bembón") and the call-and-response format heighten the emphasis of the joking tone. In particular, the constant presence of the word *bembón* in the chorus places a strategic emphasis on the very physical characteristics the man himself is trying to downplay (contrasting with the description of his fancy dress), thus simultaneously deriding him for his pretensions and celebrating his racial identity. In a poem about someone who wants to reject his blackness, the *son* rhythm provides a consistent, undeniable reminder of Afro-Cuban culture.

"Negro bembón" is significant not only for its recreation of natural-seeming speech; in four short stanzas, Guillén manages to conjure a fairly subtle and complex portrait of this individual: a dandy, a man who enjoys his free time and seems disinclined to work, who cares for his appearance to the extent that he rejects certain characterizations of himself even as he lashes out at negative stereotypes. Nancy Morejón characterizes "Negro bembón" as offering a "poetics" of *Motivos de son*: "[R]esume, sintetiza la esencia del juego verbal" ("Prólogo" 11) [It sums up, synthesizes the essence of the verbal play]. This ability to create a rich portrait in few words is what characterizes the other seven poems of the collection; for this reason, these intimate portraits gain strength from being read as a group, as the layering of these various voices produces a polyphonic portrait of at least a slice of a working-class Cuban community.

In 1931, just a year after the appearance of *Motivos de son*, Guillén published *Sóngoro cosongo*, a longer and more diverse collection of Afro-Cuban-oriented verse. In it, Guillén expands his use of Signifyin(g), moving beyond verbal *choteo* to a deeper rhythmic, social, and intertextual dialogue. His ideas with regard to race shift along with his expanded use of form. In the prologue to this collection, Guillén articulates more definitively the need to subjugate the representation of blackness (and the presence of race) to the construction of a racially mixed national identity and a poetic form able to represent that hybridity. He is now intent on creating a "poesía criolla" (Creole poetry), a truly unique national poetry, and while this cannot be done without including Afro-Cuban culture, he clearly privileges the process and product of racial (and cultural) mixing: "Opino por tanto que una poesía criolla entre nosotros no lo será de un modo cabal con olvido del negro. El negro—a mi juicio—aporta esencias muy firmes a nuestro coctel" (*Obra poética* 1: 96). [I believe that a Creole poetry among us will not be complete if we forget the black man. The black man—in my opinion—contributes very strong essences to our cocktail.] Yet perhaps the gentleman doth protest too much. Despite Guillén's emphasis on hybridity in the Prologue, *Sóngoro cosongo* is, if anything, more concerned with both representations of blackness and the situation of black Cubans than its predecessor. Despite Guillén's declaration that he wishes to create a "poesía mulata" (mulatto poetry), the visibility of blackness often proves to be a stronger presence in the poems than this intended hybridity implies.

In *Sóngoro cosongo*, Guillén relies much more on other kinds of verbal play than he does on the conversational, "doing-the-dozens" form of the *choteo*, in part because few poems from the collection employ a first-person poetic voice. Figurative language, which in *Motivos* was spare and simple, is now more lyrical, often to the point of strangeness. While *Motivos* used the *son* form (two verses, a chorus, a final verse) to shape the construction of the poems, music becomes thoroughly interwoven into *Sóngoro cosongo* as theme, structuring force, and leitmotif. Guillén frequently plays with the expectations of the reader (or listener) with regard to structure, beginning with what seems like a *son*, only to riff on this—or other established musical or poetic forms—to create something entirely new. One could almost argue that in this way, in *Sóngoro Cosogno* Guillén

Signifies on his early work. A reader familiar with *Motivos* might expect him to repeat the formal gesture he employed in that collection; Guillén's new poems thus toy with, disrupt, frustrate, and finally move beyond the reader's expectations. As in musical improvisation, Guillén's poems, no longer faithful to such a rigid structure as the *son*, build on established rhythmic patterns and expectations, moving outward towards unexpected sonorities and unpredictable rhyme schemes. While the reader who possesses a thorough knowledge of the original form may best grasp the improvised elements of the poem's structure, Guillén's Signifyin(g) opens the door both verbally and rhythmically to a kind of intentional multiplicity, positing different ways of meaning.[12]

In his poem "Secuestro de la mujer de Antonio" (The Kidnapping of Antonio's Wife, *Obra poética* 1: 109–110), Guillén not only plays with traditional or established rhythms but also Signifies on other popular texts. The poem's title makes reference to an actual *son* song, "La mujer de Antonio," first popularized by the Trío Matamoros in the 1920s.[13] In his reworking, however, Guillén does not merely reproduce the *son* structure, but rather elaborates and thus transforms both the form and content of the original. The original song describes a woman—Antonio's wife—as she returns from the market, and it emphasizes the way she walks through the chorus's repetition—"La mujer de Antonio / camina así" [Antonio's wife / walks like this]. Although Antonio's wife remains the focus of Guillén's poem, the scene is no longer the morning market but a late-night dance floor. One could argue that the poem's title refers to two symbolic "kidnappings"—that of Antonio's wife (swept off her feet to dance with the poem's speaker) and Guillén's intertextual literary "kidnapping" of the original song, which he remakes to serve his purposes. A reader familiar with Miguel de Matamoros's original piece both understands the racial identity implicit in the *son* reference and senses the new ways in which Guillén plays with both form and content.

Guillén himself calls "Secuestro" "un pequeño cuadro popular" (a small popular sketch, *Prosa de prisa* 1: 41), but this time what communicates the local, Cuban feel of the poem is not the recreation of popular dialogue but the play on musical form and on stereotypical images of Cubanness. As in "Negro bembón" (and in contrast to the Trío Matamoros song), the speaker of "Secuestro" speaks directly to Antonio's wife. The joking and sarcasm are gone, replaced by a lyricism and passionate intensity:

Te voy a beber de un trago,
como una copa de ron;
te voy a echar en la copa
de un son,
prieta, quemada en ti misma,
cintura de mi canción.

Záfate tu chal de espumas
para que torees la rumba;
y si Antonio se disgusta
que se corra por ahí:
¡la mujer de Antonio tiene
que bailar aquí!

Desamárrate, Gabriela.
Muerde
la cascara verde,
pero no apagues la vela;
tranca
la pájara Blanca,
y vengan de dos en dos,
que el bongó
se calentó . . . (*Obra poética* 1: 109)

[I'm gonna drink you up in one gulp
like a shot of rum;
I'm gonna pour you into a cup
of *son*,
black girl, burnt by your own spirit,
my song's refrain.

Take off your shawl of foam
so you can move like a bullfighter with this rumba;
and if Antonio gets mad
he can just leave:
Antonio's woman's
gotta dance here!

> Let go, Gabriela.
> Bite down
> on the green rind,
> but don't put out the fire;
> trap
> that white bird,
> and come two by two,
> cuz the bongo's
> starting up ...]

In the original song, Antonio's wife is watched by a nosy (or lustful?) neighbor; in Guillén's poem, the speaker is male and the gaze one of desire. The first lines play with the double meaning of "to drink," encompassing both the drinking (ostensibly taking place) and the speaker's desire "to drink in" the women with his eyes. Guillén elaborates the metaphor so that Antonio's wife is thrown into the "cup of *son*," as she becomes the speaker's interlocutor and the focus of his own song. While the original song identifies Antonio's wife only by her relationship to Antonio, Guillén gives her a name—Gabriela—thus identifying her as an individual, and revealing an interest in her beyond the idle observation of her physical beauty. In this first multileveled metaphor, this woman is "sweet enough to drink," maybe strong like liquor—simultaneously a description of her attractiveness (in the eyes of the speaker) and a reference to her skin color (communicated by comparing her to a glass of rum). In the second stanza she becomes the dancer to the poem's rhythm, as he tells her, "Záfate tu chal de espumas/para que torees la rumba" (*Obra poética* 1: 110). [Take off your shawl of foam/so you can move like a bullfighter with this rumba.] The use of the verb *torear* (literally, to bullfight) in the context of a rumba dance implies that this dancing has a vital force, perhaps of anger, perhaps of sexual energy, behind it. It interjects the idea of a contest of wills, a charged—and potentially dangerous—encounter between two people, into the scene. Through this imagined coupling, the poem thus communicates an energy quite different from that of Antonio's wife returning from the market in the original song.

Music makes its presence felt in "Secuestro" from the beginning, yet unlike the poems of *Motivos*, this text does not imitate the *son* form of a verse followed by a repeated chorus. While there is an emphatic rhythm to the poem, each stanza maintains its own rhyme scheme; as the poem goes on, the rigidity of the rhyme scheme breaks down so that the force of the rhythm comes to the fore. The first three stanzas can be seen as the invitation to a dance: the end of the first shows the woman as the song, the second stanza calls on her to dance, the third portrays the beginning sounds of the drums as the speaker calls the dancers to come "two by two." The internal rhymes in these stanzas (the "ma's" of *quemada* and *misma*; *muerde* and *verde* in the third stanza) sustain the sonority of the imagery.

In the fourth stanza, the rhythm becomes more frenetic, and the end of the last stanza reveals a total polyphonic breakdown, interweaving single lines from previous parts of the poem to create an increasingly intense counterpoint between these lines and the chorus:

> Mulata, mora, morena,
> que ni el más toro se mueva,
> porque el que más toro sea
> saldrá caminando así;
> el mismo Antonio si llega,
> saldrá caminando así;
> todo el que no esté conforme,
> saldrá caminando así ...
> Repique, repique, pique,
> repique, repique po;
> ¡prieta, quemada en ti misma,
> cintura de mi canción! (*Obra poética* 1: 109–110)

> [Mulatta, mora, black girl
> not even the biggest bull among us'd better move,
> cuz whoever's the biggest bull
> is gonna go out like this;
> even Antonio himself, if he shows up,
> is gonna go out like this;
> whoever isn't happy about it,
> is gonna go out like this ...
> Grind it down, down
> grind it, grind it, hey;
> black girl, burnt by your own spirit,
> my song's refrain!]

The appearance of the chorus as every other line of the last stanza both conveys the force of the speaker's emotions and echoes the rhythm of the chorus of the original *son* ("La mujer de Antonio / camina así"). However, while in the song Antonio's wife remains the sole person doing the walking, in Guillén's poem the identity of the walker shifts to the speaker's "opponent," variously "el que más toro sea" [whoever's the biggest bull], Antonio himself, and anyone who doesn't agree (implicitly, the spectators). The reader is also reminded of Guillén's narrative of "los que protestaron contra el *son*" [those who protested the *son*] in the statement "todo el que no esté conforme, / saldrá caminando así" [whoever isn't happy about it / is gonna go out (walking) like this]; just as those voting against the *son* could not help turning their rejection votes into a song, even those against Gabriela's dancing will in the end be drawn into the dance themselves. This gesture adds a performative dimension to the text that was not there in the original; if the Trío Matamoros song appeals to a potential group of observers of Antonio's wife, Guillén's Signifyin(g) in "Secuestro" includes the observer (and thus the reader) in the dance.

While music is the central device around which Guillén develops "Secuestro," he also plays with stereotypical images of Cubanness in his use of typically Cuban products. Rum, sugar, and coffee all appear in the poem as metaphors for female sensuality. Gabriela is described first as a glass of rum. Later in the poem, the dark seeds of her eyes "darán sus frutos espesos" (*obra poética* 1: 109) [will show a bountiful yield], a description suggesting coffee. The musicality of the poem and the image of the woman dancing combine with these metaphors of national produce perfectly in the fourth stanza, in which the woman's sweat from dancing is described in terms of the sugar harvest: "aquí molerán tus ancas / la zafra de tu sudor" (*Obra poética* 1: 109) [your haunches will grind down / the harvest of your sweat]. Since many of Guillén's poems are explicitly critical of the difficult working conditions created by the system of sugar production in Cuba, (including "Caña" ["Sugar Cane"], the poem which immediately precedes "Secuestro" in *Sóngoro cosongo*), the portrayal of Gabriela's sweat as liquid sugar produced by her movements is especially interesting. In the sensuality of the dance, another kind of harvest is produced, a production equally natural and equally Cuban.

While "Secuestro" plays with the Trío Matamoros *son*, other poems in Guillén's collection Signify on the work of other *negrista* writers. The poem "Rumba," for example, takes as its subject the iconic Afro-Cuban dance (which in the 1930s was still far from accepted by mainstream Cuban society).[14] A number of *negrista* poets, principally José Z. Tallet and

Ramón Guirao, had already published poems dealing with this theme.[15] Whereas Tallet and Guirao focus on the figure of the female *rumba* dancer, Guillén's poem personifies the *rumba* dance itself.

As his use of racially identified play expands, Guillén's poems find themselves stuck in something of an ideological impasse. On the one hand, blackness is, if anything, more visible in this collection than in *Motivos*. On the other hand, Guillén is—as he himself states time and again—trying to use blackness as a step towards the idea of a single Cuban hybrid "race." In a slightly later essay "Cuba, negros, poesía" ("Cuba, Blacks, Poetry," 1937), Guillén explains the celebration of black culture—in both his poetry and that of *negrista* writers—as an intermediate stage that "facilitates" the ultimate creation of an authentic, hybrid Cuban culture:

> Por lo pronto, señalemos el hecho de que el movimiento negro fue dando a cada atmósfera social una temperatura lírica diversa... De manera que al llegar hasta la Isla aquella onda exótica, no fue una novedad sorprendente: antes bien, abrió de un solo golpe el camino propio, permitiendo comprender que por la expresión de lo negro era posible llegar a la expresión de lo cubano; de lo cubano ya sin matiz epidérmico, ni negro ni blanco, pero integrado por la atracción simpática de esas dos fuerzas fundamentales en la composición social isleña. (*Prosa de prisa* 1: 100)

> [As a beginning, let us highlight the fact that the black movement little by little gave each social atmosphere a different lyrical temperament... So that by the time this exotic phase arrived on the Island, it was no longer a surprising novelty. Well now, in one blow it opened a new path for itself, allowing it to be understood that through black expression it was possible to reach Cuban expression: Cubanness now without different skin tones, neither black nor white but integrated by the sympathetic attraction of these two fundamental forces in the social composition of the island.]

For Guillén, it seems obvious—and perhaps necessary—that visible phenotypic differences are disappearing and must disappear. But he does not expand his discussion here to explore what this might mean for accompanying cultural differences ("these two fundamental forces"), which he constructs as a black/white dialectic. In *West Indies, Ltd.*, the poetry collection that followed this essay, Guillén increasingly returns to this black/

white racial binary, the most obvious instance being that of the two grandfathers in "Balada de los dos abuelos" ("Ballad of the Two Grandfathers"), although it is also visible in poems such as "Dos niños" (Two Children) which compares the situation of two equally destitute children, one black, one white. In these examples, there is an attempt at a critique of human suffering that goes beyond race: "Dos niños, ramas de un mismo arbol de miseria" (*Obra poética* 1: 129) [Two children / branches of one same suffering tree of poverty]. Yet the presence of this binary, if anything, continues to make blackness visible.

Blackness continues to be an issue that appears in the intersections between form and content. If Guillén had previously Signified on such existing popular forms as the *son*, in *West Indies, Ltd.*, he also moves in the opposite direction to play with (and thus comment on) high literary forms. "El abuelo" ("The Grandfather"), another poem in the collection, offers a paradigmatic example of Guillén's exploration of this kind of Signifyin(g). A four-stanza sonnet, "El abuelo" deals with the issue of racial passing. The poem's subject is a beautiful woman whose every physical characteristic identifies her as white, and the first two four-line stanzas describe her perfect European appearance: blonde hair, straight nose, "snow-white" skin. Yet in both the last two lines of the first stanza and the last two lines of the poem, the poetic voice reveals that this woman has a black grandfather. What stands out is the contrast created within the language of the poem whenever blackness is mentioned:

> Esta mujer angélica de ojos septentrionales,
> que vive atenta al ritmo de su sange europea,
> ignora que en lo hondo de ese ritmo golpea
> un negro el parche duro de roncos atabales.
>
> Bajo la línea escueta de su nariz aguda,
> la boca, en fino trazo, traza una raya breve,
> y no hay cuervo que manche la solitaria nieve
> de su carne, que fulge temblorosa y desnuda.
>
> ¡Ah, mi señora! Mírate las venas misteriosas;
> boga en el agua viva que allá dentro te fluye,
> y ve pasando lírios, nelumbios, lotos, rosas;

que ya verás, inquieta, junto a la fresca orilla,
la dulce sombra oscura del abuelo que huye,
el que rizó por siempre tu cabeza amarilla. (*Obra poética* 1: 127)

[This angelic lady with eyes from the North,
who follows the beat of her European blood,
knows not that in this rhythm's thorough flood
a black man beats dark drums that are hoarse.

Beneath the straight course of her small, Nordic nose
her mouth traverses a thin, delicate line;
no crow flies to stain the solitary snow,
of her skin with its tremulous, naked shine.

Oh, my lady! Behold the mysteries below,
ride the live waters that deep inside you flow,
and watch lilies, lotuses, and roses as you go;

on the fresh shore, restless, you will then see
the sweet dark shadow of the grandfather flee,
he who curled your yellow head indelibly.][16]

The poem's vocabulary is sophisticated, almost overly so, and it carefully maintains a perfectly consonant rhyme scheme. Yet "el parche duro de roncos atabales" ("the dark drums that are hoarse") interrupts this precision with its sonorous "o's," suggesting the "hard drum skin" whose rough sounds cannot stay hidden within the softly elegant surface of the rest of the poem. This contrast prepares the reader for the *choteo* created in the last lines of the poem. As in "Negro bembón," the poem's speaker addresses his subject directly: "Ah, mi señora! Mírate las venas misteriosas" (127) [Literally: Ah, my lady! Look at your mysterious veins]. The apostrophe of "mi señora" is almost overly courteous, as the speaker proceeds to set up the shock of the contrast: the "agua viva" of the woman's veins, filled with the exotic delicate flowers and a "dark shadow"—the African grandfather—lurking on the bank. Gustavo Pérez Firmat refers to Guillén's use of the love sonnet to discuss racial passing as a "transculturation of the literary tradition that animates his own poem" (74). But Guillén's strategy in "El abuelo" goes beyond simply incorporating Afro-Cuban elements into a sonnet. He uses this juxtaposition of content and form to produce both humor and social critique: blackness lurks in this whitest of poetic conventions.

The Signifyin(g) in "El abuelo" is made evident by the poem's placement in the collection, coming as it does between two poems that play much more directly with Afro-Cuban rhythms: "Sensemayá" and "Caminando." This sandwiching of the ostensibly European sonnet further emphasizes the poem's ironic message with respect to passing. Roberto González Echevarría characterizes "El abuelo" as a baroque sonnet in its use of the concept of *desengaño*, the fact that beauty (both the woman's and the poem's) "is dependent upon an untruth, or at least on an interplay of superficial signs bearing both truth and the contrived beauty that conceals it" (*Celestina's Brood* 201). And yet among the poem's several dichotomies—true/false, black/white, surface/depths—it is blackness that emerges as the woman's (and implicitly the poem's) true identity. It is as if the poem itself were "trying to pass" as "purely European" (or identifying the "purely Cuban" as European), only to be revealed for the hybrid product that it is. What stands out is not the white physical shell (of both the woman and the poem), but the blackness at the poem's center.

In "West Indies, Ltd.," (the title poem of the collection), Guillén extends the antiauthoritarian aspects of Signifyin(g) to a social critique of the postcolonial situation, using the motivated *choteo* as his primary tool for challenging the sociocultural balance of power. Since the poem is very long, I will focus here on the first three sections and on the ways in which they bring out Guillén's anger and humor, both separately and in relation to each other. The poem is constructed as if it were the narrative of a guided tour, and the reader were just descending from a cruise ship for his or her first view of a Caribbean island. The exclamation points bracketing the first words "¡West Indies!" establish a tone of excitement, sustained by the list of natural products that follows. Following this exoticizing first view, the second line presents the islands inhabitants as "un oscuro pueblo sonriente" (*Obra poética* 1: 134) ("a dark, smiling people"), the smiling (dark) natives ready to welcome the distinguished travelers. The identification of the natives as nonwhite creates an implicit division between islanders and tourists, recalling (referencing) scenes of colonialism and conquest—a performance of the official reception of the colonizer by the (about-to-be) colonized.

This atmosphere of an orchestrated performance is further enhanced by the refrain, introduced in italics between parts of the poem, "Cinco minutos de interrupción. La charanga de Juan el Barbero toca un son" (136). [Five minutes of interruption. Juan the Barber's group plays a *son*.] The purpose is entertainment, and visitors should not be given any time to get bored. Consider the contrast between this staged welcome for tourists and the first lines of the first poem in *Sóngoro cosongo*, "Llegada" ("Arrival"): "¡Aquí estamos! / La palabra nos viene húmeda de los bosques, / y un sol enérgico nos amanece entre las venas" (*Obra poética* 1: 97). [Here we are! / The words comes to us moist from the forest / and a surging sun dawns in our veins.] In the later poem, the raw energy of the earlier description of arrival has been replaced by a static scene; the islands have sold out to the invaders, not those wielding swords but those waving cash. In this way, the poem in some sense moves to Signify on the reader, who through Guillén's narration is placed in the position of the tourist, caught in the very performance (of both exoticizing and racializing the islanders) that Guillén's tone and ironic presentation act to critique.

One way in which Signifyin(g) in "West Indies, Ltd." operates is in the use of irony, as Guillén builds up these images of happiness and plenty, only to undermine them in the next lines when he reveals the poverty and degradation behind them:

Éste es un oscuro pueblo sonriente,
Conservador y liberal,
ganadero y azucarero,
donde a veces corre mucho dinero,
pero donde se vive muy mal. (*Obra poética* 1: 134)

[This is a dark smiling people,
Conservative and liberal,
cow-men and sugar-men
where a lot of money flows,
but where one lives very badly.]

The contrast between the ubiquitous presence of money and the living situation of the local people produces a dark humor. The poem continues to Signify on the island's citizens, calling them "chusma incivil de variadísima" [a truly varied uncivil crew]. Rather than praise the population's ethnic harmony, the speaker says of its diversity, "se han corrido los tintes y no hay un tono estable" (135) [the colors have run and there's no fixed tone]. These descriptions laugh at the contrast between fantasy and reality, but they are also suggestive of ways in which colonial authority has been subverted. These are not the docile natives originally envisioned, nor have they maintained the social and racial boundaries originally established.

Despite the negative portrayals of the people of this Caribbean island, the object of Guillén's Signifyin(g) is not really these individuals, but rather the social hierarchies that have been established on these islands. He finally states this directly in the last stanza of the poem's first section:

> Me río de ti, noble de las Antillas,
> mono que andas saltando de mata en mata,
> payaso que sudas por no meter la pata,
> y siempre la metes hasta las rodillas. (*Obra poética* 1: 136)

> [I laugh at you, noble Antilles,
> monkey that jumps around from bush to bush,
> clown who sweats so as not to stick his foot in it,
> and who always sticks it in up to his knees.]

The image of the Antilles as a monkey suggests the trickster of African folktales, yet this is a monkey paralyzed by its inability to act, a "clown" incapable even of imitation. The islands' original nobility has been reduced to a creature capable only of parody, whose culture has become a stage for welcoming tourists. Guillén returns here to the same critique he offered in *Motivos de son* poems like "Negro bembón" and "Tú no sabe inglés" (You Don't Know No English), this time placing it in a context that extends beyond race. By selling out to the neocolonial fantasy of what they should be, the poem suggests, societies in the Caribbean can only emerge looking ridiculous in the contrast between their aristocratic social pretensions and the islands' bleaker social reality.

Of Myths and Monkeys: Cabrera Signifies on the Afro-Cuban Folktale

In his attempt to found a "poesía criolla," Guillén's Signifyin(g) moves gradually away from a specifically Afro-Cuban focus to critique colonialism and its aftereffects more generally. In contrast, Lydia Cabrera is consistently clear in affirming (and reaffirming) the racial identity of her short fiction. She significantly titles her first collection *Cuentos negros de Cuba* instead of merely *Cuentos cubanos* or *Cuentos negros*, emphasizing that the stories are not African legends, but Afro-Cuban creations. (Her second short-story collection, *Por qué . . . Cuentos negros de Cuba*, from 1948, also carries this title.) This explicit identification of the stories has often created confusion in Cabrera's readers, many of whom, unaware of her identity as the daughter of writer and journalist Raimundo Cabrera, have assumed that the author herself was black (Rodríguez-Mangual 5).[17]

In the prologue to the Spanish edition of *Cuentos negros*, Fernando Ortiz commits another error of identification when he describes Cabrera as a "translator" rather than the author of the stories, implying that Cabrera had merely facilitated the written transcription of extant oral texts:

> Porque también el texto castellano es en realidad una traducción, y, en rigor sea dicho, una segunda traducción. Del lenguaje africano (yoruba, ewe o bantú) en que las fábulas se imaginaron, éstas fueron vertidas en Cuba al idioma amestizado y dialectal de los negros criollos . . . Y de esta habla tuvo la coleccionista que pasarlas a una forma legible en castellano, tal como ahora se estamparán. La autora ha hecho tarea difícil pero leal y, por tanto, muy meritoria, conservando a los cuentos su fuerte carácter exótico de fondo y de forma. (8)

> [Because the text in Spanish is in reality a translation, and to be fully honest, a second translation. From the African language (Yoruba, Ewe, or Bantu) in which these fables were imagined, they arrived in Cuba through the mixed and dialectal language of the black Creoles . . . And from this speech the collector had to transfer them to a legible form in Spanish, just as they are now printed. The author has taken on a difficult, but faithful, and very meritorious, task to conserve the exotic nature of these stories in both form and content.]

Ortiz mistakenly views these stories as *folklore* rather than literature; he sees them as black stories quite simply because they come from the Afro-Cuban community. Yet in some ways his identification of *Cuentos negros* as traditional folktales can be forgiven. While the collection is certainly not a literal translation of stories already in existence, there is a kind of cultural translation being performed in these stories, which insist on their blackness (and highlight that blackness as difference) in contrast to their readers, who, at least initially, would have been largely white and middle and upper-middle class.

Translation is always a process of cultural encounter in which multiple elements are adjusted, reshaped, and re-presented. As Mary Louise Pratt reminds us, the fact that translation often takes place within a loaded space and along a power differential means that it can have various possible intended—and real—outcomes: "Translation in its normative, linguistic sense seeks some form of equivalence. How helpful is it, then, to treat as translation those processes that involve the purposeful creation of nonequivalence, of new musics not mandated by the original? Musics that capture aspects of the original by being parodic, mimetic, resistant, caricaturesque, or 'accurate by exaggeration,' as one colleague put it? What about processes that muffle, absorb, appropriate, transpose, conceal?" ("Traffic in Meaning" 33). I bring up Pratt's discussion of nonequivalence here because Cabrera's stories significantly present Afro-Cuban culture without attempting to find processes of equivalence. Indeed, I argue that Cabrera's creative process intentionally results in just the kind of "parodic" or "resistant" versions that Pratt describes. As I will now show, Cabrera's use of "Afro-Cuban" elements in her writing is less a case of being faithful to the letter of the folktales than to a spirit of Afro-Cuban play. Even as Cabrera's work positions Afro-Cuban culture within the larger Cuban cultural panorama, her stories disrupt traditional narrative devices and overturn expected plot structures.

In the same way that Guillén's poems in *Sóngoro cosongo* play on his earlier *son*-inspired poetry, opening that structure up to create more free-form rhythm and rhyme schemes, Cabrera plays on (and eventually defies) the reader's expectations of the "folktale," viewed as both performed narrative and written story. By Signifyin(g) on both the form and content of the traditional tale, she interrogates the boundaries of both oral and written discourses in a new way. Her choice of the tale also indicates a particular mixing of oral and written traditions that substitutes a collective narrative for the individual poetic voice of Guillén's texts. Her stories contain many of the rhetorical elements common to traditional tales; in addition to emphasizing oral communication in general, they are filled with the repetition common to oral storytelling, with characters that Signify verbally on each other, and with conflicts that are generated, fought, and resolved through verbal trickery or finesse. Yet they also include ambiguous endings, temporal shifts, and the interweaving of multiple, sometimes discordant narratives within one single tale.

Cabrera's story "Walo-Wila," which first appeared in Spanish in the Havana magazine *Grafos* in 1938, two years before the publication of the Spanish version of *Cuentos negros*, exemplifies the ways in which Cabrera experiments with the development of the folktale even as she highlights traditional storytelling conventions. The structure of the narrative follows the traditional lines of a folktale fairly closely: a beautiful woman is pursued by several suitors, but only one can overcome both the imposed verbal disguises and physical tests to win her. Yet the text's spiritual dimensions, as well as the heavy use of *Lucumí* (the Yoruba language as it is known in Cuba), make this an unusual choice for a debut publication, especially in a magazine that could be characterized as a society journal with a literary edge.[18]

In keeping with the tradition of the oral folktale, the story is simple in both structure and plot, combining elements of the quest narrative with the archetypal tale of winning a bride. The story centers around two sisters, Ayere Kénde and Walo-Wila. While Walo-Wila stays indoors, Ayere Kénde spends her time on the balcony, attracting prospective suitors for her sister with tales of her beauty. Walo-Wila, however, manages to scare each suitor away by telling him she is ugly and diseased: "¡Ay, que yo soy fea, / Que yo soy tuerta, / Que soy gambada, / Que tengo sarna! . . ." (*Cuentos negros* 37). [Ay, but I'm ugly, / But I'm one-eyed, / But I'm bow-legged, / But I have mange!] That Walo-Wila's response to each suitor is constructed like a song is just one way in which Cabrera's presentation of the tale creates a sense of orality within the written text. Much of the story is taken up by call-and-response dialogue between the two sisters and various suitors that simulates the relationship between a storyteller and his or her audience, who would be expected to call out repeated lines or phrases. The dialogue between Ayere Kénde and the men who pass below the balcony creates a verbal pattern in which the audience (or reader) can participate, and one that continues to repeat itself with several suitors until Venado, the last suitor, finally agrees to marry Walo-Wila.[19]

Into this familiar structure, Cabrera introduces narrative complexities that disrupt facile interpretation, expanding her text's levels of meaning to include not only metaphoric and allegorical depths of the story but also religious aspects. The story's challenges to the traditional narrative development of the tale are first made apparent by its ambiguities. There is no physical description of the sisters at the beginning of the story. Neither is anything said about their relationship to each other, nor the reasons for the differences in their behavior. Although the sister who is physically visible throughout the story is Ayere Kénde, she is never wooed by any of the men who see her on the balcony. Yet she never appears jealous that it is her sister in whom the men are interested, nor is she presented as the evil or ugly counterpart to her sister's attractiveness. In fact, it is she who attempts to attract potential suitors for Walo-Wila. Walo-Wila, on the other hand, neither leaves the house nor enters the text in any physical way until the end of the story. Until Venado completes his test, not even the reader knows which of these descriptions of Walo-Wila is true. Both reader and suitors must be swayed by rhetoric, since the narrator gives nothing away. We are never sure what it is that convinces Venado that he should marry Walo-Wila; is it simply her beauty, or is there another motivation?

As indicated by the ambivalent presentation of these aspects of the plot, "Walo-Wila" presents multiple levels of meaning. The interplay of these various levels can be seen in an examination of the significance of water in the text. Water is presented first as an important element of the setting, and Ayere Kénde's offer of water is what attracts potential suitors to the balcony. But there are indications that water also serves as a link to the story's religious symbolism. Rather than retrieve the pearls that Ayere Kénde scatters in the sea (as we might expect), Venado completes his "test" by returning with a gourd filled with water from the realm of Olokun. Olokun is an ambivalent, extremely powerful and mysterious *oricha* (Afro-Cuban god). Some tales state that he or she (the gender is ambiguous) is chained to the bottom of the ocean floor, to prevent him or her from destroying mankind. Because of Olokun's destructive power, the *oricha*'s realm—the ocean depths—is often seen as a kind of underworld. Venado's quest is thus in some ways the ultimate quest, a demonstration not only of bravery (or diving skill) but also of faith; like Orpheus, he must travel to a dangerous underworld and return. Because of Olokun's connection to the ocean depths, he/she has come to be associated with the Middle Passage, and with the enslaved Africans who perished on their way to the New World. This association further connects Venado's quest with a journey to a world beyond that of the living, but it also implicitly links this mythic tale to actual journeys of trauma and loss.

Venado's journey to Olokun reveals that a text that initially seems to be one of the least Afro-Cuban-influenced of Cabrera's *Cuentos negros* is firmly anchored in the cosmology of the *Regla de Ochá* (Santería).[20] The constant repetition that Walo-Wila "moría, vivía" [was living, dying] also suggests that she is the moon, waxing and waning. As Venado prepares to dive into the ocean, the calling of Walo-Wila's name by the seashore is echoed by the sentence which follows: "Y se entró por las olas cortadas a filo de luna" (38). [And he entered the waves sliced by the moon.] When Venado brings back "sapphire-blue" water from the ocean depths, Ayere Kénde finally allows him to see Walo-Wila, and she is indeed beautiful. The story ends with the enigmatic line: "Cuando se besan la luna y el mar . . ." (38) [When the moon and the sea kiss . . .], a poetic metaphor for the meeting of the lovers. Venado's trip to the deep is thus the uniting of two elemental forces, a recognition of the connection between the moon and the tides. By bringing Walo-Wila the water she needs, Venado reestablishes a cosmic balance.

Yet this explanation does not fully account for all elements of the story. Despite the connections that Cabrera's narrative establishes with aspects of Afro-Cuban religious symbolism, the story's ending does not offer a clear reading. What is Venado's connection to the moon and tides? The deer (*venado*) is connected to Ochosi, the hunter *oricha*. A woodland animal—"hijo de la Madreselva" (37)—he is connected to the outdoors, and thus at odds with Walo-Wila, who in the story's first part is confined to interior space. Does his trip to the ocean depths also suggest the union of disparate spaces? And what (or who) does Ayere Kénde represent in this interpretation? Despite its mythic structure, Cabrera's mysterious tale leaves us with as many questions as answers.

Some of the ambiguity in Cabrera's stories may not, in fact, be an innovation but rather a gesture towards the historical function of stories and the storyteller in the Caribbean. As Patrick Chamoiseau and Rafael Confiant explain, the (Afro-)Caribbean storyteller in plantation society occupies a role that simultaneously places him in a position of authority (as a recognized speaker) and makes him the voice of the subaltern, of an enslaved people (59–60). This somewhat paradoxical position demands a number of narrative strategies, many of which utilize tactics of presentation designed to both relay and hide the tale's true message. These strategies are verbal examples of Glissantian "diversion," a practice of which the storyteller is a master. The storyteller disguises his message, using what Chamoiseau and Confiant call the "voix pas claire" (the unclear voice), a series of techniques designed to evoke or suggest, rather than declare, multiple meanings. Chamoiseau and Confiant emphasize the performative elements of the storytelling experience; the question becomes how one might be "drawn in" by the "unclear voice" of a written story. Cabrera employs a "voix pas claire" as her narrative voice in "Walo-Wila," drawing in readers in the same way that Walo-Wila's suitors are drawn to rumors of her mysterious beauty. Only those readers familiar with the function of Olokun in the *Lucumí* pantheon will recognize the spiritual aspects of Venado's quest, but the ambiguous ending and the unstated references to the Middle Passage (through Olokun) offer up multiple levels of meaning, perhaps levels not meant to be captured by all of the story's readers.

In its brevity and its focus on one particular story, "Walo-Wila" is largely faithful to many of the conventions of oral storytelling. In "Taita Hicotea y Taita Tigre" (also from *Cuentos negros*), Cabrera broadens the range of her "dissembling" as she plays with narrative structure, temporal range, and Signifyin(g) within and upon the text. As with some other stories by Cabrera, this text is really constructed as a series of tales, much as an oral storyteller might add in stylistic digressions.[21] These first narrations come in such rapid succession that they create a layering of images, almost a collage of mininarratives or interconnected myths. Cabrera's structural explorations allow her to include content that more directly references Cuba as she challenges the norms of the folktale.

One of the most important ways in which Cabrera Signifies on the folktale's narrative structure in "Taita Hicotea y Taita Tigre" has to do with the way in which she explores time in the story. Glissant has argued that whereas myths begin in a time of origins and establish a connection with a sense of history, the Caribbean folktale is "anti-History," in that it deals with ordinary symbols but does not anchor them within a progressive concept of time (*Caribbean Discourse* 85). Cabrera's story plays not only with both these temporal constructions but also with references to historical time, complicating not only the structure of the text itself but also the multiple ways in which it can be read.

At the beginning of "Taita Hicotea," Cabrera's use of time leans more toward the mythic. The opening phrase, "Cuando la tierra era joven" (*Cuentos negros* 41) [When the Earth Was Young], locates the first episodes of the story in a time of origins, implying a linear relationship between these occurrences and the time of the narration. While there are elements of the anthropomorphic fantastic—Mosquito stinging the mountain, Elephant marrying the Ant, the story of how the Hare winds up in the eye of the

Moon—most of these are "por qué" (why) stories that use the time of origins to explain a current situation. The story finally introduces two of the central characters, Hicotea (Snapping Turtle) and Venado (Deer). Venado, also called "Pata de Aire" (Air-foot), is fast and powerful, but credulous and somewhat naïve; Hicotea, trickster figure par excellence, is the crafty thinker of the two. With their animal names (and characteristics), it seems as if the story will now shift to a more traditional folktale mode.

As Venado and Hicotea cross the ocean, however, Cabrera further complicates the temporal location of the story by introducing a concrete temporal marker. We are no longer in a mythic nameless land; instead, the two animals land in a specific place—"las orillas de una isla feliz" [the shores of a happy island]—and at a very specific moment, 1845. This is very different from Glissant's argument that the folktale presents time as both fragmented and unconnected to any kind of linear construction, that within the structure of the tale "time cannot be conceived as a basic dimension of human existence" (*Caribbean Discourse* 84). Clearly, Cabrera's story can no longer be seen to be "anti-History," since the year 1845 places the action of the story firmly in the prime years of colonial Cuba. This shift from mythic to concrete time significantly occurs over the transatlantic journey, perhaps signaling the shift from the mythic permanence of life in West Africa to life under slavery in the Caribbean. Effectively, the story itself performs a kind of Middle Passage. In placing the action within a concrete historical framework, Cabrera Signifies on the intentions and format of the traditional tale. By introducing a precise temporal location for her story, she creates a text which has the feel of oral literature but which also carries the narrative charge of a historicizing written text. The tale may have mythic dimensions, but giving the action a date connects it to the course of history and to the temporal location of the reader.

Together with a multilayered temporal setting, the story further subverts expectations of narrative authority through its treatment of race and gender. Just as the first section of the story chronicles the development of certain natural phenomena, it also presents the development of a binary idea of race in the form of two very different origin myths. While the first black man, "el Padre de todos los negros" [the Father of all black people], is made black when he comes too close to the sun, the first white man becomes white by traveling to the cold land of the moon. Already a dichotomy has been established; the black man is associated with the sun, with daylight, and with happiness: "La alegría es de los negros" (43).

[Happiness belongs to black people.] The white man, in contrast, is influenced by the moon, which is cold, and is sad by nature: "Son tristes . . . todo se explica" (43). [They're sad . . . everything can be explained.] Despite the assertion that this myth "explains everything," the silence of the above ellipsis points to something that cannot be narrated. This space of the unsaid seems to point to the trauma of slavery, so that even as the story itself never directly addresses the issue, the history of that experience is always in the framework of the tale. Yet within the context of slavery, one might expect the blacks to be sad. So what does the sadness of the whites explain?

The silence of that ellipsis with regard to race is an absent presence throughout the rest of the tale. After having introduced the issue of race so provocatively in the first section, the subject is dropped as the story crosses the ocean; nevertheless, the introduction of race in an origin myth presents race as a fundamental sign of difference. Given that many of the characteristics of the new island on whose shores Venado and Hicotea land identify it as nineteenth-century Cuba, the idea of slavery, while never explicitly mentioned, hangs over the text. The society into which Venado and Hicotea arrive is fundamentally capitalist; the two friends are quick to understand the new system of ownership in which "la tierra no era del que la tomaba y se decía su dueño, sino de quien la compraba" (47) [the land did not belong to him who took it and declared himself the owner, but to him who bought it]. Details of society on the island fluctuate between characteristics that correspond to the Caribbean of 1845 and a situation suggestive of the mythic time of the beginning of the story. "¿Has oído? ¡Aquí vamos a ser hacendados!" (47) [Have you heard? We're going to be landowners!], Hicotea tells Venado, yet there is no mention of the labor on their haciendas. Indeed, the story makes it appear as if Hicotea and Venado work the land entirely themselves.

The island is described first as a kind of paradise; the animals are sure that "ninguna desgracia podía ocurrirles bajo aquel cielo nuevo que era como una caricia" (47) [no harm could come to them under that sky that was like a caress]. The women, in a similar vein, are compared to flowers. The description of the men, however, is fascinating in its ambiguous tone: "[Y] muchos hombres parecían mujeres, las caderas blandas y el pie menudo. Vestían de blanco y hablaban con la voz azucarada" (47) [And many men resembled women, with soft hips and small feet. They dressed in white and spoke with sugary voices]. In their form of dress these men recall rich, white plantation owners, but rather than connecting power and masculinity, these society gentlemen are described as effeminate fin de siècle dandies. Since it is anthropomorphic animals that populate the story, this description seems to be referring to these animals.

If the narrative voice already disrupts prescribed gender and racial identities, the character of Hicotea further challenges the norms of his new island community through his trickster identity. Gates argues that in Signifying Monkey tales the real King of the Jungle is not the Lion but the Monkey, the trickster figure, who gains power over even the Lion through his verbal manipulations and mental skill (Gates 63). With his ability to trick his fellow animals, Hicotea embodies this antiauthoritarian sentiment, as most of his tricks intentionally disrupt social organization and the distribution of power. In an economy that explicitly operates on monetary exchange, he wins Venado's land through an unfair bet. While he preys on nearly all of the animals in the community, Hicotea reserves his cruelest jokes for Tigre (Tiger), who is portrayed in the story as an "Animal Grande que tiene en sus muelas la autoridad y con las muelas la mantiene" (58). [Big Animal who carries his authority in his molars and maintains it with his molars.] Hicotea's abuse of Tigre upsets the balance of power in a community where power is clearly wielded by the physically strong.

In many respects, Hicotea appears as the Cuban version of the Signifying Monkey that Gates analyzes. He triumphs not because of his natural physical gifts, but because of his ability to convince, distract, and entrap the other animals in his snares. Desirous of Venado's land, Hicotea creates a competition to see "who is the manliest," the goal of which is to withstand a brush fire. Venado jumps into the flames, convinced that Hicotea is also burning, when he is really safe in a cave. Like the Signifying Monkey, who often challenges the Lion by "doing the dozens," Hicotea trades insults with the other animals. Tigre is humiliated when he loses some toes to Hicotea's knife, but more so by the fact that Hicotea calls him *maricón* (faggot) as he does it. Even at the end of the story, when Hicotea himself has been captured, he manages to escape by charming the young Tigers into watching him dance in the river. He then makes a fake version of himself using a rock and some mud and sends that back with the Tigers.

Hicotea conforms to the classic idea of a trickster figure in many ways, but Cabrera makes it clear that he is something more. For Hicotea is not just a wily, Signifyin(g) member of the animal kingdom; he is a *Santero* and a *Palero* (ordained in the Afro-Cuban religions of both Santería and Palo Monte) who has brought his magic powers with him across the ocean, "escondida en sus pupilas, el arte de curar con las yerbas, los palos y los cantos" (48) [hidden in his pupils the art of healing with herbs, sticks and songs]. Although he often relies on his powers of persuasion, in many instances Hicotea also uses his talents as a *Palero* for his own gain. When he realizes how nice it would be to have Venado's land in addition to his own, his first action is to send his friend three *chicherekús*, possessed dolls that torment him during the night. His musical instrument, which he uses to attract (and then hurt) the other animals, is called the *cocorícamo*, which Cabrera is careful to footnote as being defined as "lo imponderable" (the unthinkable) according to Ortiz. Hicotea's powers are not at odds with his verbal skill; in many ways they seem to be interconnected, since Hicotea's magic is produced as he sings or plays. The subversive nature of his verbal trickery is thus given a special edge and an added dimension. (Perhaps suggestive of the belief in the role of Santería and Palo Monte in the Afro-Cuban communities.)

After looking at texts such as "West Indies, Ltd.," where Guillén's Signifyin(g) adds an acid intensity to the poem's explicitly political thrust, *Cuentos negros* seems almost apolitical, since the stories rarely address issues such as the social position of Santería head on. Yet Cabrera does introduce antiauthoritarian elements in her stories through Signifyin(g). In "La prodigiosa gallina de Guinea" ("The Prodigious Guinea Hen," *Cuentos negros*), she uses an animal folktale to present a very real challenge to authority. The story's heroine is a guinea hen (Gallina de Guinea, capitalized as a character), who, in an effort to get food for the barnyard poultry, leads an assortment of social characters on a journey to Havana. Although the language of the first sentences of the story—"Diablos tenían a la Lluvia prisionera en una tinaja" [Devils were holding the Rain prisoner in a tub]—gives the narrative a mythic character, later elements clearly place it during the nineteenth century, when Cuba was still a Spanish colony. Like Hicotea, the Gallina de Guinea convinces people to follow her with promises of her singing, having a small boy call out, "¡Esta es la prodigiosa Gallina de Guinea que si me pagan canta, si no me pagan, no cantará!" (159) [This is the prodigious guinea hen, who sings if you pay me, and if you don't pay me, won't!] The farmer and the workers on the farm are first to follow the guinea hen, but soon she is also followed by the mayor, the prison warden, the governor, the governor's wife, and even the King and

Queen of Spain. The last people to join the dancing crowd are the *cabildos*, the Afro-Cuban cultural societies, who bring the music and costumes from their various tribes.[22] All of them continue to pay the Gallina so she will continue to sing, and the crowd dances its way into Havana and down the city's main streets.

Through the Pied-Piper journey of the Gallina, the story Signifies on the structure of colonial society. In the same way that medieval theater pieces around the "dance of the dead" showed death coming for everyone from the richest man and the most regal king to Church cardinals and bishops, no authority figure in Cuban society is safe from the charms of the Gallina's singing. These colonial leaders ignore social convention, giving her money, allowing her into the palace, and finally letting her music take over the general population, so that the story ends with a full-scale carnival. By creating a situation in which these members of Cuban-Spanish nobility sing and dance as if in an Afro-Cuban carnival *comparsa* (carnival band), the Gallina both disrupts and pokes fun at their authority; instead of being controlled by their wishes, she controls them. Yet unlike the fairy tale of "The Pied-Piper of Hamelin," in which the piper lures away the town's children, the Gallina de Guinea's dance has no negative consequences (at least none that the story shares). She herself goes from being a "pícara desvergonzada" [shameless trickster], a possible reference to her tricksterlike function within the text, to being treated like a local celebrity.

What is significant in this story is the contrast presented between the Afro-Cuban aspects of the Gallina and the European-based (colonial) authority wielded by the King, the Queen, and the governor. More than any of the characters I have examined previously, the Gallina de Guinea exhibits clearly Afro-Cuban speech characteristics. She prays to the *oricha* Yewá, uses *Lucumí* words such as *mundele* (white man, literally "master"), and her often-repeated song is based around the word *ariyénye*, an expression that Cabrera herself defines elsewhere as "satisfacción, contentura, demostración, saludo que se da con alegría" *(Anagó* 59) [satisfaction, contentment, demonstrativeness, greeting that one gives with happiness]. As in many oral folktales, this song is highly repetitive, and as the other animals and people join in, the rhythm of the story's language seems to be encouraging the reader to do so as well. In contrast to the Gallina, characters such as the Governor and the Mayor seem heavy with the trappings of authority; the Governor, in particular, is described as having "el pecho fulgurante como un altar cubierto de cruces y medallas de oro" (161) ["his chest heavy as an altar covered with crosses as gold medallions"], as if he were literally weighed down by his social role. By placing this tale in Havana, Cabrera makes more deliberate reference to Cuban society than in previous stories. Hicotea travels over the sea to reach the island in "Taita Hicotea y Taita Tigre," but the Gallina is clearly Afro-Cuban, and her triumph thus becomes much more a celebration of the place of Afro-Cuban culture within Cuban society as a whole.

While not as overtly a trickster figure as Hicotea, the Gallina does embody some trickster attributes. Trickster figures are by nature subversive and antilaw, and the Gallina's dance is a physical force that actively subverts social authority, turning the status quo of class (and racial) hierarchy upside down. While she initially begins her song as a challenge to the hierarchy of the barnyard, the lighthearted rhythm of her song breaks through the sober attitude of the ruling classes, as all the characters, regardless of ethnicity or social standing, end up dancing to the *comparsas* and the *rumbas* (dances noted for their Afro-Cuban origins). Unlike the chaos that is created by Hicotea's abusive schemes, however, the Gallina's actions serve to unite people rather than ridicule or destroy them. The story creates a socially harmonious vision through this antilaw stance: as the people dance, "Hasta la guardia civil odiada parecía buena" (162). [Even the hated civil guard seemed good.] Like the carnival that theorist Mikhail Bakhtin analyzes, the upsetting of the social order is not only tolerated but rather celebrated, perhaps because this disruption is a temporary state.

The utopian scene that the Gallina's dancing stages in the story's ending makes clear references to a real historical situation. For much of the eighteenth and nineteenth century, and even well into the period in which Cabrera was writing, the Cuban government censored and even outlawed many practices associated with Afro-Cuban religions, in particular the public performance of Afro-Cuban *comparsa* music.[23] The Gallina's citywide carnivalesque dancing thus very literally disrupts colonial law. As she flouts the authority that would prevent this musical coming together, the Gallina's singing creates a situation that not only gives Afro-Cuban music a space for full expression, but allows all of Havana—"bozales, ladinos, criollos, rellollos, negros, blancos y amarillos" (162) [African-born blacks, Creoles, blacks, whites and yellows]—to participate in it. As the *cabildos* present the various dances and folkloric performances, their place in Cuban society is legitimated and their role in Cuban culture is revealed to be a fundamental one.

The Gallina's inclusive dance stages a performance of Cubanness in which Afro-Cuban music is the uniting element. Yet this celebration of Afro-Cuban culture is temporary; the reader can assume that as the effects of the Gallina's performance wear off, Havana society will return to normal. The performance of this antiauthoritarian gesture within a colonial setting also raises a number of questions with regard to the place of Afro-Cuban culture at the time *Cuentos negros* was written. Are we meant to take the Gallina's performance as an allegorical gesture, one that suggests that Afro-Cuban culture is to be equally celebrated in the Cuba of the 1930s? Or does the fact that this trickster-orchestrated celebration occurs in a historical time and place suggest that Afro-Cuban culture can be most safely acknowledged and celebrated when viewed from within a context bounded by history and social class?

The Prodigious Guinea Hens

As Cabrera's Gallina de Guinea humorously illustrates, Signifyin(g) can perform simultaneous, contradictory gestures of community formation and social critique; as the Gallina leads the colonial elite in a dance, she both brings together Havana's citizens and upsets—and contests—the social order of colonial society. Interestingly, in this gesture, the Gallina's Signifyin(g) thus performs a kind of "passing"—her creation of a (national) community involves an eliding of social (and racial) difference. This is not to say that these differences are erased; rather, it is the Gallina's performance, the verbal trickery of her Signifyin(g), that allows them to be present.

I end with this image from Cabrera's story because it captures something of the ways in which Signifyin(g) operates in Cabrera's and Guillén's work. To deal with subjects related to Afro-Cuban culture at the moment in which both writers chose to do so was to highlight an element of Cuban culture whose relationship to the dominant society was ambivalent at best. To introduce Afro-Cuban culture—and particularly Afro-Cuban orality—into Cuban literary culture thus required a particular sleight of hand. Like the "Gallina de Guinea," play in Guillén's and Cabrera's texts seems at first to be a superficial performance, but this dance ends by allowing for racial representations and social critiques, perhaps beyond even the authors' intentions. Guillén's experimentation with musicality, rhythm, and dialogue centers on (and draws from) Afro-Cuban culture, even when he is ostensibly focused on ideas of hybridity or on postcolonial critique. Through structural Signifyin(g) Cabrera interweaves Afro-Cuban elements into her texts in such a way that her stories become more than or something other than Afro-Cuban folktales.

The difference in these writers' use of Signifyin(g) has to do with their choice of temporal framework. While Guillén situates his poems in the dilemmas of modern Cuba, play in Cabrera's texts—as I have mentioned elsewhere—nearly always occurs within a colonial frame of reference. The Gallina's racialized moment of Bakhtinian carnival is—like any act of Signifyin(g)—temporally grounded in the moment; there is nothing to suggest that there will not be a return to the colonial social and racial hierarchies. The Signifyin(g) strategies in Cabrera's and Guillén's texts place blackness at the center of the literary space, yet by gesturing back towards the past Cabrera's texts act to highlight the (fixed) place of blackness in the social order.

4

GENDER, GENRE, AND ETHNOGRAPHIC AUTHORITY

Lydia Cabrera and Zora Neale Hurston

In the previous chapters of this book, I have looked at the ways in which Cuban writers drew from different ethnographic and literary strategies to include ideas of blackness in their reimaginings of the nation. My intention has been to understand how Cuba's particular postcolonial (with respect to Spain) and neocolonial (with respect to the United States) circumstances pushed the country's writers to take up Afro-Cuban culture as a basis for a national folk. However, Cuba was not the only country whose writers were trying to define the relationship between race and nation—and specifically the location of blackness within an idea of nation—in the first half of the twentieth century. Indeed, Cuba's massive English-speaking neighbor to the north was also engaged in renegotiating the place of African Americans and African American culture within a narrative of the nation. As in Cuba, this struggle took place not just on a political level but also on a cultural one. If the 1920s in Cuba saw the beginning of the vogue of *Afrocubanismo*, in America, thanks to the explosion of African American literary and artistic production that has since come to be known as the Harlem Renaissance, the decade initiated a period in which "many blacks and some whites viewed the black tradition in the arts not as a slight and inferior tributary to white culture but as a dominant influence on it, and as a separate tradition with a complex identity and history all its own" (Douglas 303). This interest in culture encompassed a broad embrace of blackness, including an interest in black history and African roots, as evidenced by Carter G. Woodson's work on African American history and the Puerto Rican intellectual Arturo Schomburg's collection of African American art, literature, and historical documents. Coupled with this increased visibility in representations of black culture, textual experimentation and free borrowing from both literary and ethnographic techniques marked the work of writers on both sides of the Florida Strait.

To understand something of the ways in which Cuba's anxiety surrounding national identity and race can be placed in the context of a broader, international interrogation of these constructions, this chapter turns to a transnational comparison of the work of Lydia Cabrera and the African American writer Zora Neale Hurston to highlight both the similarities in textual experimentation and the different results that this yielded when dealing with race. Both women writers began publishing during the 1930s and both wrote fiction and ethnography; the biographical and temporal similarities of their careers have led naturally to a comparison of their work and writing circumstances.[1] Yet I believe that a comparison of these seminal figures can tell us something new about a particular hemispheric exploration of the place of African-derived cultures in national literature(s), particularly with regard to the role of gender in negotiating the relationship between race and nation.

The Spy-glass of Anthropology

In 1927, Zora Neale Hurston, then a student of Columbia University anthropologist Franz Boas, left New York and headed to the South to collect African American folklore. Hurston was already an up-and-coming writer and a participant in the Harlem Renaissance, but this trip back to the South (where she had grown up) was the second in a series of research trips undertaken in conjunction with her studies in anthropology at Columbia University.[2] She begins *Mules and Men* (1935), the collection of folktales that was the final product of this fieldwork, with a description of her return to her childhood home of Eatonville, Florida, and of how that return was affected by her newly gained academic perspective: "In a way it would not be new experience for me. When I pitched headforemost into the world I landed in the crib of negroism. From the earliest rocking of my cradle, I had known about the capers Brer Rabbit is apt to cut and what the Squinch Owl says from the house top. But it was fitting me like a tight chemise. I couldn't see it for wearing it. It was only when I was off in college, away from my native surroundings, that I could see myself like somebody else and stand off and look at my garment. Then I had to have the spy-glass of Anthropology to look through at that" (1). According to her own observation, Hurston's academic training gave her a new way of seeing which, together with geographic distance, reframed her own African American Florida culture. Her newly acquired methodological approach not only provided her with the tools for looking at a culture from a different perspective; it also endowed her with an authority different from that of the native informant, the person immersed in the culture ("in the crib of negroism"), and this new authority in turn altered her own identity as an observer. In the same way that the lens of the spy-glass creates a barrier between the eye and the object being viewed, thanks to this new analytical framework Hurston now saw even her own childhood in Eatonville as the particular cultural experiences of "somebody else."

Around the same time that Hurston was leaving New York for Florida, Lydia Cabrera, at the time a Cuban art student who had yet to discover her vocation as a writer/ethnographer, was studying East Asian iconography at the Sorbonne. In a later interview, Cabrera described how her experience as a student in Paris sparked her subsequent interest in Afro-Cuban culture:

> En mi caso, mi país, Cuba, empezó a interesarme en Francia, creo que eso puede sucederle a todo el que se aleja de su tierra natal: hay una especie de redescubrimiento de lo que está lejos. Tengo un recuerdo muy específico . . . : estudiando la iconografía del Borobudur, el templo de Java, hay un bajorrelieve en que aparece una mujer con unas frutas tropicales en la cabeza. Me dije:—¡Pero si esto es Cuba! Y claro, a la distancia había crecido en mí ese recuerdo ilusionado, esa especie de nostalgia, entonces inconsciente, que se siente fuera del país propio. Iba descubriendo o mejor, redescubriendo, lo que nunca puede verse de cerca. (Hiriart, *Más cerca* 123)

> [In my case, my country, Cuba, began to interest me in France. I think that this can happen to anyone who leaves his native land: there is a kind of rediscovery of what is far away. I have a very specific memory . . . : studying the iconography of Borobudur, the Javanese temple, there is a bas-relief in which appears a woman carrying tropical fruit on her head. I said to myself, "But this is Cuba!" And of course, from a distance there had grown in me this hopeful memory, this kind of nostalgia—then unconscious—that one feels away from his own country. I began to discover, or better, rediscover, what can never be seen up close.]

In some ways, Cabrera's experience is the opposite of Hurston's; while the African American writer's spy-glass allows her to see her own hometown as other, Cabrera finds Cuban imagery in art that is culturally foreign. Yet as it did for Hurston, distance—both cultural and spatial—enables Cabrera to focus on aspects of her own culture in a new way. When Cabrera recognizes a Cuban woman in a Javanese bas-relief, the strange becomes familiar to her and the familiar strange, as she sees Cuban culture through multiple levels of displacement: she is a Cuban expatriate living in France, a Western art student looking at Indonesian art, a Cuban woman reading racialized Cuban culture into and through tropical intersections. Although Cabrera, white and upper-class, came from a different sector of society than the Afro-Cuban communities she would study, like Hurston, her academic experience and her time away from Cuba led her, after she returned home, to begin researching Afro-Cuban religious practices in the Pogolotti and Marianao neighborhoods of Havana.

For Hurston and Cabrera, these moments chronicle a transformation of their personal way of seeing. This transformation is enacted through distance, a distance created as much by acquisition of an academic approach as by a shift in culture. One could say that these experiences mark the beginning of the formation of Hurston's and Cabrera's ethnographic gaze, as they achieve an awareness of the uses of this distance in order to view part of their own culture as material for ethnographic study. As their descriptions reveal, the writers are also conscious of the ways in which this ethnographic framing both enacts and at the same time disrupts certain structures of belonging. This chapter examines how these two writers used this awareness to construct ethnographic and narrative authority in their texts. I argue that they experiment with the structures of ethnographic authority, both textual and professional, to reveal the ways in which the ethnographic scenario impacts—and is impacted by—race and gender.

Given the historical circumstances in which these experiences of new awareness took place, the idea of belonging was particularly important for both ethnographers. Their experiences illustrate a moment when the "spy-glass of anthropology" was increasingly being focused on minority cultures within national borders in both the United States and the Caribbean. Both black and white intellectuals in the United States, as in Cuba, were struggling to define the nature of African American culture and its place within a hemispheric American context. Unlike Cuba, the

United States, even while struggling through a dire economic depression that caused enormous and widespread suffering (in the 1930s), cannot be characterized as postcolonial. Indeed, dominant voices had already constructed a national narrative that defined it as modern. Within this modern nation, however, artists and intellectuals from the 1920s onward began to look to African American culture for an idea of the American "folk," just as the Cuban writers I have examined previously in this study turned to Afro-Cuban culture as a potential source for constructing a new idea of Cubanness. As Ann Douglas notes, "The black tradition was the only folk past America could claim; black cash covered white deficits" (388). Nevertheless, comparative analysis of Hurston's and Cabrera's work reveals that while Cuban writers were not alone in borrowing textual strategies from literature and ethnography, Cuban constructions of blackness were being asked to serve the nation in a different way than images of blackness in an American context.

As women writing about particular parts of their own national cultures and, more importantly, as scholars concerned with representing this minority culture to a national reading public, Hurston and Cabrera became masters at manipulating authorial distance; both women went on to prolific writing careers in which they produced works of both ethnography and fiction. However, Hurston was black, Cabrera white. Hurston returned to the South to do research on members of her own racial and cultural community; for all her familiarity with Afro-Cuban culture, Cabrera was still separated from it by racial differences and class divisions. Furthermore, the definition of blackness was different in each location. The United States tended to maintain a binary opposition between "white" and "black" races; Cuba, on the other hand, had a large percentage of people who might define themselves as "people of color," without recognizing themselves as black.[3] Yet a closer examination of their principal ethnographies, Hurston's *Mules and Men* and Cabrera's *El Monte* (1954), reveals that while they sometimes found radically different ways of addressing some of ethnography's inherent methodological and narrative challenges with regard to race, their construction of the figure of the ethnographer—and their use of the authority this position provided—were similarly key to how they positioned themselves in their texts vis-à-vis the question of race. In this sense, their experience in racial negotiation also becomes a self-fictionalizing exercise. In the treatment of ethnographic professionalism, gender, and narrative voice in their texts, they use the formal elements of ethnographic authority to explore the limits of ethnographic representation itself.

The Professionalization of Ethnography and the Ethnographic Scenario

The stories Hurston and Cabrera tell to explain how their academic training reframed their gaze seem to echo the process of standardization that anthropology, and ethnography in particular, was undergoing in the first half of the twentieth century. In the foreword to his groundbreaking study *Argonauts of the Western Pacific* (1922), Bronislaw Malinowski makes a case for the necessity of a scientific process for ethnographic inquiry: "The research which has been done on native races by men of academic training has proved beyond doubt and cavil that scientific, methodic inquiry can give us results far more abundant and of better quality than those of even the best amateur's work" (xv). Malinowski sees the professionalization of ethnography as imperative; by contrasting the methodology of those with "academic training" with the inferior work done by "amateurs," he argues that any work of significance must be based on research accomplished according to established scientific methods, and that the standardization of the field will come from its connection to Western university systems. Significant in Malinowski's commentary is the dichotomy he establishes between the "native races" that are to be the objects of study and the (white, European) "men of academic training" who will study them. A university education, it is supposed, thus adds to the separation between the ethnographer and the culture of study, and the scientist emerges as an expert cultural interpreter due to his power as a trained observer. At the same time, the construction of a scientific identity presumes an extant separation (cultural, racial) between the scientist and those being studied.

Although some of Hurston's and Cabrera's experiences seem to corroborate Malinowski's ideas about the effect of the professionalization of ethnography, their situations differ from his conception of the fieldwork experience in three fundamental ways. First, despite the importance they place on formal education, in their relationship to their cultures and communities of study Hurston and Cabrera differ from the outset from Malinowski's conception of the ethnographer. They begin their investigations as what María Eugenia Cotera and Lynda Hoffman-Jeep (among others) term "insider-outsiders" (Cotera 38, Hoffman-Jeep 337): the role of "ethnographer" serves to establish, legitimate, and maintain a distance from these communities as well as a new framework within which to analyze and narrate what they see and experience, but they return to research a culture with which they are in many ways already familiar (Hurston certainly more so than Cabrera), to work in places in which they themselves have resided, and to encounter individuals and communities with which they already have established relationships.

Second, by dedicating themselves to the study of African American and Afro-Cuban culture (respectively), Hurston's and Cabrera's ethnographies must in some way engage with the problematic and problematized relationship of these cultures to the dominant (i.e., white) culture. While the vogue of the Harlem Renaissance and the jazz age had inspired a new interest in African American culture, at least among American artists and intellectuals, the United States was a country in which black citizens were more often the victims of segregationist Jim Crow practices than the objects of ethnographic study. Hurston, herself African American and raised in an all-black Southern town, was walking the delicate line of depending on a white system of patronage while having to answer to her African American (intellectual) peers. Funding for her research came both from institutional, academic sources (including funds from the WPA-funded Florida Writers' Project) and from private donors, in particular Charlotte Osgood Mason, a wealthy Park Avenue philanthropist.[4] These white institutions wanted to see "folklore," sometimes in its most "primitive" aspects, as the practices of ethnographic others. Many of Hurston's black peers, however, were leery of anything that might perpetuate racist stereotypes of Southern blacks as "backwards" and uneducated or present a romanticized vision of Southern black life.[5]

By the time Cabrera published *El Monte* in 1954, the influence of Afro-Cuban culture was fully apparent in Cuban music, and the vogue of *Afrocubanismo* had made images of black Cubans prevalent in literature and the visual arts as well. Yet as Cabrera herself noted later, there was still significant resistance to studying Afro-Cuban culture and identifying it as Cuban: "Así en Cuba, sin riesgos, se puede ser indianista. No hay indios. Pero sondear en el viejo, incalculablemente rico fondo cultural africano, que los siglos de la trata acumularon aquí, es tarea que muchos tachan de 'antipatriótica' y negativa" (*La sociedad secreta* 8). [So in Cuba, one can be an Indianist without risks. There are no Indians. But to plumb the depths of the old, incalculably rich African culture, which the centuries of slave trade accumulated here, is work that many deride as 'antipatriotic' and negative.] As Cabrera's observation implies, despite the visibility of Afro-Cuban culture, when she published *El Monte*, Afro-Cuban religious practice was still not well understood by many middle- and upper-class Cubans.

Lastly, Hurston and Cabrera were insider-outsiders with respect to the field of ethnography. This was in part because they were women writing in a discipline where, despite a significant number of women ethnographers writing at this time—many under Franz Boas at Columbia—both the gaze and persona of the ethnographer were assumed to be male. (Hurston chooses as her metaphor the spy-glass, an instrument long associated with the strongly masculine world of naval exploration.) These writers display a particular awareness of how being a woman shaped their fieldwork experiences. Throughout their texts, gender itself serves as another kind of "contact zone," a space of encounter that allows them to destabilize the framework of ethnographic professionalism, and thus posit alternative ways of constructing ethnography's relationship to cultural translation and national cultures.[6]

Cabrera and Hurston were also insider-outsiders with respect to ethnography as a professional, academic discipline. Besides her coursework in Art History at the Sorbonne, Cabrera had no university experience and no formal ethnographic training. Hurston, when she wrote *Mules and Men*, was not yet an academic and despite her connection to the anthropology program at Columbia, was drawn to older, "less-professional" methodologies of folklore collecting. Given their ambivalent position within the field, Cabrera and Hurston were obliged—perhaps more so than their male colleagues—to negotiate the requirements of ethnographic professionalism, constructing their authority through careful associations with the established ranks of academe. Yet I argue that paradoxically, their identity as women may have been part of what enabled Hurston and Cabrera to study African American and Afro-Cuban culture in the first place. At the time when they began writing and doing fieldwork, black culture in the Americas was only beginning to be a legitimate area of ethnographic study. Their status as professional "insider-outsiders" gave these women the space in which to focus their investigation on (and thus ultimately raise the profile of) areas of racialized culture in their own national contexts.

The development of ethnography was a twofold process: the professionalization of ethnography as an academic discipline and research methodology coincided with the development of the ethnographic monograph as a genre with its own accepted stylistic norms. The text established the ethnographer as the sole interpreter of the culture that he or she had studied, and thus as the primary narrative voice of the text itself. Yet no matter how much this process of professionalization worked to legitimate the scientific nature of the field, the ethnography was in effect a literary text, connected to the literary conventions of the other genres (such as travel writing) from which it had sprung.[7] The legitimacy of the ethnographer as a privileged and accurate interpreter of the culture of study was established through both the form and narrative voice of the ethnography, but the authority of the monograph itself also rested on how well it managed to reproduce the researcher's lived experience of a different culture within a written text, and on how well it was able to translate that culture for its readers.

Given ethnography's inherent tension between the scientific and the literary, in spite of the strong push towards standardizing ethnography (and the monographs that worked to put this methodology into practice), the first half of the twentieth century was a time of significant freedom for the field, and some published texts refused to conform to the standards of the form being developed. Hurston's *Mules and Men* and Cabrera's *El Monte* have been frequently characterized as two such texts: Lori Jirousek refers to *Mules and Men* as "a hybrid text that is more than/other than ethnography" (418), and Edna Rodríguez-Mangual sees *El Monte* as occupying a discursive space somewhere between an ethnography and a testimonial novel (70). While I would generally agree with these assessments, I disagree with critics such as Rodríguez-Mangual and Hoffman-Jeep who would characterize Hurston and Cabrera as precursors to the more consistently self-conscious ethnographic work (much of it by women ethnographers) that emerged in the 1980s.[8] Rather, I contend that their work shows us that ethnography was never as "standardized" as we imagine it to be, and that this is a moment in which Cabrera, Hurston, and others employed textual experimentation to solve—or at least highlight—some of ethnography's challenges.

In *The Archive and the Repertoire*, Diana Taylor argues for the use of the "scenario" as a category of study that can mediate between the written text (the archive) and live performance (the repertoire). For Taylor, the scenario is a useful category for connecting these spaces of enunciation because it is "an act of transfer, a paradigm that is formulaic, portable, repeatable, and often banal because it leaves out complexity, reduces conflict to its stock elements, and encourages fantasies of participation" (54). In its clear articulation of the roles of "researcher" and "informant," the participant-observer model of investigation that became the foundation of ethnographic fieldwork can be considered a scenario, in that it provided a model that would continue to be repeated by ethnographic researchers and recalled in their texts. In creating a structure for interaction between the ethnographer and his or her informants, the ethnographic scenario thus shapes the ways in which ethnographers seek and receive information. Like Hurston's spy-glass, it both clarifies and distances.

The ethnographic scenario maintains a clearly defined power structure that, as Mary Louise Pratt and Clifford (among others) have shown, connects ethnographic writing to both imperialism (and the scenarios of New World Conquest that Taylor analyzes) and the formation of national identity. Often these relationships are based on the contrast Malinowski highlights between the "men of academic training" and the "natives" being studied. As their descriptions of transformational process with which I began this chapter show, Hurston and Cabrera were aware of the constructed nature of the ethnographic scenario and the limitations this structure imposed on both the fieldwork experience and the written text. While they acknowledge the importance of a professional identity to establishing ethnographic authority, their subversion of this same authority through the inclusion of personal narrative, an emphasis on textual heteroglossia, and the use of silences allows them to both make use of and downplay their position as ethnographers, preventing a facile reading of the nature of race in their work and serving to problematize the nature of ethnography as a whole.

Establishing Professional Credentials: The Science of Ethnographic Authority

From Malinowski on, the idea of the ethnographer as a professional was based first and foremost on the concept of training; this implied both a connection to an academic institution and the knowledge and application of the appropriate research methodology, which centered on fieldwork. To identify themselves as serious researchers and have their work accepted by their peers, Cabrera and Hurston needed to demonstrate a connection to academic genealogies and to established "men of science." Given their own marginal positions, and the fact that women were more likely to be seen as amateurs or untrained dilettantes, it was even more important that they construct their authority through association with the established ranks of (masculine) academe.[9] Both writers were careful from the beginning to establish and support their credentials as a means of justifying their ability to carry out—and, more importantly, to publish—their ethnographic research. They allied themselves with influential mentors, who could vouch for their capabilities as scholars (even if these mentors themselves expressed sentiments bordering on the paternalistic). At the same time, Hurston's and Cabrera's somewhat ambivalent treatment of this authority revealed how they were working to establish independent voices, separate from those of their mentors. The space they create within their texts by downplaying their scientific methodology—emphasizing the "folkloric" aspects and the "collecting" techniques, rather than referring to fieldwork—allows them a freedom both to deconstruct their own authorial voices and to experiment with form in the construction of their texts.

The prefaces to Hurston's and Cabrera's books function as the first and primary site for establishing their academic credentials. In the case of an ethnographic monograph, a preface by a senior scholar can serve as an official space for highlighting the writer's background and training (recognizing the writer *as* an ethnographer) and allows the senior scholar to place his stamp of approval on the younger ethnographer's work. Hurston's *Mules and Men* contains a foreword written by Franz Boas, Hurston's academic advisor and the head of the anthropology department at Columbia University. Boas was at the time one of the foremost cultural anthropologists in the country and a pioneer in the development of ethnographic fieldwork. His name immediately connects Hurston to the official hierarchy of academic research, and to a particular genealogy of cultural anthropology.[10] The fact that Hurston had begged Boas to contribute an introduction, despite—or because of—the fact that the book was being published with a mainstream press (rather than as an academic monograph) indicates her awareness of the importance of this academic approbation.[11] This being so, it is interesting to note that Boas does not focus his introduction on Hurston's academic training at Columbia; instead, he proceeds to outline her qualifications for this work based on her familiarity with African American culture and its folklore. "It is the great merit of Miss Hurston's work that she entered into the homely life of the southern Negro as one of them ... Thus she has been able to penetrate through that affected demeanor by which the Negro excludes the White observer effectively from participating in his true inner life" (xiii). This statement, though complimentary, is ambivalent about Hurston's position; by saying that she entered into the black community "as one of them," it implies that this belonging is a false belonging, or a belonging that has been altered. Hurston enters "as one of them," even though in her position as an ethnographer, she is not. Boas's preface thus acts to officially corroborate Hurston's own statement at the beginning of her text that her culture fit her "like a chemise." Boas gives Hurston's work legitimacy on both personal and professional grounds; he shows she is a student of academic anthropology, as he indicates she also possesses extraordinary gifts of observation thanks to her own sociocultural background. While this introduction establishes Hurston's credentials, it simultaneously reinforces the need for academic training itself, implicitly highlighting the contradictions in the two roles that Hurston found herself playing as she became her own "native informant."

Although it is considered the central text of Cabrera's ethnographic scholarship, *El Monte* does not contain a preface written by another scholar or critic. Since Fernando Ortiz, the founding father of Afro-Cuban ethnography (and, coincidentally, Cabrera's brother-in-law) contributed an introduction to the Spanish publication of Cabrera's first book of short stories, *Cuentos negros de Cuba* (*Afro-Cuban Tales*, 1940), by the time *El Monte* was published another official introduction of Cabrera as a scholar may have been deemed unnecessary.[12] While Cabrera in no way indicates that her stories have any connection to ethnography, Ortiz establishes Cabrera's scholarly connection to him in the first two sentences of his introduction to *Cuentos negros*: "Este libro es el primero de una mujer habanera, a quien hace años iniciamos en el gusto del folklore afrocubano. Lydia Cabrera fue penetrando el bosque de las leyendas negras de La Habana por simple curiosidad y luego por deleite; al fin fue transcribiéndolas y coleccionándolas" (7). [This book is the first from a woman from Havana whom we years ago initiated into an appreciation of Afro-Cuban folklore. Lydia Cabrera slowly penetrated the forest of black legends in Havana out of simple curiosity and then delight; finally she began to transcribe and collect them.] In this description, Ortiz characterizes himself as the central guiding figure; he "initiated" her into the study of Afro-Cuban culture (a term that has a certain sexual connotation, although I doubt it was intended that way). As I discuss elsewhere in this study, Ortiz mistakenly characterizes Cabrera as the "translator" rather than the author of the stories he is prefacing. While he praises her translation work—"La autora ha hecho tarea difícil pero leal" (8) [The author has completed a difficult task, but done so faithfully]—he emphasizes her "curiosity" and "delight," qualities that imply a kind of amateur enjoyment in the study of another cultural environment. Cabrera appears in an almost infantilized position in relationship to Ortiz. As in Boas's discussion of Hurston, Ortiz's description of Cabrera as "penetrating the forest" of Cuban folklore (again, note the strongly masculine language) suggests that she too has been successful at collecting folklore, but the implication is that these gifts are "intuitive," intuition being a quality frequently identified as feminine and one that is a far cry from the rigorously attuned "scientific eye" of Malinowski's ethnographer.

As a social scientist, and an intellectual who was himself preoccupied with legitimating his own scholarship, Ortiz introduces Cabrera as a scholar rather than a creative writer. By connecting Cabrera to his own scholarly efforts, Ortiz establishes her as a presence in the field of Cuban ethnography, creating a professional place for her that undoubtedly later helped her to publish part of *El Monte* in the journal *Estudios Afrocubanos*, and may have ultimately helped with the publication of *El Monte* itself.[13] While Hurston, as an African American, uses Boas's preface to vouch for her training, Ortiz's prologue maintains Cabrera's social position. As the *author* of a collection of Afro-Cuban stories, both her whiteness and her class position are suspect; by emphasizing her role as a translator or gatherer of folklore (he calls her "the white translator"), Ortiz makes her work on Afro-Cuban folklore the result of mild academic interest.

While Boas tends less toward condescension than Ortiz, both men choose to emphasize the "natural," savantlike gifts of their female protégées rather than highlight their academic skills or talents. One could view this paternalistic attitude as denying their students their full authority as professional ethnographers, yet Cabrera and Hurston use their position as women to play with these characterizations of their professional identity, simultaneously subverting and taking refuge in them. Through the use of these prefaces, both women present themselves as students in a male-dominated academic hierarchy, a gesture that gives their texts legitimacy within the scholarly world. At the same time, they seem ambivalent about fully assuming the authority that this professionalism provides. The ways in which they downplay their scientific methodology allow them a freedom both to deconstruct (or contest) the authorial voice and to experiment with form in the construction of their texts.

Cabrera initially seems reticent to challenge Ortiz's characterization of her professional identity as "collector" and "translator." When writing her own preface, as she does for *El Monte*, she presents herself as a kind of amateur, describing her five-hundred-plus pages of dense text as mere "notes," and adding: "Las publico, no es necesario subrayarlo, sin asomo de pretensión científica. El metodo seguido, ¡si de método, aún vagamente, pudiera hablarse en el caso de este libro! lo han impuesto con sus explicaciones y disgresiones . . . mis informantes . . ." (1). [I publish them, it is unnecessary to emphasize, with no pretense to science. The method I've followed—if one can even vaguely speak of a method in the case of this book!—has been imposed by . . . my informants . . . with their explanations and digressions.] The above admission by Cabrera deliberately and deceptively obscures her own role as the writer of a dense and multilayered text. Rodríguez-Mangual argues that by seeming to downplay her training and authority, Cabrera is employing typical "tricks of the weak" (to borrow Josefina Ludmer's term), strategies that women writers have used to create a space for themselves in a male-dominated discursive sphere (Rodríguez-Mangual 71).[14] Rodríguez-Mangual suggests that this gesture "suggests a negation of traditional methodology" (71), yet the fact that Cabrera chooses to mention methodology in the first paragraph of the text indicates that she is in fact highly aware of its importance in establishing the scientific validity of her work. Both "notes" and "informants" are terms that place the text's production squarely within the ethnographic scenario, even if Cabrera's assertions point to an altering of some of the roles. She also states that she intends to offer this document to "specialists," indicating that she is conscious of writing for a professional audience as well as for a more general readership. I suggest that Cabrera uses her identity as the "white translator," as Ortiz defines her, as a kind of shield to minimize the scientific expectations regarding her undertaking. Ethnographic authority of some kind is necessary to legitimize her work (and the study of Afro-Cuban culture in general), but downplaying the "official" nature of the ethnographic persona creates a space within the text for discursive exploration.

In crediting her informants with the text's construction, Cabrera steps away from the narrative role of univocal interpreter of Afro-Cuban culture.

Rather than analyze the information provided by these *Santeros* and *Paleros*,[15] she states that she wants to let these voices be heard without passing them through what she refers to as "el filtro peligroso de la interpretación" (2) [the dangerous filter of interpretation], an image that seems on some level to undercut her very function as ethnographer. Cabrera even goes so far as to say that her Afro-Cuban informants are the texts' "true authors."[16] While this declaration is, on one level, an acknowledgement of the importance of these individuals, it fuses the scene of ethnographic observation with the task of writing by removing Cabrera—the writer—from her key position as cultural translator. One could say that Cabrera's statement performs her removal from the ethnographic dilemma; even if the narrative is her careful construction, her rhetorical gesture insists on the authenticity of the reader's own translative experience. With this statement, there is no temporal delay in the production of a mediated text; all is implicitly performance, information compiled at the very moment of its recounting.

Unlike Cabrera, Hurston seems intent on presenting herself as the central scientific voice in her text, but she too places herself in an ambiguous position vis-à-vis her own narrative authority. She begins *Mules and Men* with the statement, "I was glad when somebody told me, 'You may go and collect Negro folklore'" (1). The "someone" she is referring to is most probably Charlotte Osgood Mason, who had funded the trip, yet given Boas's preface, it seems (to a reader unfamiliar with Hurston's particular situation) to refer to her academic advisor. While her statement thus (implicitly) emphasizes her participation in an academic hierarchy (the project had garnered legitimate, scholarly approval), it also suggests that her research endeavors were in part based on the desires, needs, or direction of others, and contingent upon their outside approval.[17] As bell hooks observes, this attitude downplayed the significance of Hurston's own insistence on the importance of studying African American folklore: "Hurston's declaration implies that she was merely following orders; in actuality she had defined the terrain" (138).[18] Even as she locates hers as the central narrative voice in the text, Hurston is cautious about presenting herself as the initiator of the project, and she is careful to refer to her project in mundane rather than academic terminology. Her emphasis on the process of "collecting folklore" both hearkens back to older forms of anthropological investigation and suggests a less formally scientific research methodology; folklore collecting was a job less defined by professional connections, more easily seen as a field for amateurs.[19] Like Cabrera's use of the term "translator," Hurston's own characterization of her methodological approach belies her awareness of the subtle difficulties of her ethnographic terrain.

The figure of the ethnographer that both Hurston and Cabrera construct through their introductions—and their mentors' prefaces—is complicated, for both writers clearly want their work to be recognized as academic and professional, even if their texts are geared towards other audiences (in the case of Hurston) or will go on to challenge standard discursive models. For Hurston and Cabrera, however, this ambivalent construction of their professional identity goes beyond literary rhetoric; an understanding of their position as women and a knowledge of how to use their identities as women to their advantage become key factors in their fieldwork experiences. In addition, they prove to be particularly important with regard to how these writers choose to represent race in their texts.

The Personal Is Professional: Gender and the Authorial Voice

While Cabrera and Hurston rely on their connection to established (masculine) academic space to legitimate their work in a professional sense, their awareness of their position as women enables them to establish an ambivalent relationship with the ethnographic authority that this professional identity represents. The way in which they manipulate their identity as women in their texts allows them to further question ethnographic authority through the ways in which they play with the balance between personal and professional ethnographic narratives. Despite Malinowski's assertion that ethnography must be an objective, scientific process, Pratt sees a tension between personal narrative and objective description as inherent to ethnographic writing: "Personal narrative mediates this contradiction between the engagement called for in fieldwork and the self-effacement called for in formal ethnographic description" ("Fieldwork in Common Places" 33). For both Hurston and Cabrera, calling attention to the importance of gender—and the particular negotiation required by their position as women—provides a way to highlight the contradictions of ethnographic authority. The writers present themselves as limited in their access to knowledge and implicated in the set of gendered social relationships within which fieldwork takes place, but to very different ends. While Hurston's self-centered narrative emphasizes her (racial and class) connection to her ethnographic subjects, Cabrera uses the hierarchies of domestic space to emphasize (and maintain) her position as an outsider.

Mules and Men is presented as a collection of African American folklore, but Hurston constructs a metanarrative around her own fieldwork experiences, so that each folktale surfaces in the context of a particular storytelling session.[20] This allows Hurston to solve the contradiction between formal ethnographic description and personal experience by placing the reader, as well as herself, at the scene of the fieldwork process. In particular, Hurston's first-person narration of her own research experiences allows her to explore and reveal social gender roles as she herself is impacted by them. The primary keepers of folktales in the black communities where she does her research are men. As an educated woman (coming directly from a Northern academic setting), Hurston presents a potential threat to their authority on a number of levels when she sets out to collect folklore, a process that involves both initiating herself into the male social environment and recording (possessing) their knowledge. What Hurston does not mention in her narrative in *Mules and Men* is that her first attempt to collect folklore—when she approached her Eatonville friends and neighbors in full display of her role as an "educated ethnographer"—had been a dismal failure.[21]

As she tells it, to gain her informants' confidence, Hurston makes the interesting (from a narrative standpoint) but problematic decision to work herself into their storytelling situations without revealing her education or academic background. In Hurston's hometown of Eatonville, she is universally recognized and welcomed as "Lucy Hurston's daughter, Zora" (2), but as she moves away from the place where she already possesses an identity, she must find a way to reinsert herself into society and can only do so by abiding by gendered social roles. Her most challenging research location is perhaps the lumber mills of Polk County, where she stands out as someone with money (evidenced by her car and city clothes) and as a stranger. As a woman without a visible connection to the lumber company (or to any of the male workers), she is immediately the object of some suspicion: "That night the place was full of men—come to look over the new addition to the quarters. Very little was said directly to me and when I tried to be friendly there was a noticeable disposition to fend me off" (60). Despite Boas's assertion that Hurston entered these African American communities "as one of them," here is a situation in which gender and class trump race as gatekeeping elements. She is able to gain some measure of acceptance after she passes herself off as a bootlegger's woman; yet as Graciela Hernández observes, this fabricated identity gets her into trouble, since both her false persona and her attractiveness, "... charge her with a sexual energy ... Ironically, her perceived sexual accessibility leaves her vulnerable to the attacks of Ella and Lucy, two women in the Polk County community" (158). While it can seem in the text as if the balance has tipped and the focus is not on the folktales themselves but on Hurston's own adventures, rather than serving as a distraction, these anecdotes emphasize that the ethnographic scenario is not a one-way exchange but a series of complex encounters in which Hurston does not necessarily hold the upper hand. Indeed, in the gendered politics of the work camp, the feminine identity she constructs for herself turns out to be as much of a liability (in a very different way) as revealing her professional motives might have been. Hurston may be a cultural insider, but her understanding of these gendered problematics does not necessarily make navigating them any easier.

In contrast to Hurston's experience in the male-centered world of Southern storytelling, the community of practitioners that Cabrera presents in her texts is one in which women are respected both as holders of knowledge and as anchoring the practice. Cabrera's interaction with these women—one of the few ways in which she enters the narrative—shows how race and class intersect with gender in these exchanges. While Cabrera had been exposed to Afro-Cuban culture from childhood, as a white woman of a privileged background, divisions of race and class initially kept her from anything but a superficial awareness of these cultural practices. Her first real connection to the community of Santería and Palo Monte practitioners is a woman whom she refers to as "Teresa M." or "Omí-Tomí," a seamstress to Cabrera's mother and grandmother from the time Cabrera was a small girl. Omí-Tomí initially rebuffs Cabrera's questions about Afro-Cuban religion, insisting, "De negros no sé nada" (21) [I know nothing about black people], a telling observation for the way in which race is equated with religious practice, but when she becomes convinced that Cabrera's interest is genuine, she introduces her to a series of important religious elders. This initial connection reveals how much Cabrera's work owes to the informal domestic sphere and to interactions between women in that environment. Cabrera is able to gain the other woman's trust because of the preexisting bond between them, and because of Omí-Tomí's position in Cabrera's father's household. The professional relationship (ethnographer-informant) might have been impossible without trust established through the personal one. As much as she must rely on her professional connections for recognition of her work as legitimate, Cabrera's entrance to the practice of ethnographic fieldwork takes place because of connections established through a gendered encounter, within a feminine domestic sphere.

Yet this domestic encounter is not a friendship between social equals. Cabrera's ethnographic relationship with Omí-Tomí is based on a prior one of familial patronage. Afro-Cuban religious practices may be taking place outside her back door, but the borders of racial and cultural belonging (and thus potentially the borders of contamination) are maintained by structures of class. Hurston wants to blend in, resorting to a kind of playacting to gain her informants' trust. Cabrera seems comfortable as an outsider, albeit a privileged one. Although she states in *El Monte*'s preface that she has chosen to remove her voice from the narrative as much as possible, this does not mean that she entirely effaces her presence from the text. Yet when she is visible as an actor in any scenes described, she most frequently characterizes her position as that of a novice, a visitor who does not yet know the ropes. In one particularly vivid anecdote, Cabrera describes an early visit to a "fiesta lucumí" (a Santería ritual), in which a large woman, on being possessed by the *oricha* (Afro-Cuban divinity) Changó, falls to the floor with a heavy thud. Cabrera, worried that the woman might actually have been killed by the fall, observes,

> En un segundo imaginé todas las complicaciones desagradables a que me exponía mi presencia en el "bembé" por la muerte de aquella mujer monumental. La salida de la habitación estaba obstruída por numerosa concurrencia, y ninguno de los presentes demostró el espanto que debió leer en mis ojos mi acompañante al detenerme por el brazo. "No es nada, niña. Es un santo de verdad." (37–38)

> [In a second, I imagined all the disagreeable complications to which my presence at the "bembé" would expose me thanks to the death of that monumental woman. The room's exit was obstructed by numerous guests, and none of those present showed the fear that my

companion, on grabbing my arm, must have seen in my eyes. "It's nothing, girl. It's a true saint."]

By showing how frightened she was at her (first) viewing of a spirit possession, Cabrera creates a situation in which everything can be explained to her, since she too knows nothing. Her "companion's" voice validates the authenticity of the experience; he (or she), rather than Cabrera, confirms that the woman has truly been possessed by one of the *orichas*.[22] This (assumed) naiveté creates a space for the voices of her informants to be present, but it also positions Cabrera on the side of her (uninitiated) readers. She is afraid because she, too, in that moment knew nothing about these kinds of experiences. Beyond her fear of the unknown, however, lies a fear of being "caught" somewhere she is not supposed to be. While Hurston must hide her educational superiority and her investigative intentions from her informants, as an upper-class white woman who is from the same city (and often, the same part of the city), Cabrera here acknowledges that she is breaking social taboos from the perspective of her peers. This detail, more than anything, highlights the differences of race and class that separate the ethnographer from her informants.

Cabrera is careful to delineate her presence as an outsider, appearing frequently in the text as a listener or an observer, rarely as an authoritative cultural interpreter. Furthermore, she seldom characterizes her knowledge as definitive. At the end of a tale in which a woman is asked by a spirit haunting her house to pay for thirty Gregorian masses for him, Cabrera adds: "El lector, advertido de qué fuente procede el relato queda en libertad, como siempre, de creer lo que mejor le parezca. Por mi parte me inclino a aceptarlo como verídico, pues soy testigo de otros hechos que parecerán tanto más o igualmente inverosímiles" (60). [The reader, warned of the story's source, is free, as always, to believe what seems best to him. For my part, I'm inclined to accept it as true, since I've been witness to other equally or more uncommon occurrences.] Cabrera bases her opinion in part on her experience as a researcher, but she suggests that hers is in no way the *only* valid opinion. In this way, she not only characterizes the voices of her informants as experts in their own right but also refuses to present any interpretation as definitive. This places Cabrera's construction of herself within the text in stark contrast to Malinowski's ideal of the modern ethnographer, for it privileges cultural experience over both scientific background and academic interpretive skill.

Staging the Scenario: Performance and Ethnographic Authority

Hurston and Cabrera further underscore the limitations of the actual position from which writing occurs through an emphasis on the performative basis of the ethnographic scenario. The strong presence of oral material within their texts highlights the acts of enunciation of their informants, seeming to alter the need for "expert" interpretation (and obscuring the fact that it is the text itself which is simulating performance).[23] Henry Louis Gates Jr. identifies Hurston's novel *Their Eyes Were Watching God* as what he calls a "speakerly text," in that its literary strategy centers on highlighting the oral elements from which it is formed (181). It is this narrative strategy, albeit in a modified form, that Hurston—and, I argue, Cabrera—employ in their ethnographically inclined texts.

Apart from the stories (and even frequently within the stories themselves), the focus of Hurston's text is on dialogue. Each of the folktales in *Mules and Men* surfaces out of a particular social context, a scene that sets up and frames the stories, frequently interacting with the theme or message of the tales themselves. The story of "Why Women Always Take Advantage of Men," for example, comes up during an argument about gender relations and male vs. female superiority. Susanna Pavloska observes that the narrative register of Hurston's voice is constantly shifting, so that she addresses her readers in formal English and her informants in dialect (88). I would argue that beyond addressing different audiences, Hurston uses these linguistic differences as markers of belonging, to switch allegiances, and to shift the focus away from her role as the ethnographer. Although many of the stories are told specifically for her benefit, Hurston, as she records these voices, presents herself as merely one more listener, including herself as a character in the dialogue as it unfolds. At the moment of the storytelling, this places her voice on a par with those of the others in the community, and Hurston's own voice shifts so that it more closely resembles the dialect and language of those around her. In Polk County, for example, she talks to one of the men about a particular song:

"What's dat you singing, Box-Car?" I asked.

"'Ah' Gointer Loose dis Right-hand Shackle from 'Round my Leg.' Dat's a chain-gang song. Thought everybody knowed dat."

"Nope, never heard it. Ain't never been to de gang. How did you learn it?"

"Working on de gang."

"Whut you doin' on de gang, Box-Car? You look like a good boy, but a poor boy." (153)

In this brief exchange, Hurston's tone and dialect—as she chooses to represent it in the text—is nearly indistinguishable from that of her interlocutor. By including herself in the sociolinguistic community of her informant, she leaves behind the authority of being a writer that allows her to maintain a sense of separation, and in so doing erases the power differential that her more scholarly narrative voice would have created within the text. Were it not for her pointed questioning, it would be difficult to pick out Hurston as the outsider in the exchange. Despite the problems this sometimes creates for Hurston as a researcher, it means that even the scene of the ethnographic "interview" becomes a dialogue among equals. Indeed, one might question whether an "ethnographic scenario" is truly being played out, given the ways in which Hurston attempts to disguise herself and to hide her real intentions from her informants.

While Hurston is careful to set the folktales themselves off from the text of her own experiences of collecting them, Cabrera's text is a truly polyphonic narrative that blends myths about the *orichas*, Cabrera's own commentary, commentary from informants, and anecdotes of the experiences of different individuals, frequently quoted directly. As Rodríguez-Mangual points out, Cabrera's narrative position with respect to her informants does not remain fixed: "The narration does not ground itself between an 'I' and a 'they'; rather, 'they' soon turns into 'us' and then the pronoun is changed back again" (74). One paragraph may weave together several statements that appear to be from various informants. While the contributors are frequently identified, sometimes they are not. The result is that although Cabrera's voice is still the central narrative thread to which the reader returns, the large amount of space that she gives to the input of her informants keeps her voice from dominating.

In addition to the use of direct discourse, there are a number of instances where Cabrera constructs the text itself as a performance. Cabrera begins her discussion of *El Monte* as if staging an entrance into the bush, so that a reader of her text comes to understand *el Monte* by participating in it. At the beginning of the first chapter, she warns the reader of the difficulty of entering *el Monte*: "Para que el Monte sea propicio al hombre y le ayude en sus empeños, es menester 'saber entrar en el Monte'" (14). [So that *el Monte* will act favorably toward man and help him with his tasks, it's necessary "to know how to enter *el Monte*."] Given that *El Monte* is the title of the book itself, Cabrera seems to be simultaneously referring to *el Monte* as physical space ("the bush"), as the knowledge at the heart of Afro-Cuban religious traditions, and as the text of the ethnography itself. Several chapters later, Cabrera will describe herself as having made an offering to *el Monte* in the form of "el montón de tarjetas en que anoto las informaciones de los que saben propiciarse al dios Osaín y comprar efectivamente la voluntad inteligente de las plantas" [the pile of cards on which I write down the information from those who know how to pray to the god Osaín and effectively buy the plants' intelligent will] (141). Following the image of the note cards to its logical conclusion, we could say that *El Monte* (the book) itself represents a symbolic offering to the *orichas*. Cabrera's "offering up" of her note cards turns the ethnographic scenario in on itself: while her note-taking process transforms oral exchange into written text (into part of the archive), as a ritual offering to the *orichas*, the archive itself becomes part of the performance.[24] Through this metaphor, Cabrera further erodes the boundary between observer and participant: to seek knowledge about the *orichas* is also to engage the *orichas*, to deal with them on their terms.

The Use of Silences: Or, Race and Ethnographic Authority

Throughout both Cabrera's and Hurston's texts, race is often the elephant in the room. Neither book declares itself to be a treatise on race—these are studies of cultural practices, even if that culture is racialized—yet both writers use the destabilizing of ethnographic authority to highlight race as an important element that significantly affects the power dynamics of the ethnographic scenario. Race is a difference that cannot fully be erased for either writer; it is something that must be accounted for in describing a national subculture. Cabrera's and Hurston's texts further destabilize interpretive authority and highlight the challenges in crossing racial boundaries and in representing race through what I will call their "deceptive clarity." While both writers structure their presentation of information in a way that would seem to indicate that it can be easily understood and interpreted, their texts also present evidence that this may not be the case.

By indicating "what is not said" or "what cannot be said," both writers construct race as fundamental difference.

When Hurston places herself and her own experiences at the center of the text, she creates a situation whose intimacy seems to promise the reader that she will tell all. Yet this textual honesty is deceptive; Hurston leaves clues within her text that indicate that her own authorial honesty is not as straightforward as it would appear. At the beginning of her text, Hurston discusses the difficulties of doing fieldwork in the African American community:

"[T]he Negro, in spite of his open-faced laughter, his seeming acquiescence, is particularly evasive. You see we are a polite people and we do not say to our questioner, 'Get out of here!' We smile and tell him or her something that satisfies the white person because, knowing so little about us, he doesn't know what he is missing... The Negro offers a feather-bed resistance. That is, we let the probe enter, but it never comes out. It gets smothered under a lot of laughter and pleasantries" (3). Given that Hurston herself is African American, the description serves in some part to support her own qualifications for this particular ethnographic project. Presumably, she will be able to get around the superficial pleasantries that would have stumped a white ethnographer in a similar position. Yet with the use of the first-person plural "we," Hurston also deliberately includes herself in this description of African American behavior, implying that she herself may be holding something back from her readers (many of whom would presumably be white). Her statement warns the reader not to expect a complete disclosure and signals that a full understanding may, in fact, be impossible. Through this gesture, she identifies race as a border of belonging that cannot fully be crossed. This supports Pavloska's assertion that Hurston was not interested in clarifying black culture for a white audience, but rather in "isolating African-American culture from the accretions resulting from years of appropriation by the white cultural mainstream" (79). As much as Hurston locates herself as the cultural interpreter within the text, her allusion to silences reveals that she identifies more with her black community than with the profession. (The spy-glass, after all, is just a tool.)

The possibility that there are things that Hurston chooses not to disclose (or that cannot be said) is reinforced by the deliberate silences that appear in other parts of *Mules and Men*. Many of these appear in the final section on Hoodoo, the section that is most descriptive and least narrative. This would at first appear to be the section where Hurston would have most to say, since she learns about various Southern Hoodoo practices by apprenticing herself to several Hoodoo doctors. Yet she says of Hoodoo, "It is not the accepted theology of the Nation and so believers conceal their faith . . . Nobody can say where it begins or ends . . . The profound silence of the initiated remains what it is" (185). This passage is notable for the distinction it establishes between African American culture and the dominant American culture ("the Nation"). Hurston does not explain this silence; rather, she performs it through the absences of description in the text. As one of the initiated, she chooses to maintain this silence within her own narrative. She mentions events leading up to her several processes of initiation, but leaves out the key experiences, recipes, or rituals. Of her initiation with Luke Turner in New Orleans, which required her to lie face down on a couch, she says, "For sixty-nine hours I lay there. I had five psychic experiences and awoke at last with no feeling of hunger, only one of exaltation" (199). While Hurston describes her physical position, she reveals nothing about the nature of these psychic experiences, nor of how they affected her. By placing herself center stage in this section, she performs the experience of intimacy without revealing any details, replicating the strategy of African American resistance to white curiosity that she herself lays out at the beginning of the book.[25]

By highlighting the existence of African American silences, Hurston creates a distance between the ethnographic scenario and the reader, which finally results in a breakdown of the scenario itself. The interpretative authority established by the ethnographer supposes an effort to achieve an eventual cultural transparency, since the end result of the ethnographic scenario is cultural translation or understanding. Hurston, by refusing to deliver that end result, frustrates the goals of the scenario. She will not violate the "profound silence of the initiated" (185); instead, by showing us that it is there she reminds us of the cultural differences that cannot be erased. In revealing the impossibility of the absoluteness of ethnographic authority, she communicates that there will always remain a certain part of a culture that cannot be told, the story that cannot be narrated, and she offers her own alternative strategies for manipulating the structure of the discipline itself.

As a white woman writing for a largely white readership, Cabrera speaks from a different place than Hurston. If race serves as a border of belonging, she finds herself curiously straddling the divide. She cannot necessarily orchestrate the silences in the same way that Hurston chooses to do. But she too shows an awareness that her informants can employ similar kinds of strategies. In the introduction to *El Monte* she includes a brief discussion of the challenges that her informants presented. She mentions the necessity of gaining their trust, the need to understand their language and to learn (and learn from) their thought processes. But she also mentions the need to exercise patience with regard to a particular narrative tactic:

> [S]i queremos saber, por ejemplo, por qué la diosa Naná "no quiere" cuchillo de metal sino de bambú, conformamos con que nos cuenten en cambio, cómo el gusano hizo llover y la araña se quemó el pelo que tenía en el pecho. Dos o tres meses, acaso un año después, si repetimos la misma pregunta a quema ropa, se nos dirá "que por lo que le pasó con el Hierro," y ya en posesión de algunos fragmentos de la historia más tarde se nos contará el resto... (2)

> [If we want to know, for example, why the goddess Naná "doesn't want" a metal knife but rather a bamboo one, we must be content instead to let them tell us about how the worm made it rain and the spider burned the hair on its chest. Two or three months, maybe a year, later, if we repeat the same question point-blank, they will say, "because of what happened with the Iron," and now, in possession of some fragments of the story, later they will tell us the rest...]

I think it is possible to see something of the African American strategy of evasion that Hurston describes in the circuitous explanations of Cabrera's informants, which point to how much information these *Santeros* and *Paleros* may be withholding. By including this description in her introduction, Cabrera shows that she herself is aware of the shortcomings of her interpretive position. She may also be subtly commenting on the structure of her own ethnographic narrative, signaling that a reader approaching her text may need patience as well.

Ortiz identifies Cabrera as a translator, working both across cultures and across languages, yet Cabrera is in fact careful not to translate everything.

She is content to allow for various levels of understanding within the text. José Quiroga identifies Cabrera's strategic use of silences as a "localized praxis," a technique that rather than disguising or hiding, "is a form of speech that is transparent in different terms for different members of the reading audience, who have been initiated into one of its many circuits of meaning" (*Tropics of Desire* 80). The boundaries of initiation are cultural, but also implicitly racial. In the polyphony of its narrative, the density of its construction, the sheer quantity of the material presented, and the use of a plethora of technical and religious terms in the African dialects such as *Lucumí* (Yoruba) and *Congó* (Bantu) spoken in Cuba, Cabrera's text is something of a "catch-22"; that is, it is impossible for a reader to fully understand the book without understanding much of the material beforehand, yet for an outsider it is only possible to understand the material by reading the book. Through its multiple kinds of translation—or lack thereof—Cabrera offers a text that can only be understood on certain levels by the initiated. She does little to mitigate the complexity of her text, I believe, because she is more interested in presenting the cultural information as she has received it than in creating a clear and facile narrative for the average reader. Like Hurston, this strategy to some extent both abdicates ethnographic authority and signals the limitations of the ethnographic enterprise itself. Yet while Hurston locates herself on the side of her African American informants, Cabrera's position is more ambiguous. There are certain things she *may* know and *may* have learned, but others remain unknowable from her position as a [white] outsider. The uncertain nature of "the truth" in Cabrera's text (as I have discussed it above) is another way of signaling a kind of failure or incompleteness of all interpretation. If there is no "definitive" story, no absolute interpretation, then we must be prepared to accept that there are things that we as readers cannot fully understand, just as there are things that an ethnographer may not know or may be unable (or unwilling) to say. As *El Monte* provides a glimpse into the multiplicity (or instability) of Afro-Cuban cultural truths it also becomes a meditation on the inadequacies of perception and interpretation.

Ethnographic Authority and National Projects

Hurston's and Cabrera's refusal to pick up the burden of ethnographic authority and deliver an easily assimilatable picture of African American or Afro-Cuban culture is significant when one considers that they were writing in an era that desired them to do just that. While Malinowski dreams of professional ethnography as a kind of pure science, Hurston's and Cabrera's texts point to the ways in which the fundamental instability and fluidity of the genre, far from crippling it, instead open it to complex and subtle adaptation and even subversion. In an age in which "men of academic training" were supposed to demonstrate the conclusive fruits of scientific inquiry, their texts highlight the ambiguities, impossibilities, and difficult relationships and knowledge involved in this endeavor. Through their destabilization of ethnographic authority, experimental textual structure, polyphonic narrative voice, and use of silences, both Cabrera and Hurston seem in different ways to be challenging ethnography's ability to render a culture transparent for its readers, and thus knowable and understandable for a nation.

Because of their experimentations with form, narrative voice, and ethnographic authority, Hurston and Cabrera have frequently been seen as exceptions to ethnography's rules, as professional outsiders who took unusual risks, or as feminist ethnographers *avant la lettre*. I have argued that rather than viewing them as exceptional in the ways they play with the ethnographic scenario, perhaps we should see their work as more proof that at the time in which they were writing, the ethnographic scenario itself was by no means as solidified as it has sometimes been understood to be. It is interesting to note, however, that neither writer found the readership or appreciation, either general or professional, of their work at the time of its publication that it has subsequently acquired. This may have something to do with the fact that Cabrera and Hurston were women writing in a genre that defined itself through the presentation of a masculine academic voice.

As I have shown, these writers were particularly aware of how being a woman limited and shaped their fieldwork experiences, as well as their relationship to the academy and academic mentors; their writing strategies reveal a deliberate response to this awareness. While their texts deal with a cultural environment defined in large part by race, both writers reveal a nuanced understanding of the role of gender in defining social relations, and their work ultimately illuminates the importance of gender in these same environments. Cabrera and Hurston are conscious of the "contact zones" in which they are operating, and the complex constructions of their texts are their way of attempting to mitigate the power differential of their position as ethnographers.

It is important to recognize, however, that the contact zones in which Hurston and Cabrera are operating are not the same, nor are their positions within them. They were both in some ways "insider-outsiders," but at different cost. As an African American woman from the South, even one with a Northern education, Hurston was being asked to represent aspects of her own culture for a white audience (and particularly for white mentors) and for her black literary peers; she could not escape the significance of this racial divide. Given the social and political position of African Americans, particularly in the South, it is unlikely that she felt a particular obligation to a white image of nation; yet she clearly understood the delicacy of her role as a culture-broker. By framing her study of African American folklore as a tale about herself and her experiences, she allows her textual persona to distract from the more critical gestures at work in her writing. The sociocultural negotiations that "Zora the ethnographer" undergoes in the field are sleights of hand meant to distract us from the ways in which Hurston the writer is mediating the reader's access (or lack thereof) to certain kinds of information.

By establishing herself as a cultural outsider within the text and deliberately calling attention to her own position as an upper-class white woman, Cabrera never runs the risk of being mistaken for one of her informants. She can allow her informants to "speak for themselves" precisely because the social divisions created by race and class keep her position—and theirs—intact. This is not to discount from the significance of her project; *El Monte* does present Afro-Cuban religious traditions—in all of their complexity—to an audience not familiar with them, and insists on the fundamentally "Cuban" nature of these traditions. Yet since Cuba is not necessarily seen as "white," the important maintenance of divisions of class and race are what enable Cabrera to bring Afro-Cuban religion safely into the space of nation without identifying the nation itself as "black." Her gestures signal the diversity and integrity of Afro-Cuban religious practice, but they also act to reinforce the boundaries separating it from other aspects of Cuban culture.

The difference between Cabrera's and Hurston's positions comes back to one of distance and perspective. Hurston, as a minority writer charged with explicating the traditions of her own culture, performs a complicated, fictionalizing autoethnography as she attempts to both simultaneously present black culture to a white audience and protect certain parts of it. Despite being in possession of the spy-glass, her loyalties are divided. While Cabrera may be a culture-broker, her ultimate loyalty is to Cuba as a whole. Her awareness that Afro-Cuban culture is not a "minority" culture, and her attempts to help it enter the space of nation, are what make her text so compelling and so contradictory.

Epilogue

TEXTUAL STRAITS

Race and Ethnographic Literature since the Cuban Revolution

The overthrow of Cuban president and dictator Fulgencio Batista in January of 1959 and the triumph of the 26 of July Movement and its charismatic leader Fidel Castro initiated a radical restructuring of many aspects of Cuban society. Determined to do away with the systemic inequalities in operation under Batista, the new revolutionary leadership took immediate, large-scale steps intended to promote a more even distribution of wealth: land and property were expropriated and industries were nationalized. The Revolution also worked to dismantle what its leaders perceived as the decadent, tourist-focused aspects of Cuban society by outlawing gambling, closing casinos and nightclubs, and in the process doing away with a large number of related industries and professions (Pérez, *Cuba* 252). In response to these measures, thousands of Cubans—largely the wealthy white elite and the middle class—left the country, many of them settling ninety miles across the Florida Strait in Miami.[1] In the space of two years, both the make up of the Cuban body politic and the idea of what Cuba was underwent an abrupt, dramatic transformation. Even as the possibility of a single coherent national project became all the more vexed, ethnographic literature was a part of this dramatic transformation of the Cuban imaginary.

Cuban writing prior to 1959 had produced a fertile textual dialogue around the role of race in the construction of an idea of Cuba as a nation, as writers drew from both literary and ethnographic textual strategies to reframe Afro-Cuban culture in a way that would make it a productive part of a new national narrative. While not explicitly collaborators (or revolutionaries themselves), writers such as Fernando Ortiz, Alejo Carpentier, Nicolás Guillén, and Lydia Cabrera, whose work I have explored in this study, were all interested in negotiating the relationship between intellectual and literary discourse and Afro-Cuban (popular) culture. Despite the many differences in the ways that they choose to present this encounter, their texts privilege elite cultural (and literary) forms as they locate blackness within a narrative of Cuban cultural authenticity. These texts also share a sense of literary experimentation and ideological endeavor in their approach to Afro-Cuban culture.

That particular moment of literary and intellectual exploration around questions of race and nation ended with the arrival of the Revolution. With the dramatic transformation of Cuba's political system and its adoption of a socialist outlook on policies, the very relationship between elite literary production and popular culture was called into question. As a result, the ways in which Cuban writers employed ethnographic and literary strategies to talk about race—and their reasons for doing so—concomitantly changed significantly.

Textual experimentation with elements of both ethnographic and literary discourses by Cuban writers did not end with the Revolution, but these new textual experiments were now closely linked to conflicting ideas about the Revolution itself and the construction of new national narratives centered either for or against the Revolution. The representation of blackness and the use of Afro-Cuban culture to construct an "authentic" Cuban "folk" culture were rearticulated in light of new revolutionary and counter-revolutionary projects (on the island and by writers in exile). This rearticulation was only partly the result of revolutionary rhetoric; it moreover reflected an ideological (and geographic) split among the authors who had been and were engaged in these writing practices. Of the writers who had participated in or been influenced by *Afrocubanismo*, some, such as Carpentier and Guillén, went on to occupy cultural or diplomatic positions in the new government.[2] Others, such as Cabrera, left the country for exile in Miami. Yet for all of these writers, their identity as scholars and the work they had done in the spirit of *Afrocubanismo* were reevaluated (and reshaped) in the context of the Revolution and the new writers who emerged from it.

As the Revolution produced innovations in both the theoretical approach to culture and the techniques that were used to construct cultural narratives in Cuba, it also altered the ways in which the previous generation of texts incorporating Afro-Cuban culture was read and understood. The reshaping of the relationship between literature and ethnography that occurred in the wake of 1959 is clearly visible in the work of Miguel Barnet, a student of Fernando Ortiz and a writer educated by the Revolution, and in the ethnographic writing of Lydia Cabrera—both in the reframing of the texts she published both prior to the Revolution and in work she produced in exile. In particular, two introductions—Barnet's introduction to his *Biografía de un cimarrón* (1966), and Raimundo Respall Fina's 1993 preface to Cabrera's *El Monte*, illustrate the ruptures, continuities, and reappropriations that the Revolution produced in the use of ethnography and literature to construct a narrative of Cuba.

Race and the Revolution

Racial prejudice was high on the list of social inequalities the revolutionary leadership explicitly sought to address in the first months of the Revolution. In a speech given on March 22, 1959, Fidel Castro, who had emerged as the Revolution's charismatic leader, declared that racial discrimination was one of the principal social inequalities in Cuba that must be changed (de la Fuente, *A Nation for All* 263). To that end, in the months following Castro's speech, the revolutionary leadership launched several antiracism campaigns, and the country began a slow process of desegregating public spaces and professional environments. Other policies of income redistribution initiated in the first years of the Revolution, such as a nationally mandated decrease in rents, were also intended in part to ease racial inequalities (de la Fuente, *A Nation for All* 276–78).

Having undertaken these and other steps aimed at ending racial discrimination in the labor force and reducing income disparity between black and white Cubans, the revolutionary leadership declared as early as 1962 that Cuba had succeeded in eliminating racial discrimination. As de la Fuente notes, "This became the dominant theme in public discourse, echoed in official documents, journalistic pieces, and even scholarship" (*A Nation for All* 279). Thanks to actions of the Revolution, this discourse stated, Cuba had achieved a racial democracy. By asserting that race was no longer an issue, revolutionary rhetoric effectively closed the space for discussing race, since to mention race (or racism) was to insist on imposing a social division that—according to the Revolution's narrative—no longer existed. The Cuban people, Fidel and other leaders insisted, had been united through the Revolution and its work towards the elimination of social inequalities.

By foregrounding the class struggle above all other vectors of conflict save imperialism (understood as a global extension of class conflict), the Revolution thus created a new national narrative that displaced previous intellectual investigations into the source of Cuban authenticity. In contrast to those who viewed the Revolution as a break or rupture, this new narrative saw the Revolution as the culmination of Cuba's historical trajectory, the final step in its evolutionary development as an independent nation. The overthrow of Batista in 1959 was the realization of a fight for independence that had begun in 1865; full national freedom had not been achieved merely through independence from Spain but rather by ending the neocolonial relationship Cuba had maintained with the United States. This revolutionary narrative did not express the same need for a "folk" culture; Cuba's coming into being was defined by (and viewed through) political [class] struggle. The nation now required "a people" defined as a revolutionary working class, not an authentic folk.

This shift in the need to position Afro-Cuban culture within a national narrative, coupled with the revolutionary leadership's assertion that a racially harmonious society had been achieved, profoundly affected the perspective from which interested writers approached Afro-Cuban culture. The young writers and ethnographers educated after 1959 privileged the Revolution, seen as generated and created by the Cuban people, as the ultimate realization of an authentic Cuban culture. While Afro-Cuban culture did not cease to be a subject of interest, it was no longer needed to occupy the role of the "folk"; race and racially identified culture thus came to occupy a subordinate position in relation to national narratives.[3] In his essay "Diálogos imaginarios" (Imaginary Dialogues, 1972), ethnographer Rogelio Martínez Furé defines folklore as "la más auténtica creación de las masas" (*Diálogos imaginarios* 268) [the most authentic creation of the masses], a truly egalitarian cultural product. According to Martínez Furé, in the context of the Revolution folklore is undergoing something like a transculturative process: "El folklore no desaparece sino que se transforma, y con ello nutre nuestra verdadera cultura nacional revolucionaria" (269). [Folklore doesn't disappear; it is transformed, and our true national revolutionary culture is nourished by it.] While Martínez Furé does not explicitly mention race in his initial discussion of folklore, he describes folklore's parameters in order to define national culture as racially hybrid and, to use Ortiz's concept, transculturated: "[Es un] proceso de síntesis ... que podemos contribuir a acelerar revolucionariamente" (272). [It's a synthesizing process ... that we can help accelerate revolutionarily.]

Unlike bourgeois capitalism, which sees folklore as a "minor cultural form" in contrast to "universal" bourgeois art (267), Martínez Furé argues that Cuban folklore is itself the ultimate—and central—expression of the revolutionary transculturative process.[4] While folklore is not identical to "revolutionary national culture," for him the two concepts are mutually beneficial and intimately linked, evolving simultaneously.

Revolutionary Ethnography: Barnet's *Testimonio*

The work of Miguel Barnet illustrates the ways in which literature and ethnography after the Revolution would continue to privilege a narrative of temporal development—even while developing new textual forms. Barnet is credited as the creator of the genre of the *novela-testimonio* (testimonial novel), now known as *testimonio*, which critic George Yúdice defines as: "an authentic narrative, told by a witness who is moved to narrate by the urgency of a situation. . . . Emphasizing popular, oral discourse, the witness portrays his or her own experience as an agent (rather than a representative) of a collective memory and identity" (44). However, a key difference of the *testimonio* genre is that the witness is generally not the actual writer of the tale himself; instead, he is aided by another writer (or social scientist), who collects his life story and creates a coherent and compelling narrative from it. *Testimonio* draws from a fundamental ethnographic relationship: that between an ethnographer and his or her informant. Yet instead of using the informant's story as but one piece of evidence for a scholarly argument or explanation, in creating a testimonial novel, the ethnographer facilitates the presentation of the informant's life story as the central—and most often only—narrative of the text. Although the reader is presented with an individual, first-person speaking subject (as in a novel), as John Beverley observes, this individual's life story is understood to be representative of the situation or experiences of a collective whole (35), and is thus imbued with a meaning beyond that of individual experience.

The testimonial subject is thus both an "ordinary individual" and a person whose life experiences are of particular significance. According to Barnet, the testimonial subject proposes "un desentrañamiento de la realidad" [an unveiling of reality] by narrating significant collective or national events from a first-person perspective (*Fuente viva* 20). In a later essay on *testimonio*, he declares, "I aspire to be a sounding board for the collective memory of my country" ("Alchemy of Memory" 205). In *testimonio*, compelling stories experienced by someone who is truly "one of the people" replace the novel, the expression of a bourgeois cultural environment, to create a new kind of national literature.

As Barnet tells it, his first *testimonio*, *Biografía de un cimarrón* (*Biography of a Runaway Slave*, 1966, hereafter *Biografía*) came about thanks to a chance occurrence. In 1963, while researching a project on Afro-Cuban religious traditions, Barnet came across a newspaper article that mentioned Esteban Montejo, a 104-year old Afro-Cuban man who stated he had been a *cimarrón* (runaway slave). His curiosity piqued, Barnet went to meet Montejo at the home for veterans where he was living and spent hours interviewing the elderly man, learning about life under slavery and Montejo's experiences as a runaway slave and a soldier in the War for Independence (*Biografía* 9). Barnet decided that Montejo's story should be recorded in written form. From their taped conversations, Barnet then crafted a written narrative of Montejo's life, giving it a linearly coherent structure (which the original conversations had not had) but narrating it in the first person "de manera que no perdiera su espontaneidad, pudiendo así insertar vocablos y giros idiomáticos propios del habla de Esteban" (*Biografía* 8) [so that it wouldn't lose its spontaneity, in this way being able to insert words and idiomatic turns typical of Esteban's speech]. The result is a text that reads as if Montejo himself were recounting the story of his life in a more or less direct manner.

Barnet's introduction to *Biografía*, which he included in the first edition of the text, does not merely introduce Montejo or his story; instead, it focuses on the genre of *testimonio*, and on describing both its genesis and function to the reader. Barnet makes it clear that *Biografía* is a new kind of text, produced with a new writing technique. His essay highlights the way he has sought to balance (narrative) storytelling and ethnographic technique in both his relationship with Montejo and in the structuring of the text itself. At the beginning, he states, "No fue difícil lograr un diálogo vivo, utilizando, desde luego, los recursos habituales de la investigación etnológica" (7). [It wasn't difficult to achieve a lively dialogue, making use, of course, of the customary resources of ethnographic investigation.] Barnet begins by identifying himself as an ethnographer, and yet as he tells it, the text emerges as a collaboration in which Montejo contributes just as much to the direction of the conversation—and thus to the book's focus—as Barnet. Despite the fact that the text he produced was in fact a carefully mediated reconstruction, Barnet states that his intention—in the text itself, but particularly in his description of it in the introduction—is that Montejo's story should seem as "natural" as possible. The intellectual takes a back seat to the narrator-protagonist.

Ironically, in spite of Barnet's explanation of his methodology in his introduction, *Biografía*'s central narrative—Montejo's life story—remains a text that hides the process of its construction. Although Barnet admits in the introduction that he had to "paraphrase" much of what Montejo told him, since the narrative relates everything using Montejo's "voice," Barnet's paraphrasing is not at all apparent. *Biografía* presents its story as "true," despite the fact that it is a heavily mediated—and in this sense "fictionalized"—product. As Elzbieta Sklodowska points out, Barnet's explanation of his methodology in the introduction is intended precisely to bolster the "truthfulness" of the text itself ("Spanish American Testimonial Novel" 88). On the other hand, Montejo is an authority only in the sense that he is a witness—or, from an ethnographic standpoint, an informant. His story achieves meaning from the construction of the authenticity of his lived experience, and by showing the importance of this experience within a larger sociohistorical context. Barnet's authority lies in his ability to communicate the significance of this authentic, revolutionary, and most importantly, national story.

Barnet states in the introduction that what "most impressed him" about Montejo's story and drew him to record it were Montejo's experiences as a runaway slave (*Biografía* 7). This aspect of Montejo's story has historical significance; as Barnet states, prior to his discovery of Montejo, the experiences of runaway slaves had been little documented, and it was thought that in the last decades of slavery in Cuba (the 1860s and 1870s) they had largely ceased to exist (*Fuente viva* 147). Montejo's story thus brings to light an obscured chapter of Cuba's colonial history. As both Sklodowska and Gerard Aching observe, however, Barnet was also interested in Montejo's experience as a *cimarrón* for its symbolic possibilities. Aching argues that in Barnet's text *cimarronaje* (marronage, a slave's running away) "is recruited to serve the nation" through the way that Barnet "invites the reader to identify Montejo's marronage with Cuban attempts to rid the island of Spanish rule" ("On the Creation" 38). I would argue that Barnet goes even farther, connecting Montejo's rebelliousness (something Montejo himself defines as fundamental to his character) not only with the struggle for independence from Spain but with the Cuban Revolution of 1959. In a later reflection on the making of *Biografía*, Barnet observes, "El hombre cubano, el ser humano que vive en esta isla, tenía necesidad de que le dijeran estas cosas que se dicen en el libro, que van más allá de ser el relato etnográfico de la vida de un cimarrón" (*Fuente viva* 147). [The Cuban man, the human being that lives on this island, needed to hear the things that are said in this book, which goes beyond an ethnographic history of the life of a runaway slave.] If Cuban revolutionary discourse sees the Revolution as the full realization of the Cuban nation's coming into being, Barnet constructs Montejo's desire for freedom and his refusal to submit (to slavery) as emblematic of a spirit of Cubanness essential to the Revolution's success.

Barnet intends that the reader see Montejo's story as pointing to something universally Cuban. However, his reading of the significance of the story through the official revolutionary narrative risks sublimating the issue of race and the fact that Montejo's situation and his experiences were in large measure a result of his blackness. It is interesting, then, to observe the ways Montejo's narrative pushes back against Barnet's attempts to contain it. As Aching notes, there are moments in the text, as in the description of the struggle for independence, when Montejo distinguishes between all Cubans generally and the experiences of black Cubans ("On the Creation" 38). Montejo frequently speaks in a metonymic narrative "we," but this first-person plural voice is often racially marked; it is almost always "we blacks" or "blacks" (in general). Montejo also insists on his ability to be silent or to *not* comment: "Lo que más me ha salvado es que me he callado porque no se puede confiar. El que confía mucho se hunde solo" (*Biografía* 179). [What has saved me the most is that I have been quiet, because you can't trust people. He who trusts too much betrays himself.] As I have discussed elsewhere in this book, this insistence on the value of and need for silences (in particular, the repeated mention of silence), is, as Doris Sommer has observed, a deliberate textual strategy that signals the boundaries of understanding.[5] In the *testimonio*, Barnet offers the Revolution a genre designed to give voice to the experience of "the people." Yet if Barnet wants to see Montejo's life as symbolic of Cuba's progress as a nation, through these and other gestures Montejo insists on blackness as a category of difference and on his own particularity, which is not applicable to a raceless narrative of national identity. Through his use of silences, he also points to the existence of (cultural) information that cannot be shared within the representational space of the nation.

Rereading Cabrera's *El Monte*

Given the ways in which Barnet's innovations—in his creation of *Biografía* and the genre of *testimonio*—were placed in service of revolutionary national culture, Lydia Cabrera and her work posed a peculiar problem for ethnographers working on Afro-Cuban culture in the wake of the Revolution. Cabrera left the island in 1960, part of the first wave of exiles, and she remained strongly critical of both Castro and the Revolution until her death in 1991. However, while Cabrera herself might be criticized as antirevolutionary, Barnet and other writers working on Afro-Cuban culture could not ignore her groundbreaking ethnographic work. The challenge for these revolutionary writers was to re-frame Cabrera's prerevolutionary work so that it, too could be seen to be contributing to the postrevolutionary context.

"Abriendo monte" ("Brush Clearing," literally "opening the forest"), Cuban critic Raimundo Respall Fina's preface to the 1993 Letras Cubanas edition of *El Monte*, illustrates the ways in which the postrevolutionary generation could reject Cabrera (the exile) while embracing—and in the process reenvisioning—her scholarship. With its use of the verb "to open," the prologue's title suggests that the text itself *needs* interpretation, that it is waiting to be "opened" by a knowing reader (or a helpful prologue). Respall Fina begins his introduction to Cabrera's study with an anecdote of the first meeting of Alejo Carpentier and Cabrera at a Santería ceremony. Fernando Ortiz (also in attendance) facilitated the meeting of the two writers. As with Ortiz's preface to Cabrera's first book of short stories, this detail allows Respall Fina to legitimate Cabrera's work through association with senior male colleagues (and faithful revolutionaries).

Respall Fina then characterizes Cabrera's work as "una extensa colección de testimonios" [an extensive collection of testimonies], a turn of phrase that in 1993 directly called to mind Barnet's work. Given the way that *testimonio* (as Barnet defines it) illuminates the oral history of an informant, it could be argued that Barnet's development of this form extends the very ethnographic techniques that Cabrera employs in *El Monte* (1954) and *La sociedad secreta abakuá* (1959), and Edna Rodríguez-Mangual has shown that Cabrera's "ethnographic" texts in fact do share a number of key elements with testimonial narrative (67–74). In these ethnographies, Cabrera not only weaves together long sections of quotes from her informants, often reproduced in the first person; in her introduction to *El*

Monte she insists on the importance of "allowing the voices of these men and women to come through" (3). The sense that informants' "voices" are of supreme interest and paramount importance links Cabrera's pioneering ethnographic literature to later textual projects such as Barnet's.

There is a crucial difference, however, between the function of an ethnographic informant and the role of a protagonist. For Cabrera, the elderly Afro-Cubans who have shared their knowledge with her are "the book's true authors" because of the knowledge they possess (3). While some of these informants are identified by name, the text's focus is not on their life stories but on their understanding of Afro-Cuban religious traditions. We are not asked to identify with them so much as we are asked to recognize their authority as knowledgeable cultural elders. Cabrera includes these voices in a text that presents a number of other voices (and sources of authority), including her own. To some extent, she makes the seams of the text's construction visible—or gestures towards a certain kind of visibility. Yet to call *El Monte* a *testimonio* is to assume that Cabrera intends something for her text—or for her informants—that she never articulates. She is not uninterested her informants' life stories, but ultimately she is more interested in the information they can provide.

If Respall Fina emphasizes the "testimonial" aspects of *El Monte*, this is, I believe, because these parts of the book represent the folkloric Cuba, the "authentic" Cuba that has now become folded into—and superseded by—revolutionary Cuba. By emphasizing informant testimony, as a post-1959 critic, Respall Fina can better distance the 1954 text from the subsequent (post-1959) actions of its author, who left Cuba in 1960. *El Monte* can be identified (rehabilitated) as "revolutionary," even if its author ultimately was not.

For Respall Fina, Cabrera's decision to leave revolutionary Cuba is inexplicable, particularly given her work on Afro-Cuban culture. He observes, "No alcanzo a comprender cómo Lydia Cabrera no reparó en meterse en el monte y, sin embargo, se espantó ante una Revolución que vino a consolidar definitivamente lo cubano, cómo no pudo entender este trascendente acontecimiento nacional" (9). [I cannot understand how Lydia Cabrera was unafraid to go into *el monte* and yet was frightened when faced with a Revolution that was able to definitively consolidate what is Cuban, how she couldn't understand this transcendent national event.] Given Cabrera's inability to understand the Revolution, for Respall Fina, the only work of Cabrera's that counts is her work before 1959.

According to him, in the texts that she produced in Miami she was "plagiarizing herself" (10), recompiling passages from previous texts. Since for Respall Fina the essential value of Cabrera's work lies in what she reveals of Afro-Cuban culture itself, it is as if for him, once Cabrera writes outside of Cuba, she has nothing to offer.

Gestures of Exile: *Yemayá y Ochún*

In exile in Miami, Cabrera was cut off from both her focus of study (the Afro-Cuban religious communities of Havana and Matanzas) and from Cuban society as she had known it. For a writer whose work prior to 1959 had focused on portraying the space of Afro-Cuban culture and religious practice, her physical separation from the island was in many ways a devastating predicament. If Cabrera's central intention in her earlier ethnographic texts had been to present an existing system of social practices in its entirety and its complexity, her post-1960 work indicates that she sees herself as the "keeper of the flame." She must make real in the text a now-inaccessible geographic space and render intelligible a body of practices for a new generation of readers (and practitioners), many of whom are coming of age in the distant spatial and temporal reality of urban United States.

As they highlight the spatial and temporal dislocation of Cabrera herself, her ethnographies also serve to highlight her own experience of disruption and loss. In doing so, however, these texts become simultaneously (and perhaps paradoxically) more rigidly "ethnographic"—more preoccupied with documenting culture, and making it transparently possible to understand—and increasingly dominated by Cabrera's peculiar vision, which is even more revealing of her class position than her previous work had allowed. At the same time, Cabrera's insistence on ethnographic framing actively resists a (revolutionary) narrative that would subsume these racialized practices into a homogenized national folklore or see them as part of a single national trajectory.

Yemayá y Ochún, significantly the text that Respall Fina mentions in his introduction to *El Monte* as a "plagiarization," in fact differs dramatically from Cabrera's earlier text in its organization, focus, and outlook. Ostensibly a study of the role of the female *orichas* (goddesses) Yemayá and Ochún within the Santería pantheon, and in Cuban culture more broadly, the text begins with both a spatial and temporal rupture: "El ocho de septiembre—antes de Castro—era una fecha importante en la devoción del entonces alegre y despreocupado pueblo habanero" (9). [The eighth of September—before Castro—was an important religious date for the then-happy and carefree people of Havana.] In this, the book's first sentence, the phrase "before Castro" stands out (both visually and discursively), clearly identifying the Revolution as the rift that marks the book's narrative, and separating the temporal space into a "before" and an "after." The sentence does not clearly articulate the nature of this "after," and yet the description of the people of Havana as "*entonces* alegre" (then-happy) implies a downturn in the well-being of Havana's citizens. The text thus already positions itself along a line of temporal displacement, in which both the reader and (implicitly) the narrator are separated from this Havana and inscribed in the text's tale of loss.

Having identified the Revolution and the arrival of Castro as a fundamental historical break, Cabrera begins her discussion of Nuestra Señora de Regla (Our Lady of Regla), Havana's patron saint and the Catholic equivalent of the *oricha* Yemayá, much earlier, tracing the history of the sanctuary in Regla from its founding in 1690. This diachronic approach further emphasizes the sense of temporal and physical separation, since it presumes a reader with neither a historical nor a cultural context within which to situate the saint/*oricha*. Yet it also shifts the text's focus to an event from a more remote cultural past. If the 1959 Revolution is implicitly the moment of rupture, the moment of Cuban wholeness to which Cabrera returns is not the Cuba of 1958 or even 1901, but rather the colonial era, certainly an integral time in Cuba's formation but also the time of slavery and a rigid division of both labor and social power.

Cabrera's retelling of the history of the worship of Our Lady of Regla also helps to explain why she chooses to focus on this particular pair of *orichas*. The Catholic saints connected to Yemayá and Ochún (Our Lady of Regla and Our Lady of Charity of El Cobre, respectively) are the patron saints of Cuba, and to travel between the churches considered their sanctuaries—one in Regla, outside Havana, the other in El Cobre, near Santiago, in Oriente province—one must traverse nearly the entire island. This narrative of the two *orichas* acts as a remapping of the contours of Cuba itself, a reinsertion of the physical space of Cuba into this supposedly temporally structured narrative. The decision to focus on Yemayá and Ochún is also significant when one considers that these are the *orichas* that represent/are connected to water—Ochún to lakes and rivers (fresh water) and Yemayá to the ocean. By beginning her text with a discussion of Yemayá, Cabrera emphasizes Cuba's island nature and the importance of the ocean for the people there; the sea is what gives Cuba its identity as an island.

But the practice of worshipping Yemayá through Our Lady of Regla also references the idea of sea crossings: first the literal crossing of the bay to get from Havana to Regla, but also, implicitly, two far less pleasant journeys: the Middle Passage experienced by so many Africans who came to Cuba as slaves, and the journey of Cuban exiles (including Cabrera) across the ninety miles of water separating Cuba from south Florida. Cabrera emphasizes Yemayá's connection to Olokun, the spirit of the ocean depths who, according to legend, is chained to the ocean floor to prevent him from destroying the earth, as he does in one tale. If Yemayá is the sea as maternal origin, Olokun represents the unpredictable destructive power of the ocean waters, a symbol of the ambivalent power of these spiritual and natural forces.

Despite the dangerous power of Olokun, Yemayá is most often invoked as a kind of mother figure among the *orichas*—a caring, maternal feminine presence. This characterization gives added significance to Cabrera's choice to begin her narrative with the worship of Our Lady of Regla, since through this introduction Yemayá thus emerges as both the "mother" and creator of the *orichas*, and as a kind of spiritual mother for the Cuban nation as a whole. If the actual ocean waters (of the Florida Strait) divide the Cuban people, Yemayá unites them symbolically. Cabrera paints the *oricha* as a universally Cuban figure, and there is a constant emphasis on racial harmony in the text. This is evident in the first chapter; Cabrera focuses not on private Santería ceremonies honoring Yemayá but on the national holiday which honors the *oricha* in her Catholic form, a day in which "negros, mulatos y blancos acudían al santuario de Nuestra Señora la Virgen de Regla" (9) [blacks, mulattos and whites would come to the sanctuary of Our Lady of Regla]. Lest her readers miss the cultural significance of a Catholic celebration honoring an *oricha*, Cabrera ends this first chapter by characterizing the holiday as an example of religious syncretism and observing that "nos muestra la influencia sutil, incalculable, en un aspecto ontológico, que los africanos ejercieron y ejercen en innumerables cubanos de raza blanca" (19) [it shows us the subtle, incalculable, in a way ontological influence that Africans exercised and exercise on innumerable white Cubans]. The racial harmony implicit in this expression of religious syncretism is an idea to which Cabrera will return in numerous small gestures and statements throughout the text.

While Cabrera's preexile texts acknowledged that Afro-Cuban religions are practiced by white Cubans was well as those of African ancestry, Cabrera's insistence in *Yemayá y Ochún* on the varied racial backgrounds of Cuban Santería worshippers comes to seem like an expression of anxiety, a concern to communicate that religious practices can fundamentally unite her compatriots, even if politics has separated them. The theme of racial harmony is only further emphasized when Cabrera turns to explaining the *oricha* Ochún, for the Virgen de la Caridad del Cobre (Our Lady of Charity of El Cobre, Ochún's Catholic equivalent) has an origin story in which these previous threads resurface. According to popular legend (and as recounted by Cabrera in the text), the statue of the Virgin was found floating in the Bay of Nipe (near Santiago) in the early 1600s by three men, two Indians and one black man, and was declared Cuba's patron saint in 1916. Her appearance is emblematic of racial harmony, and her official recognition, achieved after Cuban Independence, is a symbolic affirmation of the emergence of the nation itself.

In keeping with its desire to unify Cuba, *Yemayá y Ochún* is perhaps the most straightforwardly organized of Cabrera's ethnographic texts. After a number of chapters devoted to the characters of Yemayá and Ochún and their relationships to other *orichas*, the book's second half explains the process of initiation into the *Regla de Ochá* (another name for Santería in Cuba) in a more or less step-by-step fashion. The orderly narrative of initiation that Cabrera constructs in this section of the text is in direct contrast to the more rhizomatic structure of her earlier ethnographies. This adds to the sense that rather than meditating on a set of practices that can be observed in other contexts, the text attempts to record practices that are in the process of changing. While earlier texts such as *El Monte* were open to the ambivalent nature of "truth" in the *Regla de Ochá*, one senses in *Yemayá y Ochún* that there is a "right" way and a "wrong" way to go about these practices, and that one can find both charlatans and serious practitioners of the religion. The book is written to inform the reader in the present, but by seeking to (correctly) educate Santería initiates and practitioners on both sides of the Florida Strait, it also concerns itself with the future of these religious practices. Without the spatial grounding of Cuba itself, *Santeros* are in danger of going astray. Cabrera's exile text radiates a temporal anxiety that, despite Cabrera's rejection of the Revolution, ironically comes to echo its nationalist claims.

Ethnographic Memories: Folklore from the Past

Barnet chooses to celebrate postrevolutionary Cuba; Cabrera mourns prerevolutionary Cuba. Yet for both of them, the Revolution's reframing of national narrative—both by casting the Revolution of 1959 as the culmination of a national struggle and through its insistence on the Revolution as continual transformation rather than a finished event—sharply altered the way in which these writers approached the use of ethnographic strategies.

Barnet utilizes ethnographic fieldwork techniques, namely the intensive interviewing of a key informant, to reconstruct a personal narrative that belongs to national history. While he may have been drawn to Montejo as an exceptional individual, Barnet is most interested in how Montejo's story can be made to illuminate less exceptional kinds of communal (national) experience. In this way, his *testimonio* shares with Cabrera's exile ethnographic texts a preoccupation with the past; he too locates racial difference and racialized inequalities in historical time (even if his subject, Montejo, does not). For Barnet, Montejo not only offers a valuable lesson in the historical experiences of the Cuban people; he allows Barnet to show the great distance Cuba has come (since the Revolution) in creating an egalitarian society.

While ethnography has often been accused of a kind of imperialist preemptive nostalgia, a documenting of cultures "as they are disappearing," Cabrera uses her exploration of a moment of Afro-Cuban religious practice (as it is no longer) to recall older, more restrictive—but more established—social structures. By insisting on Afro-Cuban culture as something that must be preserved—rather than transformed—her exile texts resist a narrative that would celebrate any subsuming of these practices into a national narrative.

Both Barnet and Cabrera to some extent perform a kind of "archaeological ethnography," returning to analyze a cultural environment that no longer exists in precisely the same way. Yet their postrevolutionary textual experiments would not have been possible without those of the prerevolutionary period. In his construction of a revolutionary folklore, like Barnet, Martínez Furé draws on a history of representing Afro-Cuban culture that reaches back to Fernando Ortiz. As with Alejo Carpentier's writing in the 1930s and 1940s, Barnet too struggles with the desire to be innovative (if not avant-garde), while identifying his literary innovations as "national." Cabrera, on the other hand, finds herself in her post-1959 work mining ethnographic material she had gathered decades previously. While she does not "plagiarize herself," as Respall Fina suggests, deprived of a national space from which to write, her exile writing continues to return to the scene of her earlier, more experimental texts.

Writers such as Guillén, Carpentier, and Cabrera all choose—at least in their prerevolutionary work—to explore the productive possibilities of experimentation, employing (and playing with) ethnographic and literary elements in their work as a means for bringing blackness into the space of the national imaginary. Post-1959 revolutionary discourse, on the other hand, returns to the narrative as a means of "resolving differences." As much as the emergence of the *testimonio* as a new genre of ethnographic literature highlights a change in and an evolution of textual forms, its use of a narrative of the experience of (racial) solidarity as a means of incorporating race into the national imaginary returns in many ways to the strategies employed by the foundational fictionalizing of the nineteenth-century novel that Doris Sommer has analyzed. A return to these kinds of narratives points to the ways in which the location of blackness within Cuba's national narrative remains unresolved. It also reaffirms the ultimate importance of the prerevolutionary literary moment, when racial anxieties produced conflicting and contradictory but experimentally daring new textual constructions in the search to understand the role of blackness within Cuban culture.

NOTES

Introduction: A Folklore for the Future: Race and National Narrative in Cuba

1. This translation and all others mine, unless specifically stated.
2. The terms "black" and "Afro-Cuban" are often used somewhat interchangeably, yet each term expresses slightly different meanings in the Cuban context. While North Americans tend to identify anyone with some African heritage as "black," racial identification in Cuba depends on a variety of factors, including phenotype, color, social class, and region. My use of "black" or "blackness" in this study thus refers to individuals who have been identified (or who have self-identified) as black within this more fluid context. Afro-Cuban, on the other hand, is used to refer more generally to anyone with African heritage or to cultural practices of African origin.
3. González y Contreras was a Salvadoran writer who found himself in exile in Havana during the decade of the 1930s. He was an occasional contributor to Cuban periodicals such as *Grafos* and *Revista Bimestre Cubana*.
4. This movement also included the work of painters Jaime Valls Díaz, Eduardo Abela, Antonio Gattorno, and Carlos Enríquez, and the incorporation of Afro-Cuban themes in classical music compositions of composers such as Alejandro García Caturla, Amadeo Roldán, and Gilberto Valdés (Arnedo-Gómez 1–3, 21–41). For more of *Afrocubanismo* in Cuban popular music, see Kutzinski, *Sugar's Secrets* 155–62 and Moore, *Nationalizing Blackness*, 198–202, 220–221.
5. Diarmuid O'Giolláin observes that folklore "is more an ideological than a scientific concept," given that it comes into use in the nineteenth century, just as industrialization is creating a division between "traditional societies" and "modern(izing) societies" (32).
6. For an excellent analysis of Arozarena's use of Afro-Cuban imagery in his own poetry, see Thomas F. Anderson.
7. I take this term from Rama's *The Lettered City (Post-Contemporary Interventions)*. Although the book's original Spanish title (*La ciudad letrada*) has been translated as *The Lettered City*, I believe that John Beverley's translation of it as "the republic of letters" in some ways captures the expansive function of the written word (and its connection to the construction of colonial society) more fully than "city."

8. In *Foundational Fictions*, Sommer posits that nineteenth-century Latin American novels often attempt to resolve issues of national difference through the trope of the romance. In her reading of *Sab*, Sommer argues that the novel presents Sab as a doomed character; his love for Carlota, daughter of a white plantation owner, will remain unrequited thanks to their differences in race and class.

9. According to Partha Chatterjee, postcolonial nations are implicitly denied the ability to fully shape their own national discourses: "If nationalisms in the rest of the world have to choose their imagined community from certain 'modular' forms already made available to them by Europe and the Americas, what do they have left to imagine? History, it would seem, has decreed that we in the postcolonial world shall only be perpetual consumers of modernity" (5).

10. While nation-states were ostensibly sovereign units existing in fraternal relation to one another, the transnational political economy of the time was in fact still grounded in colonial and neocolonial relations, and the relative status of subordinate nations was adjudicated by powerful ones, namely the United States and those of northern Europe. This sometimes contradictory political situation in which Cuba and other Latin American nations found themselves was intimately connected to the (sometimes contradictory) way in which intellectuals in these countries approached discourses of intellectual and cultural modernity.

11. For a discussion of the plantation system as modern, see Mintz, and Trouillot, *Global Transformations* 41–46.

12. Modeled after Spanish religious *cofradías* (brotherhoods), some *cabildos de nación*, as they were first known, dated from as early as the sixteenth century, although they grew in size and number as the Afro-Cuban population increased in the nineteenth century (Howard, Brown). As Scott argues, after slavery ended, however, there was increasing pressure for the *cabildos* to become civic-type organizations rather than religious centers (Scott 264–78, Brown 55–57).

13. See Pérez, *On Becoming Cuban* for an in-depth examination of the close relationship between Cuba and the United States from 1901 onward.

14. U.S. War Department, *Report on the Census of Cuba, 1899* (Quoted in Scott 64–65). As Scott observes, slavery in Cuba ended in phases, beginning with the Moret Law of 1871, which declared that all children born to slaves from 1868 onward were to be declared free.

15. American arguments for Cuba's racial inferiority were based on pseudoscientific theories of racial inferiority (particularly a belief that racial miscegenation resulted in "mongrelization") coupled with the impression held by many Americans that a majority of the island's population was nonwhite (de la Fuente 40–45).

16. As Ferrer points out, loyalty to Cuba as a nation was seen to transcend not only racial difference but also the threat of a black rebellion: "Even with weapons in his hands, the black insurgent of pro-independence writings respected the norms that relegated him to an inferior social status" (120).

17. Trans. Esther Allen 295.

18. In 1892, Juan Gualberto Gómez founded the Directorio Central de las Sociedades de la Clase de Color, "an umbrella organization designed to bring together black and mulatto organizations in order to advocate publicly for the concession of civil rights to Cubans of color" (Ferrer 129).

19. Some of these organizations, such as the *Club Atenas*, also put out their own journals (Kapcia 85).

20. For more discussion of the middle-class disavowal of Afro-Cuban traditions, see Andrews 124–25.

21. The most notable case was the carnival *comparsa*, which was outlawed in 1913 when a rivalry between two *comparsa* groups turned violent, and was not legalized again until 1937 (Moore, *Nationalizing Blackness* 62–86).

22. The most famous of these cases was the abduction and murder of the "niña Zoila," in 1904, in which a young white girl was abducted and supposedly murdered so that her bones could be used in an *embó* (spell). An Afro-Cuban *brujo* known as Bocourt and an "accomplice" were eventually arrested, tried, and executed for the crime. Prior to their execution, they also became two of the "informants" for Fernando Ortiz's early study *Hampa afrocubana: Los negros brujos* (1906), which I discuss in greater detail in chapter 1 of this book. For a more detailed analysis of the "niña Zoila" case and similar cases, see Bronfman, *Measures of Equality* 37–65 and Palmié 237–59.

23. For a discussion of these and other early republican texts on Cuban identity, see Rojas, *Isla* 125–166.

24. Cubans were not alone in this anxiety. Other Caribbean intellectuals would bemoan the particular postcolonial conditions of island societies—including the climate—as producing a weak or inferior population. A notable example of this "negative insularity" is Puerto Rican writer Antonio S. Pedreira's *Insularismo* (*Insularity*, 1934).

25. An influential text for Cuban (and other Latin American) intellectuals writing in the early 1920s was Oswald Spengler's *The Decline of the West* (1918), in which Spengler proposes a cyclical theory for the rise and fall of world civilizations. Spengler posited that western Europe was already well into its decline, an argument that many Latin American and Caribbean intellectuals took as an indication that Latin American civilization might, in fact, be on the rise. See a further discussion of Spengler's significance for Latin American avant-gardes in Rosenberg (22) and Alonso, *The Burden of Modernity*.

26. Alonso argues that the search for the autochthonous, or locally authentic, in Latin American culture has itself become a "vehicle for the validation and generation of cultural production in the region" (*The Spanish American Regional Novel* 17). That is, culture is produced precisely because of and thanks to what he defines as the "crisis" of what is regionally or nationally authentic. The autochthonous is thus defined as it is brought into being.

27. For a further discussion of Glissant's concepts, see De Ferrari 3, 18–22.

28. Jorge Coronado explains that while *indigenista* texts may "[evoke] an indigenous

object," this very process "reflects the gap between Hispanic society and indigenous cultures" (17). Coronado observes that *indigenismo* was also sometimes marshaled to serve regional as well as national purposes, particularly in countries such as Peru where power hierarchies were split along regional lines: "Within the Andes, regionalisms have been strong enough . . . to mount a considerable response to the homogenization of a given geopolitical space proposed by nationalism. In turn, of course, regionalisms have proposed their own homogenization across class, race and culture in alternative geopolitical spaces" (12).

29. Alonso notes that Creole intellectuals performed the same temporally distancing operation with regard to Spanish culture post-independence: "Spaniards were simply written out of [the narrative of Creole hegemony] by being subsumed under the mantle of the preterit, by being assigned to what from the perspective of the narrative of the future could only be described as the *non-place* of the past" (*The Burden of Modernity* 16).

30. Until very recently, the consensus seemed to be that the indigenous *Taíno* (Arawak) population had been almost entirely exterminated within the first two centuries of a European presence on the island. While recent scholarship by José Barreiro and others has revealed that a small indigenous population is still present in certain isolated communities in the provinces of Bayamo and Guantánamo, at the turn of the twentieth century, the indigenous presence, while acknowledged by some scholars as a cultural influence, was not a visible one.

31. In this, Cuba was most similar to Brazil, with which it shared a history of slavery, a late date of manumission, and a large black and mixed-race population. (See Andrews.) Brazil, however, also had a significant indigenous population (mainly in the Amazon), and Brazilian intellectuals turned to both indigenous and Afro-Brazilian populations to construct an idea of the folk. (See Gabara, *Errant Modernism*.)

32. For a discussion of the modernness of African American cultures and cultural practices, see Palmié 51–52 and Trouillot, *Global Transformations* 12–18.

33. "Ethnography will become a form of exegesis that has not ceased providing the modern West with what it needs in order to articulate its identity through a relation with the past or the future, with foreigners or with nature" (xxvii).

34. Clifford notes that the professionalization of ethnography corresponded to a codification of a new "ethnographic subjectivity" that emerged in the early twentieth century: "Modern anthropology—a Science of Man linked closely to cultural description—presupposed the ironic stance of participant observation. By professionalizing fieldwork anthropology transformed a widespread predicament into a scientific method" (*Predicament of Culture* 93). (See also Cotera 28–29.)

35. Clifford and Marcus's edited volume *Writing Culture: The Poetics and Politics of Ethnography* was one of the first and most significant collections to inaugurate the self-conscious turn in ethnography. *Writing Culture* was followed by Behar and Gordon's *Women Writing Culture*, which explored the gendering of ethnography in both professional and methodological terms.

36. Pratt adds that autoethnographic texts, "involve a selective collaboration with and appropriation of idioms of the metropolis or the conqueror. These are merged or infiltrated to varying degrees with indigenous idioms to create self-representations intended to intervene in the metropolitan modes of understanding" ("Arts" 35).

37. Many Latin American elites studied with European eugenicists, and then sought to apply what they had learned in Europe to the environment of their home countries. Some nations—Brazil and Argentina, in particular—adopted policies that were directly influenced by these ideas. They encouraged European immigration in hopes of "whitening" the population, and often employed "scientific" evidence as justification for limiting social and political equality of racial minorities (Helg, "Race" and Leys Stepan 45–46).

38. The idea of "homiculture" was an elaboration on French eugenicist Adolphe Pinard's idea of "puericulture," or the improvement of society through a focus on mother-and-child health, particularly through the control of adverse environmental factors in the period between conception and birth (Leys Stepan 76–78). Hernández and Ramos expanded this idea to include cultivation of the whole individual. Thanks largely to Ramos's efforts, the Pan-American Conference on Eugenics was held on the island in 1927, although it could be argued that by that time interest in eugenics in Cuba was on the wane.

39. By "avant-garde" here I am referring primarily to the artistic and literary production of the first decades of the twentieth century, in particular that of the period between the two World Wars (what in English literary studies is also referred to as Modernism). Speaking of Latin America's vanguards, Vicky Unruh defines the early twentieth-century avant-garde generally as "a multifaceted cultural activity, manifested in a variety of creative endeavors and events and seeking to challenge and redefine the nature and purpose of art" (2). I am well aware, however, that "avant-garde" as an idea emerges much earlier, with Baudelaire, and that it is made up of more aesthetic *and* political movements, statements, and gestures than my glossing of it can communicate here. For further discussion of this term and the artistic movements associated with it, see Berman, Brandon, Breton, Paz, Pavloska, Poggioli, Rosenberg, and Unruh.

40. See González Echevarría, *Myth and Archive* and Fass Emery. López-Baralt approaches the relationship between anthropology and literature from an even broader perspective, as she argues that an ethnographic gaze is evident even in colonial Latin American literature.

41. Cuba in not the only nation in Latin America to have used hybridity as what Joshua Lund terms "a critical tool in the service of emancipatory, cultural affirmation" (xiii). Notable examples are Mexican writer José Vasconcelos's *La raza cósmica* (1925: *The Cosmic Race*, 1997) and the writings of the Brazilian sociologist Gilberto Freyre. For more on the complex development and theoretical implications of discourses of hybridity in Latin America and the Caribbean, see Rama, *Transculturation*, Lund, and Miller.

42. For a more complete discussion of Caribbean theories of hybridity, see De Ferrari

12–14. Jamaican cultural critic Stuart Hall takes the idea of transculturation even further when he declares identity itself as "a 'production' which is never complete, always in process, constituted within, not outside representation" ("Cultural Identity" 222).

43. See Gutiérrez, González Mandri, Mateo, Rodríguez-Mangual.

44. Both Rodríguez-Mangual and González Mandri see Cabrera as utilizing a self-conscious ethnographic methodology that was ahead of her time (González Mandri 41). Rodríguez-Mangual argues, "[T]he black cosmogony re-created in [Cabrera's] work becomes a place of enunciation of an alternative national identity that exposes the limits of official discourse" (20).

45. For more on these women ethnographers, see Behar and Gordon, *Women Writing Culture*, and Cotera.

Chapter 1. Locating Afro-Cuban Religion: Fernando Ortiz and Lydia Cabrera

1. See Ortiz Herrera 4, and Coronil, "Introduction" xvi–xvii.

2. See González Mandri 49–52 for a discussion of Cabrera's use of Ortiz's early work.

3. The exception to this is the work of Rómulo Lachatañeré, who published two short works on Santería, *Manual de Santería* (*Santería Manual*, 1942) and "El sistema religioso de los lucumís" ("The Lucumí Religious System," published serially in *Estudios Afrocubanos* [1939 and 1940]). While Lachatañeré's critique of Ortiz's use of the word *brujo* (witch) in "El sistema religioso de los lucumís y otras influencias africanas en Cuba" is interesting, I have chosen not to include a discussion of Lachatañeré's work here both because of its brevity and in order to more fully elaborate the connections between the work of Cabrera and Ortiz.

4. Ortiz declared that he had "initiated" Cabrera into the study of Afro-Cuban folklore, and Cabrera did dedicate *El Monte* to her brother-in-law. Yet actual correspondence between the two scholars remains scarce and somewhat brief. The Fernando Ortiz archives at the José Martí National Library in Havana contain a scant half dozen examples of letters by Cabrera addressed to Ortiz, and these are brief and conversational, with little mention of any scholarly projects. There is certainly no evidence of explicit collaboration between them.

5. Ortiz completed his undergraduate education at the University of Havana (1895–1898), but shortly thereafter left for Spain, where he pursued his postgraduate education in both Madrid and Barcelona. His first ethnographic studies focused on traditions of the different cultures within Spain. See his "Para la agonografía española: Estudio monográfico de las fiestas menorquinas," in *Fernando Ortiz y España: A cien años de 1898*, 17–45.

6. For more information on Ortiz's education and early work in Europe, see Naranjo Orovio and Puig-Samper Mulero.

7. For an example of such a narrative, see Henri Dumont, *Antropología y patología comparadas de los negros esclavos* (1876). This study by a French doctor attempts to

distinguish between the various African ethnic groups represented among the Cuban slave population from a medical/criminological perspective. His only discussion of African religious practices is to say, "Los africanos son todos fetichistas. . . . Los sacrificios humanos y la antropofagia se practican en honor de los ídolos en algunos tribus de la Nigricia austral y de la Nigricia central" (53) [Africans are all fetishists. . . . Human sacrifice and cannibalism are practiced to honor the idols in some tribes of eastern and central Niger]. For an analysis of Dumont see Lane 182–87.

8. As discussed in the introduction, two notable proponents of the ideas of biological determinism were Luis Montané of the Cuban Anthropological Society and Arístides Mestre of the anthropology department at the University of Havana. See Bronfman, *Measures of Equality* 28-29.

9. The most significant example of "armchair anthropology" is, of course, James Frazer's *The Golden Bough* (1890), a comparative examination of mythology and religion from various modern and ancient cultures. Frazer did no field research for his two-volume tome. Rather, he relied on previous writing on these traditions, analyzing them via a comparativist approach.

10. It was common for ethnographers to seek a population in relative cultural isolation. Franz Boas's work on the Kwatkiutl, Bronislaw Malinowski's study of Polynesian gift-giving, and E. Evans Pritchard's work on the Nuer are all examples of classic ethnographic studies.

11. See Bronfman, "Poetry in the Presidio" for an exploration of the connections between *Los negros brujos* and Ortiz's later work on the Cuban penal code. Bronfman shows that in fact, Ortiz's interest in criminology may have been more important to his later work than has previously been noted.

12. Mullen notes that Ortiz's original intention was to write a series of studies on black Cuban culture, a goal that was only partially realized with the publication of *Los negros esclavos* (1916) and, posthumously, *Los negros curros* (1986) (Mullen, "A Re-examination" 115).

13. In his study, Duno Gottberg traces the negotiation of race and culture in Cuba through the development of narratives of hybridity. While his discussion is certainly useful to my exploration here, I prefer not to begin my discussion with hybridity, since the use of the term runs the risk of glossing over the different kinds of negotiation with which Ortiz engages in his negotiation of questions of race.

14. Lombroso had pioneered the concept of the "born criminal," the idea that criminals could be identified through certain physical traits. He had also advanced the idea that criminal tendencies were largely the result of heredity and reinforced these ideas of racial superiority by arguing that criminal tendencies were most pronounced in "inferior peoples," races who had not yet fully left a primitive evolutionary state behind (Bronfman, *Measures of Equality* 31). His work is illustrative of the ways in which anthropology at the turn of the twentieth century was connected to such pseudosciences as eugenics.

15. "A Unamuno," *Entre cubanos*, 11–13. See also Mañach *La crisis de la alta cultura en Cuba*, 15–50.

16. Ortiz's desire to produce "exportable material" has much in common with Brazilian writer Oswald de Andrade's *Manifesto Antropófago* and *Manifesto da Poesia Pau Brasil*. But I doubt that Ortiz at this early stage in his writing career necessarily envisions the production of "authentic" Cuban writing as the kind of "cannibalistic" process of combining and reworking. In this first text, some thirty years from the production of *Contrapunteo cubano*, Ortiz is more interested in something (Cuban) that can be held up to European standards of literature and scholarship.

17. "Civilization and barbarism" were first introduced into Latin American intellectual discourse by Argentine intellectual Domingo Faustino Sarmiento in *Facundo: civilización y barbarie en las Pampas argentinas* (1845), ostensibly a biography of the Argentine *caudillo* Juan Facundo Quiroga. For Sarmiento, "civilization" (represented by the urbanizing city) stands in direct contrast to the "barbarism" of the undeveloped countryside. According to Sarmiento, that the characteristics that allowed Facundo to triumph in the rough land of the Pampas—brutality and the use of violence to maintain control—simultaneously stood in the way of progress and civilization. For Sarmiento, this problem was in some way endemic to Argentine society, since these "barbaric" elements of the Argentine character were, he felt, a response to the conditions of life on the Pampas.

18. Positivism in Latin America had its origins in the work of French philosopher Auguste Comte. In its most basic form, Comte's positivism argues for social progress through scientific development. In nineteenth-century Latin America, intellectuals combined Comtian positivism with elements of social Darwinism to advocate a kind of national positivism, in which they argued that the nation would progress through education and scientific development. They supported eradicating "outmoded" or "backwards" beliefs and practices through education. See Bethell.

19. *Brujería* is Ortiz's general term for all varieties of Afro-Cuban religious practice. In this text, Ortiz does not differentiate between the different kinds of Afro-Cuban religious practice (Santería, Palo Monte, and Abakuá), largely because of a lack of information prohibits him from distinguishing between them.

20. For more on the history of the Chinese in Cuba, see López-Calvo.

21. Ortiz remarks on the scarcity of outside sources in his introduction as one of the obstacles he encountered in his research, others being the difficulty of conducting research on the "underworld" as well as the time he himself had spent away from Cuba.

22. It should be noted that Nina Rodrigues was himself informed by a criminologist methodology. Roger Bastide, in the 1958 introduction to his *Le Candomblê de Bahia*, observes that "Nina Rodrigues croyait à l'infériorité du Nègre et à son incapacité à s'intégrer dans la civilisation occidentale" (33). [Nina Rodrigues believes in the inferiority of the black man and in his incapacity to integrate himself into Western civilization.] He also vouches for the veracity of his information, however: "Malgré

toutes ces failles, il n'en reste pas moins que les ouvrages de Nina Rodrigues restent encore peut-être les meilleurs qui aient été publiés, d'abord parce que ses informateurs appartenaient au *candomblé* le plus traditionnel, le plus purement africain de son époque . . ." (34). [In spite of all his faults, Nina Rodrigues's works remain perhaps the best that have been published, since his informants were practitioners of the most traditional, most African *candomblé* of their era.]

23. *Collares* are ritual necklaces, one for each of the *orichas*, given to practitioners who have completed a kind of preliminary initiation by making a series of offerings to each of the *orichas*.

24. Cuban musicologist Argeliers León, in his prologue to Ortiz's *Los bailes y el teatro de los negros en el folklore de Cuba*, observes that Ortiz's lecture on Yoruban music in Cuba in 1937 was the first time that he made special use of informants: "Cierto que desde sus trabajos más tempranos de búsqueda informativa, Ortiz recurrió a muchos viejos, algunos africanos que quedaban ya muy ancianos, pero fueron más en el plano de entrevistas muy generales y como para corroborar algún que otro dato, que el trabajo más amplio que abordó, para aquella conferencia, con los tamboreros, y conocedores de los cultos de santería . . ." (León, "Prólogo" 15). [It's true that from his earliest works of informative research Ortiz consulted many elders, some of them Africans who were already very old, but he did so more in the way of general interviews, and to corroborate an occasional fact. For the larger work, for that conference, he consulted the drummers and experts in Santería cults.]

25. Translation, Harriet de Onís.

26. Rómulo Lachatañeré's collection of *patakíes* (*Regla de Ochá* legends about the *orichas*) *¡¡Oh, mío Yemayá!!* was published in 1938, two years before *Cuentos negros de Cuba* would be published in Spanish, but two years after the initial publication of Cabrera's text in French by Gallimard.

27. See Price Mars, Landes, Zora Neale Hurston's *Tell My Horse* (1938), and the work of Melville Herskovits, Alfred Metraux, Roger Bastide, and Pierre Verger.

28. "Hubo un tiempo, hasta el cese de la trata, en que los cultos debieron conservarse relativamente en su originalidad africana; pero a partir de esta época, cuando las relaciones con Africa se rompieron, todos los cultos se falsearon más o menos" (*Los negros brujos*, 27). [There was a time, until the end of the slave trade, in which these cults must have remained true to their African origins; but from that era on, when the ties to Africa were broken, all these cults became more or less impure.]

29. The historical perspective is frequently added as simply another comparison of the variation in methods of cultural practice, a kind of "before and after."

30. "[P]rima la coherencia por encima de la inteligibilidad; la metáfora misma traza un circuito espacial y lo hace inteligible dentro de sus propios términos, sin que haya necesidad de salir de ellos" ("Lydia Cabrera, invisible" 100). [Coherency takes precedence over intelligibility; the metaphor itself traces a special circuit and makes it intelligible within its own terms, without the necessity of leaving them.]

Chapter 2. Beyond Bongos in Montmartre: Lydia Cabrera and Alejo Carpentier Imagine Blackness

1. The term *solar* in the Cuban context refers generally to a tenement house, particularly those erected in central and old Havana in the nineteenth century. *Solares* are usually Spanish-style buildings constructed as a number of subdivided apartments built around a center courtyard. However, in this case, the "Solar del Arará" seems to be a *cabildo*, a mutual-aid organization for Africans and African-descended Cubans, which often functioned as spaces for religious practice. This is further implied by Carpentier's description that this was where white elites went to ask for an *embó* (a spell or witchcraft) to be worked on their behalf. I translate *embó* as "potion" here, following Ortiz, who suggests that an *embó* is not the spell itself but rather the medium through which the spell is transmitted (*Glosario de afronegrismos* 186). However, it should be noted that *embó* can also be understood to mean a *limpieza* or spiritual cleansing, intended to ward off negative influences rather than enact spells.

2. "—¿Conque usted es cubano?—os preguntan las francesas, encantadas de conocer vuestra nacionalidad—. ¿Cubano? ¡Enséñeme a bailar la rrromba!" (296). ["So you're Cuban?" The French women ask you, charmed at knowing your nationality. "Cuban? Teach me to dance the rrrumba!]

3. While Paris has long been considered the center of the French intellectual scene in the interwar years, Nicholas Hewitt observes that "Marseille was the only great provincial city that could constitute a convincing cultural counterweight to the capital" (61).

4. Unpublished correspondence, dated June 16, 1933. The Lydia Cabrera Collection. The Cuban Heritage Collection. Miami University.

5. Another writer to study Afro-Cuban culture in these early decades was Israel Castellanos, who published a number of articles between 1914 and 1915 with a criminological focus in the health and social science journal *Vida nueva* (Moore, *Nationalizing* 32; Marques de Armas).

6. For more on images of blackness circulating in France at the *fin de siècle*, see Smalls. He observes that the 1900 Universal Exposition was particularly significant for constructing blackness as a spectacle, in part thanks to Gaston Bergeret's fictional *Journal d'un nègre á l'Exposition de 1900* (351).

7. André Breton, one of Surrealism's founders, characterized the moment as one in which "a new morality must be substituted for the prevailing morality, the source of all our trials and tribulations" (*Manifestoes* 44).

8. Dirks observes that for colonized populations, "Colonial historiography increasingly conceded to anthropology the study of historical subjects which had not yet entered modernity" such that "by the late nineteenth century, anthropology became quite literally the history of the colonized" (57).

9. *Documents* was founded by Marcel Mauss, along with Georges Bataille, former members of the Surrealist movement who had split with André Breton (Clifford, *Predicament of Culture* 129–34).

10. *Documents* became a space for exploring "sousrealism," what Archer Straw has described as the "abstracted hell somewhere beneath mainstream surrealism" (143).

11. "Légitime défense" was included as an introduction to a journal with the same title. Intended as a Surrealist call to arms, the authors directly address their fellow (Afro-)Caribbeans: "Emerging from the French mulatto bourgeoisie, one of the most depressing things on earth, we declare (and we shall not retract this declaration) that, faced with all the administrative, governmental, parliamentary, industrial, commercial corpses and so on, we intend,—as traitors to this class—to take the path of treason as far as possible" (Richardson 43).

12. These included the Chilean poet Vicente Huidobro, Argentine writer Jorge Luis Borges, the Uruguayan Juan Carlos Onetti, and Miguel Angel Asturias from Guatemala, among many others. (See Weiss.)

13. In a letter addressed to composer Alejandro García Caturla dated March 13, 1931, in which he asks García Caturla for some information regarding an Abakuá ritual, Carpentier states, "No tengo la retencion, desde luego, de describir una ceremonia que no he visto," (*Obras completas* 1: 293). [I don't have the retention, in any case, to describe a ceremony that I haven't seen.] García Carranza affirms that "Carpentier conocía la vida de los negros cubanos, jamaicanos y haitianos que trabajaban las plantaciones de azúcar de Santiago de Cuba . . ." (51). [Carpentier was familiar with the life of the black Cubans, Jamaicans and Haitians that worked the sugar plantations in Santiago de Cuba.] For her part, Cabrera began doing informal ethnographic fieldwork on her return to Cuba in 1930, with the help of Calixta García, an elderly member of the Santería community whom Cabrera had met through a family servant (*Páginas sueltas*, 207–17; *El Monte* 24–27).

14. Carpentier began his career as a journalist while he was still young, contributing to a number of commercial Cuban publications such as *Hispania, Discusión,* and *Social,* as well as *Carteles.* This work included authoring the women's fashion column in *Social* under the pseudonym Jacqueline. See Pancrazio's *Logic* and Sifuentes-Jáuregui for readings of Carpentier's "Jacqueline" texts.

15. The Grupo Minorista, so called because of "el corto número de miembros efectivos que lo integran" ("Declaración" 249) [the small number of members of which it is composed] was a group of Cuban young writers and intellectuals dedicated to the renovation of Cuban arts and letters. While their own work focused on literature, the group was politically engaged, left-leaning, and according to Esperanza Figueroa met regularly in the bar of the Ambos Mundos Hotel in Old Havana (280). In their 1927 manifesto, "Declaración del Grupo Minorista" ("Declaration of the Minorist Group"), also known as the Minorista Manifesto, written as a protest against then-dictator Gerardo Machado, they declared themselves to be "por la revision de valores falsos y gastados" [for the revision of false and worn-out values] and "por el arte nuevo en todas sus manifestaciones" [for new art in all its forms], but they called for a revision of primary education, Cuban economic independence, and an end to American imperialism and dictatorships everywhere ("Declaración" 249–50).

16. See Birkenmaier's *Alejo Carpentier*, García-Carranza, and Hernández Adrián for discussion of both the genesis and the texts of Carpentier's ballets *La rebambaramba* and *El milagro de Anaquillé*.

17. Despite these connections to the French avant-garde, in interviews that she gave throughout the course of her life Cabrera resolutely insisted that she had never been "officially" part of any group or movement. In an interview with Suzanne Jill Levine, she states, "Pero ya en los años 20, conocía el movimiento surrealista—tenía mucho respeto por lo que hacía Breton, entre otros, como es natural—, pero no tuve contacto personal con los surrealistas" (3). [But in the 1920s, I was already familiar with the Surrealist Movement—I had a great deal of respect for what Breton, among others, was doing—, but I never had any personal contact with the Surrealists.] While Cabrera was never an official member, her insistence on her distance from the group is not entirely correct, given that she at one time translated (although, to my knowledge, never published) *Le Mirroir du merveilleux*, Pierre Mabille's classic surrealist work on myth.

18. As Sylvia Molloy notes, while Cabrera and de la Parra's relationship would be recognized as lesbian today, the two women themselves never explicitly identified their relationship as such. For a detailed analysis of their relationship, see Molloy.

19. Alonso writes, "The result is that even while arguing for the adoption of the ideology of modernity and its values, Spanish American writers also moved simultaneously to delimit a space impervious to that rhetoric as a strategy to address the threat with which the discourse of modernity unremittingly confronted their discursive authority" (*The Burden of Modernity* 26).

20. In addition to rhythms such as the *danzón* and later the *son*, composers such as Alejandro García Caturla and Ernesto Lecuona, whose work was more classical in nature, were incorporating Afro-Cuban motifs in their compositions. Carpentier collaborated with composer Amadeo Roldán on two ballets (*La rebambaramba*, 1927 and *El milagro de Analquillé*, 1937) and with composer Alejandro García Caturla, also Cuban, on a comic opera (*Manita en el suelo*, 1931). Interestingly, the Carpentier/Roldán ballets were not staged until after the Cuban Revolution (García-Carranza 61).

21. See Bronfman's *Measures* and Palmié (237–59).

22. For a more detailed discussion of *comparsas*, see Moore, *Nationalizing Blackness* 62–86.

23. Afro-Cuban religious gatherings and rituals were frequently raided, and the religious objects being used were confiscated. The criminalization was due in part to the prevailing popular understanding that religious practitioners robbed graves and even abducted and murdered children to obtain the human bones necessary for their religious rites. (Bronfman, *Measures* 37–66.)

24. While the term *ñáñigo* was often used in the nineteenth and early twentieth centuries to refer to any kind of Afro-Cuban initiate, particularly one engaged in casting spells, the term refers more specifically to members of the Abakuá order, an all-male religious society composed primarily of Africans from the Efik peoples and their

descendents. One of the most comprehensive explorations of this religious order is still Lydia Cabrera's *La sociedad secreta abakuá narrada por viejos adeptos* (1959). See also her *La lengua sagrada de los ñáñigos* (1988).

25. See Arroyo (110) and González Echevarría (*Alejo Carpentier* 69, 75).

26. Sklodowska points out that in his recourse to negative stereotypes in his portrayal of the Haitian workers, Carpentier fails to deal with the initial stirrings of a pan-Antillean labor movement taking place in the sugar industry in these years (*Espectros* 89).

27. Arroyo has shown the ways in which Carpentier borrowed from Ortiz's *Los negros brujos* in his descriptions of Afro-Cuban rituals. Here the narrative's description follows the criminological methodology on which Ortiz relied to gain many of his informants (107).

28. For a definition of *solar*, see note 1 from this chapter. *Solares* were a frequent destination for migrants from rural Cuba arriving in Havana.

29. "On the one hand, ethnographers, especially those who have taken communicative approaches . . . have always acknowledged coevalness as a condition without which hardly anything could ever be learned about another culture . . . But when it comes to producing anthropological discourse in the forms of description, analysis, and theoretical conclusions, the same ethnographers will often forget or disavow their experiences of coevalness with the people they studied" (Fabian 33).

30. The Haitian Revolution might have served to reframe European Enlightenment ideas even more if it had not been so significantly ignored. As Buck-Morss shows, European intellectuals and philosophers found themselves strangely silent with respect to the climactic events taking place in Saint Domingue.

31. Exoticizing descriptions of Haiti included William Seabrook's novel *The Magic Island* (1929) and Zora Neale Hurston's *Tell My Horse* (1938), both focused on the Vodou religion, as well as travel writing by Katherine Dunham and Langston Hughes. In these North American narratives, Renda argues, Haiti, characterized as the exotic, racialized other, "contributed to a defense of white supremacy conceived in terms of gender and sexuality" (305). See also the more local ethnographic studies of Vodou, such as Jean Price Mars's *Ainsi parle l'oncle* (1932), which was reviewed in *Estudios Afrocubanos* 2 (1939).

32. "Leyes de África." *Carteles*, 27 December, 1931. See also Paravisini-Gebert.

33. "Since he [Carpentier] does not share the religious beliefs of the slaves, how then can he portray the 'marvelous' aspects of the Saint Domingue uprising without resorting to the same literary 'tricks' for which he criticized the surrealists?" (Webb 31).

34. Pancrazio suggests that Carpentier's text goes so far as to suggest that maroonage as a strategy is in fact complicit with "hegemonic discourse": "Maroonage is the inverted reflection of emancipatory moralism, the basis of revolutionary praxis in Cuba: both sustain an ideology of disappearance in which being is not of this world" (*Logic* 182).

35. Rodríguez-Mangual argues something similar when she says that Cabrera "postulates a positive ontology in the representation of blackness by placing whiteness in the space of otherness" (123). However, while I agree that Cabrera centers her narrative within a black space, I want to be careful about arguing that this makes whiteness "other" in terms of a reversal of the power dynamic.

36. These tales serve both to explain the relationships of the various *orichas* to each other as well as to explain the reason for their different characteristics. In this way, the tales resemble the legends of classical Greek mythology.

37. For a more complete analysis of the function of the *calesero* in several nineteenth-century texts, see Luis 44–47.

38. Moore defines the *calesero* as "a gaudily dressed coach driver-slave who inevitably believes himself to be extremely good-looking" (*Nationalizing* 47). When slavery ended, the *calesero* became the *cochero*, a more general term for coach-driver. As Moore notes, however, the *calesero* remained a popular character type well into the 1930s.

Chapter 3. The National Art of Signifyin(g): Nicolás Guillén and Lydia Cabrera

1. In this way, the *choteo* enacts a destabilization of the social order similar to the function of carnival as identified by Bakhtin, albeit in a much briefer time and space.

2. "Así y todo, no me parece improbable que el hombre de color, por su caudal de inestrenada vitalidad, por su índole impresionable y sensual y por su carencia de aquel pesimismo que dan los trabajos seculares de la civilización, haya acentuado ciertos rasgos criollos que, en el hombre blanco, resultan propicios al choteo, al aliarse con otros factores psíquicos" (Mañach, *Indagación* 62). [Broadly speaking, it doesn't seem improbable to me that the man of color, as a result of his abundant, untried vitality, his impressionable and sensual temperament, and his lack of that pessimism that civilization's secular works confer, should have accented certain Creole characteristics that in the white man, on combining with certain other psychic factors, ended up being favorable to the *choteo*.]

3. In *Indagación del choteo* and other works, Mañach was a proponent of ideas of "negative insularity," the idea that Cuban society was inherently underdeveloped, behind, or inferior thanks to the tropical climate, a history of colonialism, and particular defects in the Cuban character. I discuss this mode of thought in greater detail in chapter one of this study.

4. My understanding of play draws on anthropologist Margaret Drewal's work with Yoruba ritual performance (Yoruba being the ethnic origin of many Africans who came to Cuba). Drewal sees play as an essentially performative activity: "In relation to ritual, what I understand Yoruba to mean by 'play' is, more specifically, that they improvise... I use the term 'improvisation'—as Yoruba use the English word 'play'—to refer to a whole gamut of spontaneous individual moves: ruses, parodies, transpositions, recontextualizations, elaborations, condensations, interruptions, interventions, and more" (20).

5. Vasconcelos may have been one of the first to criticize the incorporation of Afro-Cuban popular culture in poetry, but he was not the last. Perhaps the most notable critique comes from Cintio Vitier in his epic survey of Cuban poetry, *Lo cubano en la poesía*. According to Vitier, Afro-Cuban elements in *negrista* or *afrocubanista* poetry "nos anillaniza, en el peor sentido de la palabra. Lo cubano aquí pierde su individualidad, su perfil, para sumergirnos en una especie de difuso pintoresquismo antillano, que lo falsea todo" (297). [They "Antilleanize" us, in the worst sense of the word. Here the Cuban loses his individuality, his profile, in order to immerse us in a kind of diffuse Antillean picturesque that falsifies everything.] Vitier sees *Motivos de son* as but a stepping stone on the way to Guillén's later works, where Guillén's "Spanish roots" are finally made visible (302).

6. For a detailed analysis of these novels and their struggle to construct a national modernity, see Alonso, *The Spanish American Regional Novel*.

7. The French translation of *Cuentos negros* chooses to use the more pejorative term "negre," instead of the more neutral "noire." I do not know if this was Cabrera's choice or the editor's, as Spanish does not have the vocabulary to make this distinction.

8. Guillén was also the author of an early book of avant-garde poetry (*Cerebro y corazón*, 1923).

9. For more on the history and evolution of the *son*, see Roy 119–148.

10. Trans. Achy Obejas. I also use Obejas' translations of Guillén's poems "Secuestro de la mujer de Antonio," "Llegada," and "West Indies, Ltd."

11. Jorge Marcone suggests that performativity is in fact inherent to the definition of oral discourse: "De acuerdo con este entendimiento, 'texto oral' o 'discurso oral' deben ser pensados como *performance* ('actuación') y/o como una producción dialógica de los sujetos que interactuan a través de la comunicación oral" (37). [In accordance with this understanding, "oral text" or "oral discourse" should be understood as *performance* ("acting") and/or as a dialogic production of the subjects who are interacting by means of this oral communication.]

12. Guillén's use of Signfiyin(g) is similar to what Gates describes as operating in jazz music: "In the jazz tradition, compositions by Count Basie ('Signify') and Oscar Peterson ('Signifying') are structured around the idea of formal revision and implication.... Because the form is self-evident to the musician, both he and his well-trained audience are playing and listening with expectation. Signifyin(g) disappoints these expectations ... This form of disappointment creates a dialogue between what the listener expects and what the artist plays"(Gates 123).

13. The Trío Matamoros, one of the first Cuban *son* groups to record music, was formed in 1925 by Miguel de Matamoros, Rafael Cueto, and Siro Rodríguez, all of whom were from Santiago. The group was extremely popular, and continued to perform until they disbanded in 1960 (Moore, *Nationalizing* 107–108).

14. For more on the *son*, see Moore, *Nationalizing Blackness* 87–113.

15. Guirao's "Bailadora de rumba"("Rumba Dancer") was published in 1928 in the newspaper *Diario de la Marina*'s section "Ideales de una raza" ("Ideals of a Race"); Tallet's "La rumba" came out that same year in *Atuei* (Kapcia 80, Arnedo-Gómez 1–2).

16. Trans. Kutzinski, *Callaloo* 31 (Spring 1987): 191. Kutzinski also reprints her translation in *Sugar's Secrets*, 168–69.

17. In addition to being a well-known author and member of Cuba's literary elite, Raimundo Cabrera (1852–1923), Lydia's father was also the editor of weekly paper *Cuba y América* (*Cuba and America*).

18. *Lucumí* can refer not only to the Yoruba language (as it is spoken in Cuba) but also to cultural practices or to a person's place of origin in Africa. The Santería religion (also known as *Regla de Ochá*) is of Yoruban origin, as were a majority of the Africans who came to Cuba as slaves.

19. "Venado" is Spanish for deer. It is not clear from the story whether Venado is meant to be understood as an anthropomorphic construction ("Deer" acting as a human being), or whether this is simply a man's name.

20. Gutiérrez has written extensively on Afro-Cuban symbolism in Cabrera's work. See in particular "La armonía cósmica."

21. Chamoiseau and Confiant recognize these "digresions humoristiques" as a signature element of Caribbean storytelling (69).

22. David Brown defines *cabildos* as "social clubs and religious mutual aid societies of neo-African ethnic denomination. At the same time, the members of the heterogeneous nations took on significant aspects of a 'creole' identity, as they . . . confronted common obstacles to their advancement and liberty" (27).

23. Despite a growing interest in some kinds of Afro-Cuban music, until 1937 it was a criminal offense to perform publicly in a *comparsa* band (Moore, *Nationalizing* 145).

Chapter 4. Gender, Genre, and Ethnographic Authority: Lydia Cabrera and Zora Neale Hurston

1. See De Costa Willis and Hoffman-Jeep. De Costa Willis deals primarily with the biographical similarities that shaped the writers' relationship to their work, while Hoffman-Jeep examines Hurston's and Cabrera's folktales, focusing on what she terms "their bifocal vision as insider-outsiders within the minority cultures they represent" (338).

2. Carter Woodson's Association for the Study of Negro Life and History funded Hurston's first folklore collecting trip (Pavloska 84, Hemenway 84). Later trips (in 1928 and 1929) were funded primarily by Charlotte Osgood Mason, patron to a number of Harlem Renaissance writers. Nonetheless, Hurston was in close contact with Franz Boas, her advisor at Columbia, and the expectation was that she would write up her findings for publication (Cotera 82–89).

3. According to the 1930 U.S. Census, 11.9 million (or 9.7 percent) of U.S. citizens identified as black. Cuba at Independence had a population that was 33 percent black and *mestizo* (Helg, "Race in Argentina and Cuba" 47).

4. Hemenway estimates Mrs. Mason to have given Hurston as much as fifteen thousand dollars over the course of their relationship of patronage (104). As Hemenway

reports, "The problem with Mrs. Mason, as perhaps with all patrons, was that she expected some return on her money. In Hurston's case it was a report on the aboriginal sincerity of rural southern blackfolk" (106). Mrs. Mason was not simply funding a research proposal; she had expectations regarding both the methodology and the "results" of Hurston's research.

    5. In 1937, African American writer Richard Wright published a highly critical review of Hurston's novel *Their Eyes Were Watching God* in which he accused Hurston of pandering to white readers' stereotypes of blackness. Wright's public excoriation of Hurston occurred two years after the publication of *Mules and Men*, yet Hurston must have been aware of the difficulties of representing Southern black culture, and the potential hostility of her black peers, even as she began her fieldwork. For a full discussion of the Wright-Hurston polemic see Maxwell, 153–78.

    6. I draw on Pratt's definition of "contact zones" as "social spaces where disparate cultures meet, clash, and grapple with each other, often in highly asymmetrical relations of domination and subordination" (4). See also the discussion of the concept of the contact zone in the introduction.

    7. See Clifford's exploration of relationship between ethnography and other literary and artistic practices in *The Predicament of Culture*.

    8. Kamala Visweswaran defines feminist ethnography as both "women-centered ethnography," and a "de-centering" of established ethnographic methodologies and assumptions. She locates feminist ethnography "in the recent challenge mounted by experimental ethnography on ethnographic authority" found in the work of ethnographers such as Michelle Rosaldo and Marilyn Strathern (17), and in the "confessional fieldwork narratives" of anthropologists such as Laura Bohannon, Elizabeth Fernea, and Marjory Wolf (22).

    9. Interestingly, despite the gendering of the figure of the ethnographer as male, there were a significant number of women ethnographers and social scientists working in the early decades of the twentieth century. A significant number of them—Ruth Landes, Margaret Mead, Ella Cara Deloria, to name a few—studied at Columbia University with Hurston's advisor Franz Boas. It is also important to note that many of them had complicated professional trajectories, and have received mixed treatment by both their peers and later scholars. See Ruth Behar's "Introduction" to *Women Writing Culture*.

    10. Boas, widely considered to be the father figure of American cultural anthropology, began as a physical anthropologist in Germany, but ultimately rejected theories of biological determinism to argue that culture is shaped by a combination of biological, social, and environmental factors. He was also a pioneer against racism and what are now considered to be racist pseudoscientific methodologies in the social sciences. Boas was an early practitioner of the participant-observer method of fieldwork, yet unlike Malinowski, who argued that ethnographic subjects were seldom aware of their own culture's social structures, Boas pioneered the use of "native" or "privileged" informants, most famously in his collaboration with the Kwakiutl Indian

George Hunt (Pavloska 81). Boas was responsible for the founding of the United States' first program in anthropology (at Columbia University) in 1899. The program went on to educate some of the most well-known anthropologists in the country, among them Alfred Kroeber, Melville Herskovits, and Margaret Mead, in addition to Mexican anthropologist Manuel Gamio and Brazilian Gilberto Freyre. For a full discussion and history of Boas's ideas about race (and his relationships with many African American intellectuals), see Vernon J. Williams.

11. For an extended discussion of the publication of *Mules and Men*, and Hurston and Boas's relationship, see Cotera 87–91.

12. As well as founding the journal *Estudios Afrocubanos*, Ortiz was the first scholar to publish a monograph on Afro-Cuban religion: *Hampa afrocubana: Los negros brujos* (*The Afro-Cuban Underworld: Black Witchcraft*, 1906). I analyze Ortiz's significant role in developing Afro-Cuban ethnography as a serious field of study in chapter 1 of this book.

13. This earlier version of *El Monte* was published in *Revista Bimestre Cubana* in 1947, under the title "Eggüe o Vichichi Nfinda." It appears reprinted in *Páginas sueltas* (273–356). For a discussion of some of the differences between this earlier version and the 1954 text, see González Mandri 49–51.

14. For further discussion of the idea of "tricks of the weak," see Ludmer.

15. These are practitioners of the Santería and Palo Monte religions. Santería is descended from practices brought to Cuba by slaves from Yoruba-speaking West Africa (known in Cuba as *lucumíes*); Palo Monte refers to the religious traditions of the Bantú-speaking peoples (*congo* in Cuba), most of whom came from south-central West Africa (the area of present-day Cameroon). See Barnet, *La fuente viva*, for a more detailed discussion of Afro-Cuban religious origins.

16. This declaration would later be echoed by anthropologist Renato Rosaldo and its sentiments shared by other ethnographers in the 1980s. See Rosaldo, *Culture and Truth*.

17. In a financial sense, this was true; in funding Hurston's research, Charlotte Osgood Mason had placed certain restrictions on it, particularly on where and how Hurston could publish (Cotera 84–85).

18. While the idea of "race" was the object of much study, when Hurston began her research for *Mules and Men* she was one of only a handful of African Americans studying anthropology, and almost no research had been done on African American culture. The exception to this was Louis Eugene King, who produced his dissertation for Columbia, "Negro Life in a Rural Community," after working with both Melville Herskovits and Otto Klineberg (who were both studying black body size and intelligence). Despite early support from these scholars, King was unable to find a teaching position and spent the better part of his life working as a management analyst for the Naval Supply Depot in Mechanicsburg, Pennsylvania (Harrison 70–83).

19. See Cotera 27–39 for a discussion of the history of the split between folklore studies and anthropology. As Cotera notes, Boas and his students saw value in col-

lecting folklore as it "constituted a form of expression that revealed something about the values and belief system of a given society" (33).

20. According to Cotera, this was the result of negotiation between Hurston and her editor, Bertram Lippincott, who wanted a book closer in tone to Hurston's novel *Jonah's Gourd Vine*, which had recently been published (91).

21. "I knew where the material was all right. But, I went about asking, in carefully accented Barnardese, 'Pardon me, but do you know any folk tales or folk songs?' The men and women who had whole treasuries of material just seeping through their pores, looked at me and shook their heads. No, they had never heard of anything like that around there.... Oh, I got a few little items. But compared with what I did later, not enough to make a flea a waltzing jacket" (Hurston, *Dust Tracks* 144).

22. Because of the syncretic relationship that developed between African religious traditions and Catholicism in Cuba, each Afro-Cuban *oricha* is represented by a Catholic saint. To be initiated into the *Regla de Ochá* (Santería) is *hacerse santo* (literally, to be made a saint).

23. Cabrera may in fact overemphasize her reliance on oral material. Dianteill and Swearingen argue that there was already a tradition of Afro-Cuban religious writing before *El Monte*—mostly in the form of *libretas*, small notebooks kept by initiates, and show that Cabrera made use of these texts in the construction of her ethnography.

24. The metaphor of the ethnographer's note cards as an offering to the *orichas* is interesting on another level, given that Cabrera, for all of her attempts to identify herself as an outsider, never clearly states her own beliefs or level of initiation in the religions. A number of people I spoke with in Cuba informed me that it was rumored that Cabrera was initiated into the *Regla de Ochá* (Santería), and that she was a "daughter of Yemayá," the female *oricha* whose provenance is the sea. However, I have found no documentation to confirm this.

25. This strategy is similar to the one that Sommer recognizes in the testimonial novel *Me llamo Rigoberta Menchú* (*I, Rigoberta Menchú: An Indian Woman in Guatemala*). In that text, Menchú mentions that Indians have secrets, and then purposely withholds the actual information from the reader. Sommer argues that this refusal to reveal information constitutes a deliberate textual strategy that signals the boundaries of understanding: "The calculated result of Rigoberta's gesture for sympathetic readers is, paradoxically, to exclude us from her circle of intimates.... [I]t produces a particular kind of distance akin to respect" ("Rigoberta's Secrets" 36).

Epilogue: Textual Straits: Race and Ethnographic Literature since the Cuban Revolution

1. Roughly 200,000 Cubans left the country in the first three years of the Revolution (Pérez, *Cuba* 255).

2. Guillén had become a supporter of communism after the Spanish Civil War, well before the Revolution. He was exiled under Batista, but was welcomed back by Fidel

Castro. He was appointed the first director of the newly formed Unión Nacional de Escritores y Artistas Cubanos (the Writers and Artists Union, or UNEAC) in 1961, a position he held until 1985. Carpentier, who had also been living in exile during Batista's dictatorship (in Venezuela), returned to Cuba after the Revolution and was named the Cuban ambassador to France, a position he held until his death in Paris in 1980.

3. I am speaking here of the first decades after the Revolution. As Sujatha Fernandes and Kenneth Routon (among others) have shown, Afro-Cuban images and Afro-Cuban religious traditions, Santería in particular, have assumed a different—and more visible—role in Cuba since the economic crisis of the Special Period (1990–the present).

4. Martínez Furé's emphasis on the importance of folklore as a universal cultural product is connected to the way in which the role of the intellectual was being defined in relation to the Revolution. In his 1961 speech "Palabras a los intelectuales" (Words to Intellectuals), Fidel Castro explicitly rejected the idea of the intellectual as a voice for bourgeois or elitist class interests. The intellectual, Castro argued, must be "with the Revolution," although, as Ana Serra observes, he did not make it clear just in what way that was to be demonstrated (60). Martínez Furé's championing of folklore can thus be seen as a way to position the intellectual within the panorama of national culture. If folklore is the "authentic" expression of an entire Cuban people, the intellectual thus exists to facilitate the productive, nurturing relationship between it and "revolutionary culture."

5. See Sommers's reading of the use of textual silences in *Me llamo Rigoberta Menchú* in "Rigoberta's Secrets."

SELECTED BIBLIOGRAPHY

Aching, Gerard. "Beyond Sites of Execution: Haiti and the Historical Imagination in C.L.R. James and Alejo Carpentier." *Sisyphus and Eldorado: Magical and Other Realisms in Caribbean Literature.* Ed. Timothy J. Reiss. 2nd ed. Trenton, N.J.: Africa World Press, 2002. 103–26.
———. *Masking and Power: Carnival and Popular Culture in the Caribbean.* Cultural Studies of the Americas. Eds. George Yúdice, Jean Franco, and Juan Flores. Minneapolis: University of Minnesota Press, 2002.
———. "On the Creation of Unsung National Heroes: Barnet's Esteban Montejo and Armas's Julián del Casal." *Latin American Literary Review* 22.43 (January–June 1994): 31–50.
Alonso, Carlos J. *The Burden of Modernity: The Rhetoric of Cultural Discourse in Spanish America.* Cambridge: Cambridge University Press, 1998.
———. *The Spanish American Regional Novel: Modernity and Autochthony.* Cambridge: Cambridge University Press, 1990.
Anderson, Benedict. *Imagined Communities.* 1983. London: Verso, 1991.
Anderson, Thomas F. "Inconsistent Depictions of Afro-Cubans and Their Cultural Manifestations in the Early Poetry of Marcelino Arozarena." *Afro-Hispanic Review* 27.2 (Fall 2008): 9–44.
Andrews, George Reid. *Afro-Latin America, 1800–2000.* Oxford: Oxford University Press, 2004.
Archer Straw, Petrine. *Negrophilia. Avant-Garde Paris and Black Culture in the 1920s.* New York: Thames and Hudson, 2000.
Arnedo-Gómez, Miguel. *Writing Rumba: The Afrocubanista Movement in Poetry.* New World Studies. Charlottesville, Va.: University of Virginia Press, 2006.
Arozarena, Marcelino. "Canción negra sin color." *La palabra.* March 1935. Rpt. in *Afro-Hispanic Review* 17:1 (Spring 1998): 31–32.
Arroyo, Jossianna. *Travestismos culturales: Literatura y etnografía en Cuba y Brasil.* Serie Nuevo Siglo. Pittsburgh: Instituto Internacional de Literatura Iberoamericana, 2003.
Asad, Talal. "The Concept of Cultural Translation in British Social Anthropology." *Writing Culture: The Poetics and Politics of Ethnography.* Eds. James Clifford and George E. Marcus. Berkeley: University of California Press, 1986. 141–64.

Bakhtin, M. M. *The Dialogic Imagination: Four Essays.* Ed. Michael Holquist. Trans. Caryl Emerson and Michael Holquist. Austin: University of Texas Press, 1981.

Barnes, Sandra T. *Africa's Ogun: Old World and New.* 2nd. ed. Bloomington: Indiana University Press, 1997.

Barnet, Miguel. "The Alchemy of Memory." *Biography of a Runaway Slave.* Trans. Nick Hill. Willmantic, Conn.: Curbstone Press, 1994. 203–208.

———. *Biografía de un cimarrón.* 1966. Havana: Editorial Letras Cubanas, 2001.

———. *Biography of a Runaway Slave.* Trans. Nick Hill. Willmantic, Conn.: Curbstone Press, 1994.

———. *La fuente viva.* Havana: Editorial Letras Cubanas, 1998.

Barreda-Tomás, Pedro M. "Alejo Carpentier: dos visiones del negro, dos conceptos de la novela." *Hispania* 55.1 (March 1972): 34–44.

Barreiro, José. "Indians in Cuba." *Cultural Survival Quarterly* 13.3 (1989): 56–60.

Bastide, Roger. *Le Candomblé de Bahia (Rite Nagô).* Mouton & Co., Paris-La Haye, 1958. Terre Humaine. Paris: Éditions Plon, 2000.

Behar, Ruth. "Introduction: Out of Exile." *Women Writing Culture.* Berkeley: University of California Press, 1995. 1–32.

Bell, Michael. "The Metaphysics of Modernism." *The Cambridge Companion to Modernism.* Ed. Michael Levenson. Cambridge: Cambridge University Press, 1999.

Benítez Rojo, Antonio. "Creolization and Nation-building in the Hispanic Caribbean." *Sisyphus and Eldorado: Magical and Other Realisms in Caribbean Literature.* Ed. Timothy J. Reiss, 2nd ed. Trenton, N.J.: Africa World Press, 2002. 201–10.

———. *La isla que se repite: El Caribe y la perspectiva posmoderna.* 1989. Hanover, N.H.: Ediciones del Norte, 1996.

Berman, Marshall. *All That Is Solid Melts into Air: The Experience of Modernity.* 1982. New York: Penguin Books, 1988.

Bethell, Leslie, ed. *Ideas and Ideologies in Twentieth-Century Latin America.* Cambridge: Cambridge University Press, 1996.

Beverley, John. "The Margin at the Center: On Testimonio (1989)." *The Real Thing: Testimonial Discourse and Latin America.* Ed. Georg M. Gugelberger. Durham: Duke University Press, 1996. 23–41.

Bhabha, Homi K. "DissemiNation: Time, Narrative, and the Margins of the Modern Nation." *Nation and Narration.* Ed. Homi K. Bhabha. London: Routledge, 1990. 291–322.

———. *The Location of Culture.* London: Routledge, 1994.

Birkenmaier, Anke. *Alejo Carpentier y la cultura del surrealismo en América Latina.* Madrid: Iberoamericana Vervuert, 2006.

———. "Alejo Carpentier y Wifredo Lam: Negociaciones para un arte revolucionario." *Cuba: Un siglo de literatura (1902–2002).* Eds. Anke Birkenmaier and Roberto González Echevarría. Madrid: Editorial Colibrí, 2004. 71–90.

Blake, Jody. *Le Tumulte Noir: Modernist Art and Popular Entertainment in Jazz-Age Paris, 1900–1930.* University Park: Penn State University Press, 1999.

Boas, Franz. Preface. *Mules and Men.* By Zora Neale Hurston. 1935. New York: Harper Collins, 1990. xiii–xiv.

Bolívar Arostegui, Natalia. *Cuba: Imágenes y relatos de un mundo mágico.* Havana: Ediciones Unión, 1997.

———. *Lydia Cabrera en su laguna sagrada.* Santiago de Cuba: Editorial Oriente, 2000.

Bolívar Arostegui, Natalia, and Valentina Porras Pots. *Orisha Ayé: Unidad mítica del Caribe al Brasil.* Guadalajara, Spain: Ediciones Pontón, 1996.

Boti, Regino E. "La poesía cubana de Nicolás Guillén." *Revista Bimestre Cubana* (mayo–junio 1932): 140–46.

Boym, Svetlana. *The Future of Nostalgia.* New York: Basic Books, 2001.

Branche, Jerome C. *Colonialism and Race in Luso-Hispanic Literature.* Columbia: University of Missouri Press, 2006.

Brandon, Ruth. *Surreal Lives: The Surrealists, 1917–1945.* New York: Grove Press, 1999.

Breton, André. *Conversations: The Autobiography of Surrealism.* 1969, Paris: Editions Gallimard. Trans. Mark Polizzotti. New York: Marlowe & Company, 1993.

———. *Manifestoes of Surrealism.* Trans. Richard Seaver and Helen R. Lane. Ann Arbor: University of Michigan Press, 1962.

Bronfman, Alejandra. *Measures of Equality: Social Science, Citizenship, and Race in Cuba: 1902–1940.* Chapel Hill: University of North Carolina Press, 2004.

———. "Poetry in the Presidio: Toward a Study of *Proyecto de Código Criminal Cubano*." *Cuban Counterpoints: The Legacy of Fernando Ortiz.* Eds. Mauricio A. Font and Alfonso W. Quiroz. Lanham, Mass.: Lexington Books, 2005. 157–68.

Brown, David H. *Santería Enthroned: Art, Ritual, and Innovation in and Afro-Cuban Religion.* Chicago: The University of Chicago Press, 2003.

Buck-Morss, Susan. "Hegel and Haiti." *Critical Inquiry* (Summer 2000): 821–65.

Cabrera, Lydia. "Al aficionado a la historia de Cuba que pueda interesar..." *Diario Las Américas* Wednesday, August 6, 1980.

———. *Anagó, vocabulario lucumí. El Yoruba que se habla en Cuba.* 1957. Miami: Ediciones Universal, 1996.

———. *Ayapá, cuentos de Jicotea.* Miami: Ediciones Universal, 1971.

———. *Cuentos negros de Cuba.* 1936. Miami: Ediciones Universal, 1993.

———. *Koeko Iyawó: Aprende novicia.* Miami: Ultra Graphics, 1980.

———. *La laguna sagrada de San Joaquín.* 1973. Ediciones Erre. Ed. Isabel Castellanos. 2nd ed. Miami: Ediciones Universal, 1993.

———. *La lengua sagrada de los ñáñigos.* Miami: V & L Graphics, 1988.

———. *El Monte: Igbo Finda, Ewe Orisha, Vititi Nfinda (Notas sobre las religiones, la magia, las supersticiones y el folklore de los negros criollos y el pueblo de Cuba).* 1954. Miami: Ediciones Universal, 1983.

———. *Páginas sueltas.* Ed. Isabel Castellanos. Miami: Ediciones Universal, 1994.

———. *Por qué... cuentos negros de Cuba.* Colección Del Chicherekú En El Exilio. Madrid: Editorial Ramos, 1972.

———. *La Regla Kimbisa del Santo Cristo del Buen Viaje.* Miami: Ediciones Universal, 1986.

———. *La sociedad secreta abakuá narrada por viejos adeptos.* 1959. Miami: Editorial C. R., 1969.

———. "Y Así Fue..." *El Tiempo. Página Literaria* Sunday, January 18, 1970: 1.

———. *Yemayá y Ochún: Kariocha, iyalorichas y olorichas.* 1980. Miami: Ediciones Universal, 1996.

Carpentier, Alejo. "Correspondencia con García Caturla." *Obras completas.* Vol. 1. Mexico City: Siglo Veintiuno Editores, 1983. 278–313.

———. *De lo real maravilloso americano.* Colección Pequeños Grandes Ensayos. Mexico City: Universidad Autónoma de Mexico City, 2003.

———. *Écue-Yamba-Ó. Obras completas.* Vol. 1. Mexico City: Siglo Veintiuno Editores, 1983. 21–194.

———. *The Kingdom of This World.* 1957. Trans. Harriet de Onís. Introd. Edwidge Danticat. New York: Farrar, Straus and Giroux, 2006.

———. "Lettre des Antilles." *Bifur* (1929): 91–105.

———. "La musique cubaine." *Documents* 6 (November 1929): 324–27.

———. "Prólogo a *Écue-Yamba-Ó*." *Obras completas.* Vol. 1. Mexico City: Siglo Veintiuno Editores, 1983. 23–28.

———. "Prólogo a *El reino de este mundo*." *Vanguardia latinoamericana: Historia, crítica y documentos.* Tomo 2. Caribe, Antillas Mayores y Menores. Eds. Gilberto Mendonça Teles and Klaus Müller-Bergh. Frankfurt am Main: Vervuert; Madrid: Iberoamericana, 2002. 52–55.

———. *El reino de este mundo.* 1949. Barcelona: Biblioteca del Bolsillo, 1994.

———. "La Rue Fontaine: calle cubana." *Obras completas.* Vol. 8: Crónicas 1. México: Siglo Veintiuno Editores, 1985. 295–99.

Castellanos, Isabel. "Introducción." *Páginas sueltas.* By Lydia Cabrera. Miami: Ediciones Universal, 1994. 13–66.

Castellanos, Isabel, and Jorge Castellanos. *Cultura afrocubana 3: Las religiones y las lenguas.* Miami: Ediciones Universal, 1992.

———. *Cultura afrocubana 4: Letras, música, arte.* Miami: Ediciones Universal, 1994.

Castellanos, Isabel and Josefina Inclán, eds. *En torno a Lydia Cabrera (Cincuentenario de "Cuentos negros de Cuba," 1936–1986).* Miami: Ediciones Universal, 1987.

Castellanos, Israel. "Psicología de las multitudes." 1914. *La Habana Elegante, Segunda Época* (Summer 2004) http://www.habanaelegante.com/Summer2004/Panoptico.html.

Césaire, Aimé. *Notebook of a Return to the Native Land.* 1947. Introduction by André Breton. Trans. Clayton Eschleman and Annette Smith. Middletown, Conn.: Wesleyan University Press, 2001.

Chacón y Calvo, José María. "Del folklore cubano." *Archivos del Folklore Cubano* 5.2 (1930): 175–79.

Chamoiseau, Patrick, and Raphaël Confiant. *Lettres Creoles: Tracées Antillaises et Con-*

tinentales de la Litterature: Haiti, Guadaloupe, Martinique, Guyane. Paris: Hatier, 1991.
Chatterjee, Partha. *The Nation and Its Fragments: Colonial and Postcolonial Histories*. Princeton: Princeton University Press, 1993.
Clifford, James. *The Predicament of Culture: Twentieth-Century Ethnography, Literature, and Art*. Cambridge, Mass.: Harvard University Press, 1988.
Clifford, James, and George E. Marcus, eds. *Writing Culture: The Poetics and Politics of Ethnography*. Berkeley: University of California Press, 1986.
Cordones Cook, Juanamaría. "Prologue." *Mirar adentro/Looking Within: Selected Poems, 1954–2000*. By Nancy Morejón. Detroit: Wayne State University Press, 2003. 13–66.
Coronado, Jorge. *The Andes Imagined: Indigenismo, Society, and Modernity*. Pittsburgh: University of Pittsburgh Press, 2009.
Coronil, Fernando. "Challenging Colonial Histories: *Cuban Counterpoint*/Ortiz's Counterfetishism." *Critical Theory, Cultural Politics, and Latin American Narrative*. Eds. Stephen M. Bell, Albert H. Le May, and Leonard Orr. South Bend, Ind.: University of Notre Dame Press, 1993.

———. Introduction. *Cuban Counterpoint, Tobacco and Sugar*. By Fernando Ortiz. Durham and London: Duke University Press, 1995.
Cortés-Roca, Paola. "Etnología ficcional: brujos, zombis y otros cuentos caribeños." *Revista Iberoamericana* 75.227 (abril–junio 2009): 333–47.
Cotera, María Eugenia. *Native Speakers: Ella Deloria, Zora Neale Hurston, Jovita González and the Poetics of Culture*. Austin: University of Texas Press, 2008.
Cuervo Hewitt, Julia. *Aché, presencia africana: Tradiciones yoruba-lucumí en la narrativa cubana*. New York: Peter Lang, 1988.
Dash, J. Michael. *Literature and Ideology in Haiti, 1915–1961*. Basingstoke, U.K.: Macmillan, 1981.

———. "The Madman at the Crossroads: Delirium and Dislocation in Caribbean Literature." *Profession* (2002): 37–43.
Davis, Catherine. *A Place in the Sun? Women Writers in Twentieth-Century Cuba*. London: Zed Books, 1997.
De Anhalt, Nedda G. "Lydia Cabrera, la Sikuanekua." *Rojo y naranja sobre rojo*. Mexico City: Editorial Vuelta, 1991. 35–60.
de Certeau, Michel. *The Writing of History*. Trans. Tom Conley. New York: Columbia University Press, 1988.
De Costa Willis, Miriam. "Folklore and the Creative Artist: Lydia Cabrera and Zora Neale Hurston." *College Language Association Journal* 27:1 (1983): 81–90.
De Ferrari, Guillermina. *Vulnerable States: Bodies of Memory in Contemporary Caribbean Fiction*. New World Studies. Charlottesville: University Press of Virginia, 2007.
de la Fuente, Alejandro. "Myths of Racial Democracy: Cuba, 1900–1912." *Latin American Research Review* 34.3 (1999): 39–73.

———. *A Nation For All: Race, Inequality, and Politics in Twentieth-Century Cuba*. Chapel Hill: University of North Carolina Press, 2001.

de Melo, Alfredo Cesar B. "A face de Janus no ensaísmo latinoamericano." *Chasqui* 36.1 (May 2007): 121–32.

"Declaración del Grupo Minorista." 1927. In *Manifiestos, proclamas y polémicas de la vanguardia hispanoamericana*, ed. Nelson T. Osorio. Caracas: Biblioteca Ayacucho, 1988. 248–51.

Desnos, Robert. "Introduction." In "La musique cubaine" by Alejo Carpentier. *Documents* 6 (November 1929): 324.

Dianteill, Erwan and Martha Swearingen. "From Hierography to Ethnography and Back: Lydia Cabrera's Texts and the Written Tradition in Afro-Cuban Religions." *Journal of American Folklore* 116.461 (2003): 273–92.

Díaz Quiñones, Arcadio. "Fernando Ortiz y Allan Kardec: Espiritismo y transculturación." *Catauro* 1.0 (July-December 1999): 14–31.

Dirks, Nicholas B. "Annals of the Archive: Ethnographic Notes on the Sources of History." *From the Margins: Historical Anthropology and Its Futures*. Ed. Brian Keith Axel. Durham: Duke University Press, 2002. 47–65.

Domina, Lynn. "'Protection in my Mouf': Self, Voice and Community in Zora Neale Hurston's *Dust Tracks on a Road* and *Mules and Men*." *African American Review* 31.2 (Summer 1997): 197–209.

Douglas, Ann. *Terrible Honesty: Mongrel Manhattan in the 1920s*. New York: The Noonday Press, 1995.

Drewal, Margaret Thompson. *Yoruba Ritual: Performers, Play, Agency*. 2nd ed. Bloomington: Indiana University Press, 1992.

Duany, José. "After the Revolution: The Search for Roots in Afro-Cuban Culture." *Latin American Research Review* 23.1 (1988): 244–55.

Du Bois, W.E.B. *The Souls of Black Folk*. 1903. Ed. Donald B. Gibson. New York: Penguin Books, 1989.

Dumont, Henri. *Antropología y patología comparadas de los negros esclavos*. 1876. Trans. Israel Castellanos. Havana: Colección Cubana, 1922.

Duno Gottberg, Luis. *Solventando las diferencias. La ideología del mestizaje en Cuba*. Frankfurt am Main: Vervuert; Madrid: Iberoamericana, 2003.

Edwards, Brent Hayes. *The Practice of Diaspora: Literature, Translation, and the Rise of Black Internationalism*. Cambridge, Mass.: Harvard University Press, 2003.

Ellis, Keith. *Cuba's Nicolás Guillén: Poetry and Ideology*. Toronto: University of Toronto Press, 1983.

Fabian, Johannes. *Time and the Other: How Anthropology Makes Its Object*. New York: Columbia University Press, 1983.

Fass Emery, Amy. *The Anthropological Imagination in Latin American Literature*. Columbia: University of Missouri Press, 1996.

Fernandes, Sujatha. *Cuba Represent!: Cuban Arts, State Power, and the Making of New Revolutionary Cultures*. Durham: Duke University Press, 2006.

Fernández de Castro, José Antonio. "La literatura negra actual de Cuba." *Estudios Afrocubanos* 4 (1940): 3–22.

Fernández Martínez, Mirta, and Valentina Porras Pots. *El ashé está en Cuba*. Havana: Editorial José Martí, 1998.
Fernández Retamar, Roberto. "*Entre cubanos*: Tres cuartos de siglo después." *Catauro* 1.0 (July-December 1999): 5–13.
Fernández Robaina, Tomás. *El negro en Cuba, 1902–1958: Apuntes para la historia de la lucha contra la discriminación racial*. Sociologia. Havana: Editorial de Ciencias Sociales, 1990.
Fernández Villa-Urrutia, Rafael. "En torno a la pintura de Wifredo Lam." *Revista Lyceum* (1951): 62–69.
Ferrer, Ada. *Insurgent Cuba: Race, Nation, and Revolution, 1868–1898*. Chapel Hill: University of North Carolina Press, 1999.
Fichtner, Margarita. "The Legendary Lydia Cabrera." *Miami Herald* March 14 1982, Living Today section.
Figueroa, Esperanza. "Tres vidas divergentes, Lydia, Enríquez y Carpentier." *En torno a Lydia Cabrera (Cincuentenario de "Cuentos negros de Cuba," 1936–1986)*. Eds. Isabel Castellanos and Josefina Inclán. Miami: Ediciones Universal, 1987.
Finnegan, Ruth. *Oral Literature in Africa*. Oxford: Clarendon, 1970.
Fischer, Sibylle. *Modernity Disavowed: Haiti and the Cultures of Slavery in the Age of Revolution*. Durham: Duke University Press, 2004.
Font, Mauricio A. and Alfonso W. Quiroz, eds. *Cuban Counterpoints: The Legacy of Fernando Ortiz*. Lanham, Mass.: Lexington Books, 2005.
Frazer, James George. *The Golden Bough: A Study in Magic and Religion*. One volume edition, 1890. New York: The Macmillan Company, 1948.
Freud, Sigmund. *Jokes and Their Relation to the Unconscious*. Trans. James Strachey. New York: W. W. Norton & Company, 1960.
Gabara, Esther. *Errant Modernism: The Ethos of Photography in Mexico and Brazil*. Durham: Duke University Press, 2008.
García-Carranza, Araceli. "Apuntes bibliográficos de una etapa precursora en los años jóvenes de Alejo Carpentier." *Cuba: Un siglo de literatura (1902–2002)*. Eds. Anke Birkenmaier and Roberto González Echevarría. Madrid: Editorial Colibrí, 2004. 51–70.
Gates, Henry Louis, Jr. *The Signifying Monkey: A Theory of African-American Literary Criticism*. Oxford: Oxford University Press, 1988.
Geertz, Clifford. *After the Fact: Two Countries, Four Decades, One Anthropologist*. Cambridge, Mass.: Harvard University Press, 1995.
———. "Found in Translation: On the Social History of the Moral Imagination." *Local Knowledge: Further Essays in Interpretive Anthropology*. New York: Basic Books, 1983. 36–54.
Gikandi, Simon. *Writing in Limbo: Modernism and Caribbean Literature*. Ithaca: Cornell University Press, 1992.
Gilroy, Paul. *The Black Atlantic: Modernity and Double Consciousness*. Cambridge, Mass.: Harvard University Press, 1993.

Glissant, Édouard. *Caribbean Discourse: Selected Essays.* 1981. Le Discours Antillais. Trans. J. Michael Dash. Caraf Books. Charlottesville: University of Virginia Press, 1989.

———. *Poetics of Relation.* 1990. Trans. Betsy Wing. Ann Arbor: University of Michigan Press, 1997.

González Echevarría, Roberto. *Alejo Carpentier: The Pilgrim at Home.* Ithaca: Cornell University Press, 1977.

———. *Celestina's Brood: Continuities of the Baroque in Spanish and Latin American Literatures.* Durham: Duke University Press, 1993.

———. *Myth and Archive: A Theory of Latin American Narrative.* 1990. 2nd ed. Durham: Duke University Press, 1998.

González Mandri, Flora. *Guarding Cultural Memory: Afro-Cuban Women in Literature and the Arts.* New World Studies Series. Charlottesville: Virginia University Press, 2006.

González Pérez, Aníbal. "Ballad of the Two Poets: Nicolás Guillén and Luis Palés Matos." *Callaloo* 10. 2 (1987): 285–301.

González y Contreras, Gilberto. "La poesía negra." *Revista Bimestre Cubana.* (January–February, 1936): 40–45.

Gordon, Deborah. "The Politics of Ethnographic Authority: Race and Writing in the Ethnography of Margaret Mead and Zora Neale Hurston." *Modernist Anthropology: From Fieldwork to Text.* Ed. Mark Manganaro. Princeton: Princeton University Press, 1990. 146–162.

Graff Zivin, Erin. *The Wandering Signifier: Rhetoric of Jewishness in the Latin American Imaginary.* Durham: Duke University Press, 2009.

Greenfield, Charles. "Cuba's Matriarch of Letters, Lydia Cabrera." *Nuestro,* September 1982, 13–16.

Guillén, Nicolás. *Epistolario de Nicolás Guillén.* Ed. Alexander Pérez Heredia. Havana: Editorial Letras Cubanas, 2002.

———. *Obra poética.* 1972. 2nd ed. 2 vols. Havana: Editorial Arte y Literatura, 1985.

———. *Prosa de prisa, 1929–1972.* 4 vols. Havana: Editorial Arte y Literatura, 1975.

Gutiérrez, Mariela A. "La armonía cósmica africana en los cuentos de Lydia Cabrera." *Encuentro* 4/5 (Spring–Summer 1997): 202–9.

———. *El cosmos de Lydia Cabrera: dioses, animales y hombres.* Colección Ébano y Canela. Miami: Ediciones Universal, 1991.

———. *Los cuentos negros de Lydia Cabrera: estudio morfológico esquemático.* Miami: Ediciones Universal, 1986.

———. *An Ethnological Interpretation of the Afro-Cuban World of Lydia Cabrera, 1900–1991.* Lewiston, N.Y.: Edwin Mellon Press, 2008.

———. *Lydia Cabrera: Aproximaciones mítico-simbólicas a su cuentística.* Madrid: Editorial Verbum, 1997.

Hall, Stuart. "Cultural Identity and Diaspora." *Identity: Community, Culture, Difference.* Ed. Jonathan Rutherford. London: Lawrence & Wishart, 1990. 222–237.

———. "What Is This Black in Black Popular Culture? (Rethinking Race)." *Social Justice* 20.1–2 (Spring–Summer 1993): 104–11.
Harrison, Ira E. "Louis Eugene King, the Anthropologist Who Never Was." *African-American Pioneers in Anthropology*. Ed. Ira E. Harrison and Faye V. Harrison. Urbana: University of Illinois Press, 1999. 70–84.
Helg, Aline. *Our Rightful Share: The Afro-Cuban Struggle for Equality, 1886–1912*. Chapel Hill: University of North Carolina Press, 1995.
———. "Race in Argentina and Cuba, 1880–1930: Theory, Policies, and Popular Reaction." *The Idea of Race in Latin America, 1870–1940*. Ed. Richard Graham. Austin: University of Texas Press, 1990. 37–70.
Hemenway, Robert E. *Zora Neale Hurston: A Literary Biography*. 1977. Urbana: University of Illinois Press, 1980.
Hernández, Graciela. "Multiple Subjectivities and Strategic Positionality: Zora Neale Hurston's Experimental Ethnographies." *Women Writing Culture*. Eds. Ruth Behar and Deborah Gordon. Berkeley: University of California Press, 1995. 148–65.
Hernández Adrián, Francisco-Javier. "On Tropical Grounds: Avant-Garde Imaginations of Insularity in the Hispanic Caribbean and the Canary Islands." Dissertation. New York University, 2002.
Herskovits, Melville J. *Life in a Haitian Valley*. New York: Knopf, 1937. New York: Octagon, 1975.
Hewitt, Nicholas. "'Marseille qui jazz': Popular Culture in the Second City." www.h-france.net/rude/rude%20volume%20ii/Hewitt%20Final%20Version.pdf
Hiriart, Rosario. *Lydia Cabrera: Vida hecha arte*. New York: Eliseo Torres & Sons, 1978.
———. *Más cerca de Teresa de la Parra (diálogos con Lydia Cabrera)*. Caracas: Monte Ávila Editores, 1980.
Hoffman-Jeep, Lynda. "Creating Ethnography: Zora Neale Hurston and Lydia Cabrera." *African American Review* 39.3 (2005): 337–53.
hooks, bell. *Yearning: Race, Gender, and Cultural Politics*. Boston: South End, 1990.
Howard, Phillip A. *Changing History: Afro-Cuban Cabildos and Societies of Color in the Nineteenth Century*. Baton Rouge: Louisiana State University Press, 1998.
Hughes, Langston, trans. *The Translations: Federico García Lorca, Nicolás Guillén, and Jacques Roumain*. The Collected Works of Langston Hughes. Vol. 16. Introd. Dellita Martin-Ogunsola. Columbia: University of Missouri Press, 2003.
Hurston, Zora Neale. *Dust Tracks on a Road*. 1942. New York: Harper Collins, 1996.
———. *Mules and Men*. 1935. New York: Harper Collins, 1990.
———. *The Sanctified Church*. Introd. Toni Cade Bambara. New York: Marlowe & Co., 1984.
———. *Tell My Horse*. 1938. New York: Vintage, 1990.
Ibarra, Jorge. *Prologue to Revolution: Cuba, 1898–1958*. Trans. Marjorie Moore. London: Lynne Rienner Publishers, 1998.

Jackson, Walter. "Melville Herskovits and the Search for African American Culture." *Malinowski, Rivers, Benedict and Others: Essays on Culture and Personality.* Ed. George W. Stocking, Jr. History of Anthropology, Vol. 4. Madison: University of Wisconsin Press, 1986. 95–126.

Jameson, Fredric. *The Political Unconscious: Narrative as a Socially Symbolic Act.* Ithaca: Cornell University Press, 1981.

Jirousek, Lori. "'That Commonality of Feeling': Hurston, Hybridity, and Ethnography." *African American Review* 38.3 (2004): 417–27.

Kapcia, Antoni. *Havana: The Making of Cuban Culture.* Oxford: Berg Publishers, 2005.

Kaup, Monika. "Our America That Is Not One: Transnational Black Atlantic Discourses in Nicolás Guillén and Langston Hughes." *Discourse* 22.3 (Fall 2000): 87–113.

Kelley, Robin D. G. *Freedom Dreams: The Black Radical Imagination.* Boston: Beacon Press, 2002.

Krupat, Arnold. *Ethnocriticism: Ethnography, History, Literature.* Berkeley: University of California Press, 1992.

Kubayanda, Josaphat B. *The Poet's Africa: Africanness in the Poetry of Nicolás Guillén and Aimé Césaire.* New York: Greenwood, 1990.

Kutzinski, Vera M. "Afro-Hispanic American Literature." *The Cambridge History of Latin American Literature.* Eds. González Echevarría and Enrique Pupo-Walker. Vol. 2. New York: Cambridge University Press, 1996. 164–94

———. *Against the American Grain: Myth and History in William Carlos Williams, Jay Wright, and Nicolás Guillén.* Baltimore: Johns Hopkins University Press, 1987.

———. "'Cuba Libre': Langston Hughes and Nicolás Guillén." *Cuba: Un siglo de literatura (1902–2002).* Eds. Anke Birkenmaier and Roberto González Echevarría. Madrid: Editorial Colibrí, 2004. 129–46.

———. *Sugar's Secrets: Race and the Erotics of Cuban Nationalism.* New World Studies Series. Charlottesville: University of Virginia Press, 1993.

Lachatañeré, Rómulo. *Manual de Santería.* 1942. 2nd ed. Havana: Editorial de Ciencias Sociales, 1995.

———. *¡¡Oh, mío Yemayá!!* 1938. Colección Echú Bi. 2nd ed. Havana: Editorial de Ciencias Sociales, 1992.

———. "El sistema religioso de los lucumís y otras influencias africanas en Cuba." *Estudios Afrocubanos* 3.1 (1939): 28–84.

Landes, Ruth. *The City of Women.* 1947. Trans. Introduction by Sally Cole. 2nd ed. Albuquerque: University of New Mexico Press, 1994.

Lane, Jill. *Blackface Cuba, 1840–1895.* Philadelphia: University of Pennsylvania Press, 2005.

Lang, Andrew. *Custom and Myth.* 1885. 2nd Ed. Oosterhout, Netherlands: Anthropological Publications, 1970.

Legrás, Horacio. "Hegelian Tales in the Caribbean: Production, Expression, and History in the Articulation of the Atlantic Subject." *Arizona Journal of Hispanic Cultural Studies* 5 (2001): 133–48.

León, Argeliers. "Prólogo." *Los bailes y el teatro de los negros en el folklore de Cuba*. By Fernando Ortiz. 1951. Havana: Editorial Letras Cubanas, 1993. 7–18.
Levering Lewis, David. *When Harlem Was in Vogue*. 1979. New York: Penguin Books, 1991.
Levine, Suzanne Jill. "Conversación con Lydia Cabrera." *Linden Lane Magazine* (abril–junio 1982): 3–4.
Leys Stepan, Nancy. *"The Hour of Eugenics": Race, Gender, and Nation in Latin America*. Ithaca: Cornell University Press, 1996.
López-Baralt, Mercedes. *Para decir al otro: literatura y antropología en nuestra América*. Frankfurt am Main: Vervuert; Madrid: Iberoamericana, 2005.
López-Calvo, Ignacio. *Imagining the Chinese in Cuban Literature and Culture*. Gainesville: University Press of Florida, 2008.
López Valdés, Rafael. *Componentes africanos en el etnos cubano*. Havana: Editorial de Ciencias Sociales, 1985.
Ludmer, Josefina. "Tricks of the Weak." *Feminist Perspectives on Sor Juana Inés de la Cruz*. Ed. Stephanie Merrim. Detroit: Wayne State University Press, 1991. 86–93.
Luis, William. *Literary Bondage: Slavery in Cuban Narrative*. Austin: University of Texas Press, 1990.
Lund, Joshua. *The Impure Imagination: Toward a Critical Hybridity in Latin American Writing*. Minneapolis: University of Minnesota Press, 2006.
"Lydia Cabrera: Otra descubridora de Cuba." *Revolución y cultura* 2000: 18–27.
Malinowski, Bronislaw. *Argonauts of the Western Pacific*. 1922. New York: Dutton, 1961.
———. *A Diary in the Strict Sense of the Term*. Introd. Raymond Firth. Trans. Norbert Guterman. Stanford: Stanford University Press, 1989.
Manganaro, Marc. *Myth, Rhetoric, and the Voice of Authority: A Critique of Frazer, Eliot, Frye, and Campbell*. New Haven: Yale University Press, 1992.
Mañach, Jorge. *La crisis de la alta cultura en Cuba; Indagación del choteo*. Ed. Rosario Rexach. Colección Cuba y Sus Jueces. Miami: Ediciones Universal, 1991.
Marcone, Jorge. *La oralidad escrita. Sobre la reivindicación y re-inscripción del discurso oral*. Lima: Pontificia Universidad Católica del Perú Fondo Editorial, 1977.
Marcus, George E. and Michael M. J. Fischer. *Anthropology as Cultural Critique: An Experimental Moment in the Human Sciences*. Chicago: University of Chicago Press, 1986.
Marques de Armas, Pedro L. Introduction. "Psicología de las multitudes." By Israel Castellanos. *La Habana Elegante, Segunda Época* (Summer 2004): http://www.habanaelegante.com/Summer2004/Panoptico.html.
Martí, José. "Nuestra América." *Obras completas*. Vol. 6. Havana: Editorial de Ciencias Sociales, 1975. 15–23.
———. "Our America." *Selected Writings*. Trans. Esther Allen. Introd. Roberto González Echevarría. New York: Penguin Books, 2002.
Martínez Furé, Rogelio. *Diálogos imaginarios*. Havana: Editorial Letras Cubanas, 1979.
Mateo, Margarita. "Los *Cuentos negros de Cuba*: transgresión y ruptura." *Transgresiones*

cubanas: Cultura, literatura y lengua dentro y fuera de la isla. Frankfurt am Main: Vervuert; Madrid: Iberoamericana 2006: 41–53.

Matory, J. Lorand. *Sex and the Empire That Is No More: Gender and the Politics of Metaphor in Oyo Yoruba Religion*. Minneapolis: University of Minnesota Press, 1994.

Matos Arévalos, José A. "Fernando Ortiz: Una propuesta de estudio de las ideas." *Catauro* 1.0 (July–December 1999): 32–43.

Maxwell, William J. *New Negro, Old Left: African-American Writing and Communism Between the Wars*. New York: Columbia University Press, 1999.

Meisenhelder, Susan Edwards. *Hitting a Straight Lick with a Crooked Stick: Race and Gender in the Work of Zora Neale Hurston*. Tuscaloosa: University of Alabama Press, 1999.

Menéndez, Lázara. "*El Monte* desde el monte." *Catauro* 1.1 (enero–junio 2000): 36–8.

———. *Selección de lecturas de Estudios Afrocubanos*. Havana: Universidad de Havana, 1990.

Mikell, Gwendolyn. "Feminism and Black Culture in the Ethnography of Zora Neale Hurston." *African-American Pioneers in Anthropology*. Eds. Ira E. Harrison and Faye V. Harrison. Urbana: University of Illinois Press, 1999. 51–69.

Miller, Marilyn Grace. *Rise and Fall of the Cosmic Race: The Cult of Mestizaje in Latin America*. Austin: University of Texas Press, 2004.

Mintz, Sidney W. "From Plantations to Peasantries in the Caribbean." *Caribbean Contours*. Ed. Sidney Mintz and Sally Price. Baltimore: Johns Hopkins University Press, 1985.

———. *Sweetness and Power: The Place of Sugar in Modern History*. New York: Penguin Books, 1985.

Molloy, Sylvia. "Disappearing Acts: Reading Lesbian in Teresa De La Parra." *¿Entiendes? Queer Readings, Hispanic Writings*. Eds. Emilie L. Bergman and Paul Julian Smith. Durham: Duke University Press, 1995. 230–56.

Moore, Robin D. *Music and Revolution: Cultural Change in Socialist Cuba*. Berkeley: University of California Press, 2006.

———. *Nationalizing Blackness: Afrocubanismo and Artistic Revolution in Havana, 1920–1940*. Pittsburgh: University of Pittsburgh Press, 1997.

Morejón, Nancy. "A propósito de Nicolás Guillén." *Fundación de la imagen*. Havana: Editorial Letras Cubanas, 1988. 103–34.

———. *Nación y mestizaje en Nicolás Guillén*. 1982. Havana: Ediciones Unión, 2005.

———. Prologue. *Recopilación de textos sobre Nicolás Guillén*. Serie Valoración Múltiple. Havana: Casa de las Américas, 1974. 7–30.

Mullen, Edward J. *Afro-Cuban Literature: Critical Junctures*. Contributions to the Study of World Literature 91. Westport/London: Greenwood Press, 1998.

———. "The Emergence of Afro-Hispanic Poetry: Some Notes on Canon Formation." *Hispanic Review* 56 (1988): 435–53.

———. "*Los negros brujos*: A Re-examination of the Text." *Cuban Studies* 17 (1988): 11–49.

Muñoz-Basols, Javier. "Sangre, tambores y vudú: convergencia del prólogo y la narración como alegoría de lo real-maravilloso en *El reino de este mundo*." *Céfiro* 3.2 (Spring 2003): 44–53.

Nairn, Tom. "The Modern Janus." *New Left Review.* 1/94 (Nov.–Dec. 1975): 3–29.

Naranjo Orovio, Consuelo, and Miguel Angel Puig-Samper Mulero. "Spanish Intellectuals and Fernando Ortiz (1900–1941)." *Cuban Counterpoints: The Legacy of Fernando Ortiz.* Lanham, Mass.:Lexington, 2005. 9–38.

Novás Calvo, Lino. "Los cuentos de Lydia Cabrera." *Exilio* (Summer 1969): 17–20.

O'Giolláin, Diarmuid. *Locating Irish Folklore: Tradition, Modernity, Identity.* Cork: Cork University Press, 2000.

Ortiz, Fernando. *Los bailes y el teatro de los negros en el folklore de Cuba.* 1951. 3rd ed. Havana: Editorial Letras Cubanas, 1993.

———. *Contrapunteo cubano del tabaco y el azúcar.* 1940. Havana: Consejo Nacional de Cultura, 1973.

———. *Cuban Counterpoint: Tobacco and Sugar.* Trans. Harriet de Onís. Introduction by Fernando Coronil. 1947. Durham: Duke University Press, 1995.

———. "La cubanidad y los negros." *Estudios Afrocubanos* 1 (1939): 3–15.

———. "Cuentos afrocubanos." *Archivos del Folklore Cubano.* 4.2 (1929): 97–112. Rpt. in *Catauro* 1.1 (enero–junio 2000): 118–129.

———. *Entre cubanos: Psicología tropical.* Havana: Editorial de Ciencias Sociales, 1987.

———. "Estudiemos La Música Afrocubana." *Estudios Afrocubanos* 5 (1940–1946): 7–18.

———. *Fernando Ortiz y España: A cien años de 1898.* Ed. Jesús Guanche. Havana: Fundación Fernando Ortiz, 1998.

———. *Glosario de afronegrismos.* 1924. Havana: Editorial de Ciencias Sociales, 1991.

———. *Hampa afrocubana: Los negros brujos.* 1906. Prologue, Alberto N. Pamies. Miami: Ediciones Universal, 1973.

———. *Los negros curros.* 1986. Havana: Editorial Ciencias Sociales.

———. *Los negros esclavos.* 1916. Havana: Editorial de Ciencias Sociales, 1996.

———. "Por la integración cubana de blancos y negros." *Estudios Afrocubanos* 5 (1946): 217–230.

———. "Prejuicio." *Cuentos negros de Cuba.* By Lydia Cabrera. 1940. Miami: Ediciones Universal, 1993. 7–10.

———. "Los últimos versos mulatos." *Revista Bimestre Cubana* 37.3 (May–June 1935): 321–36.

Ortiz Herrera, María Fernanda. "Fernando Ortiz, mi padre." *Cuban Counterpoints: The Legacy of Fernando Ortiz.* Ed. Mauricio A. Font and Alfonso W. Quiroz. Lanham, Mass.: Lexington Books, 2005. 3–8.

Palmié, Stephan. *Wizards and Scientists: Explorations in Afro-Cuban Modernity and Tradition.* Durham: Duke University Press, 2002.

Pamies, Alberto N. "Prólogo." *Hampa afrocubana: Los negros brujos.* By Fernando Ortiz. Miami: Ediciones Universal, 1973.

Pancrazio, James J. *The Logic of Fetishism: Alejo Carpentier and the Cuban Tradition.* Lewisburg, Pa.: Bucknell University Press, 2005.

———. "Maceo's Corps(e): The Paradox of Black *and* Cuban." *Caribe* 2.2 (1999): 83–99.

Paravisini-Gebert, Lizabeth. "The Haitian Revolution in Interstices and Shadows: A Re-reading of Carpentier's *The Kingdom of This World.*" *Research in African Literatures* 25.2 (Summer 2004): 114–27.

Pavloska, Susanna. *Modern Primitives: Race and Language in Gertrude Stein, Ernest Hemingway, and Zora Neale Hurston.* New York: Garland Publishing, 2000.

Paz, Octavio. *Children of the Mire: Modern Poetry from Romanticism to the Avant-Garde (Charles Eliot Norton Lectures).* 1974. Cambridge, Mass.: Harvard University Press, 1991.

Pérez, Louis A., Jr. *Cuba: Between Reform and Revolution.* 1988. 3rd edition. Oxford: Oxford University Press, 2006.

———. *On Becoming Cuban: Identity, Nationality, and Culture.* Chapel Hill: University of North Carolina Press, 1999.

Pérez Firmat, Gustavo. *The Cuban Condition: Translation and Identity in Modern Cuban Literature.* Cambridge: Cambridge University Press, 1989.

Pérez Heredia, Alexander. "Sobre el epistolario de Nicolás Guillén." *Epistolario de Nicolás Guillén.* By Nicolás Guillén. Ed. Alexander Pérez Heredia. Havana: Editorial Letras Cubanas, 2002. 5–13

Pérez Sarduy, Pedro and Jean Stubbs, eds. "Introduction: Race and the Politics of Memory in Contemporary Black Cuban Consciousness." *Afro-Cuban Voices: On Race and Identity in Contemporary Cuba.* Gainesville: University Press of Florida, 2000. 1–38.

Piedra, José. "From Monkey Tales to Cuban Songs: On Signification." *Sacred Possessions: Vodou, Santería, Obeah, and the Caribbean.* Ed. Margarite Fernández Olmos and Lizabeth Paravisini-Gebert. New Brunswick, N.J.: Rutgers University Press, 1997. 122–50.

Poggioli, Renato. *The Theory of the Avant-Garde.* Trans. Gerald Fitzgerald. Cambridge, Mass.: The Belknap Press of Harvard University Press, 1968.

Pratt, Mary Louise. "Arts of the Contact Zone." *Profession* (1991): 33–40.

———. "Criticism in the Contact Zone: Decentering Community and Nation." *Critical Theory, Cultural Politics, and Latin American Narrative.* Eds. Stephen M. Bell, Albert H. Le May, and Leonard Orr. South Bend: University of Notre Dame Press, 1993. 83–102.

———. "Fieldwork in Common Places." *Writing Culture: The Poetics and Politics of Ethnography.* Eds. James Clifford and George E. Marcus. Berkeley: University of California Press, 1986. 27–50.

———. *Imperial Eyes: Travel Writing and Transculturation.* London: Routledge, 1992.

———. "The Traffic in Meaning: Translation, Contagion, Infiltration." *Profession* (2002): 25–36.

Price Mars, Jean. *So Spoke the Uncle*. Trans. Magdaline W. Shannon. Washington, D.C.: Three Continents Press, 1983.
Quiroga, José. "Lydia Cabrera, invisible." *Sexualidad y nación*. Ed. Daniel Balderston. Pittsburgh: Biblioteca de América, 2000. 99–109.
———. *Tropics of Desire: Interventions from Queer Latino America*. Sexual Cultures: New Directions from the Center for Lesbian and Gay Studies. New York: New York University Press, 2000.
Rama, Angel. *The Lettered City*. Trans. and ed. John Charles Chasteen. Durham: Duke University Press, 1996.
———. *Transculturación narrativa en América Latina*. Mexico City: Siglo Veintiuno Editores, 1982.
Regazzoni, Susanna. "La ambigua realidad cubana en los cuentos de Lydia Cabrera." *Alma cubana: Transculturación, mestizaje e hibridismo*. Frankfurt am Main: Vervuert; Madrid, Iberoamericana, 2006. 143–166.
Renan, Ernest. "What Is a Nation?" 1882. Trans. Martin Thom. *Nation and Narration*. Ed. Homi K. Bhabha. London: Routledge, 1990. 8–22/
Renda, Mary A. *Taking Haiti: Military Occupation and the Culture of U.S. Imperialism, 1915–1940*. Chapel Hill: University of North Carolina Press, 2001.
Respall Fina, Raimundo. "Abriendo monte." Preface. *El Monte*. By Lydia Cabrera. Havana: Editorial Letras Cubanas, 1993.
Richardson, Michael and Krzystof Fijalkowski, eds. *Refusal of the Shadow: Surrealism and the Caribbean*. London: Verso, 1996.
Rodríguez-Mangual, Edna M. *Lydia Cabrera and the Construction of an Afro-Cuban Cultural Identity*. Chapel Hill: University of North Carolina Press, 2004.
Rojas, Rafael. "Contra el *homo cubensis*: Transculturación y nacionalismo en la obra de Fernando Ortiz." *Cuban Studies* 35 (2004): 1–23.
———. *Isla sin fin: Contribución a la crítica del nacionalismo cubano*. Miami: Ediciones Universal, 1998.
Romeu, Raquel. *Voces de mujeres en las letras cubanas*. Madrid: Editorial Verbum, 2000.
Rosaldo, Renato. *Culture and Truth: The Remaking of Social Analysis*. Boston: Beacon Press, 1989.
Rosenberg, Fernando J. *The Avant-Garde and Geopolitics in Latin America*. Pittsburgh: University of Pittsburgh Press, 2006.
Routon, Kenneth. *Hidden Powers of State in the Cuban Imagination*. Gainesville: University Press of Florida, 2010.
Roy, Maya. *Cuban Music: From Son and Rumba to the Buena Vista Social Club and Timba Cubana*. Princeton, N.J.: Markus Wiener Publishers, 2002.
Russ, Elizabeth Christine. *The Plantation in the Postslavery Imagination*. Oxford: Oxford University Press, 2009.
Said, Edward W. *Culture and Imperialism*. New York: Vintage Books, 1993.
Santana, Joaquín G. *El joven Guillén*. Havana: Editorial Abril, 1987.

Sarmiento, Domingo Faustino. *Facundo: Civilization and Barbarism: The First English Translation*. Trans. Kathleen Ross. Berkeley: University of California Press, 2003.

Schuller, R. "La etnología moderna." *Revista Bimestre Cubana*. (mayo–junio 1929): 410–17.

Scott, Rebecca J. *Slave Emancipation in Cuba: The Transition to Free Labor, 1860–1899*. Pittsburgh: University of Pittsburgh Press, 1985.

Serra, Ana. *The "New Man" in Cuba: Culture and Identity in the Revolution*. Gainesville: University Press of Florida, 2007.

Sklodowska, Elzbieta. *Espectros y espejismos: Haití en el imaginario cubano*. Frankfurt am Main: Vervuert; Madrid: Iberoamericana, 2009.

———. "Spanish American Testimonial Novel: Some Afterthoughts." 1994. Rpt. in *The Real Thing: Testimonial Discourse and Latin America*. Georg M. Gugelberger, ed. Durham: Duke University Press, 1996. 84–100.

Sifuentes-Jáuregui, Ben. *Transvestism, Masculinity, and Latin American Literature: Genders Share Flesh*. New York: Palgrave Macmillan, 2002.

Sommer, Doris. *Foundational Fictions: The National Romances of Latin America*. Berkeley: University of California Press, 1993.

———. "Rigoberta's Secrets." *Latin American Perspectives*. 18.3 (Summer 1991): 32–50.

Smalls, James. "'Race' As Spectacle in Late-Nineteenth-Century French Art and Popular Culture." *French Historical Studies*, 26.2 (Spring 2003): 351–82.

Spitta, Silvia. "Transculturation, the Caribbean, and the Cuban-American Imaginary." *Tropicalizations: Transcultural Representations of Latinidad*. Eds. Frances R. Aparicio and Susana Chávez-Silverman. Hanover: Dartmouth University Press, 1997. 160–82.

Stephens, Michelle. "What is this *Black* in Black Diaspora?" *Small Axe* 29 (July 2009): 26–38.

Stocking, George W., Jr. "The Ethnographic Sensibility of the 1920s and the Dualism of the Anthropological Tradition." *Romantic Motives: Essays on Anthopological Sensibility*. History of Anthropology, Vol. 6. Ed. George W. Stocking, Jr. Madison: University of Wisconsin Press, 1989. 208–76.

———. "Macalay, Kubary, Malinowski: Archetypes from the Dreamtime of Anthropology." *Colonial Situations: Essays on the Contextualization of Ethnographic Knowledge*. History of Anthropology, Vol. 7. Ed. George W. Stocking, Jr. Madison: University of Wisconsin Press, 1991. 9–74.

Szasz, Margaret Connell. *Between Indian and White Worlds: The Cultural Broker*. Norman: University of Oklahoma Press, 1994.

Tarica, Estelle. *The Inner Life of Mestizo Nationalism*. Minneapolis: University of Minnesota Press, 2008.

Taylor, Diana. *The Archive and the Repertoire: Performing Cultural Memory in the Americas*. Durham: Duke University Press, 2003.

Trouillot, Michel-Rolph. *Global Transformations: Anthropology and the Modern World*. New York: Palgrave Macmillan, 2003.

———. *Silencing the Past: Power and the Production of History*. Boston: Beacon Press, 1995.

Unruh, Vicky. *Latin American Vanguards: The Art of Contentious Encounters*. Berkeley: University of California Press, 1994.

Valdés Cruz, Rosa. "Mitos africanos conservados en Cuba y su tratamiento literario por Lydia Cabrera." *Chasqui* 3.1 (1982): 31–36.

Vasconcelos, José. *La raza cósmica*. 1925. *The Cosmic Race*. Trans. Didier T. Jaén. Afterword, Joseba Gabilondo. Baltimore: Johns Hopkins University Press, 1997.

Vasconcelos, Ramón. "Motivos de son." *Recopilación de textos sobre Nicolás Guillén*. Ed. Nancy Morejón. Havana: Casa de las Américas, 1974. 243–46.

Visweswaran, Kamala. *Fictions of Feminist Ethnography*. Minneapolis: University of Minnesota Press, 1994.

Vitier, Cintio. *Lo cubano en la poesía*. 1958. Havana: Editorial Letras Cubanas, 2002.

Webb, Barbara J. *Myth and History in Caribbean Fiction: Alejo Carpentier, Wilson Harris, and Édouard Glissant*. Amherst: University of Massachusetts Press, 1992.

Weiss, Jason. *The Lights of Home: A Century of Latin American Writers in Paris*. New York: Routledge, 2003.

West, Alan. *Tropics of History: Cuba Imagined*. Westport, Conn.: Bergin & Garvey, 1997.

Williams, Claudette M. *Charcoal and Cinnamon: The Politics of Color in Spanish Caribbean Literature*. Gainesville: University Press of Florida, 2000.

Williams, Lorna V. *Self and Society in the Poetry of Nicolás Guillén*. Baltimore: Johns Hopkins University Press, 1982.

Williams, Vernon J. Jr. *Rethinking Race: Franz Boas and His Contemporaries*. Lexington: University Press of Kentucky, 1996.

Wilson, Jason. "Alejo Carpentier's Re-invention of América Latina as Real and Marvelous." *A Companion to Magical Realism*. Eds. Stephen M. Hart and Wen-chin Ouyang. London: Tamesis Books, 2005. 67–78.

Yúdice, George. "*Testimonio* and Postmodernism." *The Real Thing: Testimonial Discourse and Latin America*. Ed. Georg M. Gugelberger. Durham: Duke University Press, 1996. 42–57

INDEX

Abakuá, 8, 74, 76, 84, 199n13, 200n24; Palo Monte and Santería distinguished, 56, 58–59, 196n19
"Abriendo Monte" ("Brush Clearing") (Respall Fina), 181–83, 175
"Absent presence," 3, 23, 103
"Abuelo, El" ("The Grandfather") (Guillén), 124–26
Aching, Gerard, 179–80
African American culture, 113, 143–46, 149; literature in, 105–6; place in American context, 143–44, 146–47, 167, 204n3
African art, 19, 20, 64–68, 71
African Diaspora, 43–44, 52, 70, 91
Africanía de la música folklórica de Cuba, La (*The Africanness of Cuban Folkloric Music*) (Ortiz), 30
African languages, 8, 94; *bozal*, 8; *Congó* (Bantu), 8, 169, 206n15; *Lucumí* (Yoruba), 8, 94, 131, 139, 169
African religious practices, 8, 12, 25–26. *See also* Abakuá; Afro-Cuban religious practices; Palo Monte; Santería
Afro-Cuban culture: as antimodern, 4, 38, 43; attempts at co-optation, 112; to Lydia Cabrera, 31, 33, 52–59, 68, 71, 92, 145–46; to Alejo Carpentier, 63, 66–68, 70–71, 75–79; construction by intellectuals, 1, 34; Cuban writers' relation to, 17, 20–21, 34, 108; as fundamental to Cuban culture, 1, 38, 52, 147, 149; to Gilberto González y Contreras, 3; and high culture distinguished, 3, 107; as indicator of colonialism, 14–15; *mestizaje* and, 23–24; to Fernando Ortiz, 30, 31, 42, 68; as source for Cubanness, 1, 15, 25; as unique to Cuba, 4, 20–21, 38, 91, 108. *See also* Afro-Cuban music; Afro-Cuban religious practices; Afro-Cubans
Afrocubanismo (Afro-Cubanism): 2, 112, 143; 189n4; vogue for in 1920s and 1930s Cuba, 2, 12, 35, 107, 111, 149
Afro-Cuban music, 47, 63, 66, 76, 141, 149; bongo drums, 75–76; *comparsa*, 12, 71, 139–40, 191n21, 204n23; French vogue for, 63, 66–67, 71; repression of, 12, 71, 140, 191n21, 204n23; *rumba*, 63, 122–23, 140; *son*, 12, 26, 71, 107–9, 113–18; as source of authenticity, 76, 79
Afro-Cuban religious practices: description of ceremonies, 45–46, 56–57, 77–78, 161, 165, 201n27; different practices distinguished, 56, 58–59, 196n19; importance of *el Monte*, 33, 54–57, 164–65; official repression of, 12, 47–48, 72, 140, 200n23; relationship between physical and spiritual worlds, 93, 95; as represented by Lydia Cabrera, 25–26, 30, 52–59, 92, 132–33, 146, 171; as represented by Alejo Carpentier, 77–78; as represented by Fernando Ortiz, 25–26, 34, 39–48; role in Cuban society, 52; as source of authenticity, 76, 79; visibility in Cuba since the Special Period, 208n3. *See also* Abakuá; Lydia Cabrera; Palo Monte; Santería
Afro-Cubans: agency, 32, 52, 61; definition and use of term, 189n2; geographical integration, 15; marginalization, 11, 52; middle class, 11; participation in War for Independence, 7–8; presence in national space, 1, 3–4, 71; voting rights, 11. *See also* Afro-Cuban culture; Afro-Cuban music; Afro-Cuban religious practices

228 / Index

Alonso, Carlos, 69, 191n26, 192n29, 200n19
Alrededor de nuestra psicología (*Concerning Our Psychology*) (Márquez Sterling), 12
Anagó (Cabrera), 139
Anderson, Benedict, 5, 13
Anthropology, 16–19, 112, 148, 194n34, 205n10, 206n19; African Americans and, 146–47, 206n18; Alejo Carpentier and, 83; comparative approach, 44; in Cuba, 18, 24, 34, 195n8; Zora Neale Hurston and, 144–45, 153–54; Fernando Ortiz and, 4, 29–30, 34, 43, 52, 60–61, 154, 207n12; in the nineteenth century, 43–44, 195n14, 198n8; relationship to literature, 21, 193n40. See also Ethnography
Anti-history, 134–35
Antislavery novels, 5, 99
Archer Straw, Petrine, 19, 65, 199n10
Archive and the Repertoire, The (Taylor) 151–52
Archivos del Folklore Cubano (*Archives of Cuban Folklore*), 29, 30
Argonauts of the Western Pacific (Malinowski), 148
"Armchair anthropology," 35, 195n9
Arozarena, Marcelino, 1, 3, 23; "Canción negra sin color" ("Black Song without Color"), 1, 3
Arroyo, Jossianna, 46, 76, 201n27
"Artist-ethnographers," 2–3, 4, 6, 15
Authenticity, 14, 15, 26, 191n26
Autochthony, 191n26
Autoethnography, 17, 193n36
Avant-garde (movements), 19–20, 26, 193n39; in Cuba, 20–21, 68, 69–71, 106, 108; ethnography and, 66; in Europe 19–20, 65–67, 70–71 (and the primitive, 19–21, 26, 64–67, 70–75); in Latin America, 69–70, 191n25, 193n39

Bailes y el teatro de los negros en el folklore de Cuba, Los (*Black Dance and Theatre in Cuban Folklore*) (Ortiz), 47, 197n24
Bakhtin, Mikhail, 140, 142, 202n1
"Balada de los dos abuelos" ("Ballad of the Two Grandfathers") (Guillén), 124
Ballagas, Emilio, 2, 31, 111
Bantu. See *Congó*
Barnet, Miguel, 174–75, 177–81, 187–88; *Biografía de un cimarrón* (*Biography of a Runaway Slave*), 178–81

Bataille, George, 198n9
Behar, Ruth, 192n35; *Women Writing Culture*, 192n35
Benítez Rojo, Antonio, 50
Bernabe, Jean, 23
Beverley, John, 177, 189n7
Bhabha, Homi, 13
Bifur, 69, 80
Biografía de un cimarrón (*Biography of a Runaway Slave*) (Barnet), 178–81
Biological determinism, 18, 34–36, 39. See also Criminology; Eugenics
Birkenmaier, Anke, 77, 78, 80, 86
Black Cubans: definition and use of term, 189n2. See also Afro-Cubans
"Black internationalism," 20, 67
Blackness: after Cuban Revolution, 28, 174; as antimodern, 76, 84; in Cuban letters, 3, 147; definition and use of term, 189n2; European fascination with, 19–20, 64–68, 70, 198n6; to Lydia Cabrera, 64, 73, 91–92, 103, 111, 129–30, 202n35; to Alejo Carpentier, 64, 73–74, 76, 79–82, 84–88, 102–3; to Nicolás Guillén, 107, 109, 112, 117, 123–24, 188; to Latin American writers, 20, 70; in narratives of hybridity, 23–24; to Fernando Ortiz, 25, 29, 33, 35, 39–40, 51; and primitiveness, 65, 70–71, 74, 79, 102; symbolic function, 26; in United States, 104–5, 143–47
Blake, Jody, 67, 71
"Blanco: he ahí el problema, El" ("The White Man: That's the Problem") (Guillén), 113
Boas, Franz: as ethnographer, 16, 195n10, 205n10, 206n19; as mentor, 144, 150, 153–55, 157, 204n2, 205n9. See also Zora Neale Hurston, *Mules and Men*
Bozal, 8
Branche, Jerome, 201n27
Brathwaite, Edward Kamau, 23
Brazil, 43–44, 192n31, 193n37, 193n41
"Bregantino Bregantín" (Cabrera), 91–92, 95–97
Breton, André, 68, 198n7, 198n9, 200n17
Brown, David, 204n22
Brujería (witchcraft) 39–47, 196n19
Brujos (witches), 12, 38, 47–48, 59, 191n22
Buck-Morss, Susan, 201n30

Cabildos (African cultural organizations), 8, 11, 97, 139–41, 190n12, 198n1, 204n22

Cabrera, Lydia: Afro-Cuban music and, 92, 139–41; Afro-Cuban religion (representation of, 25, 33, 92, 132–33, 164–65) (research into, 30–31, 160–65, 168, 181, 186, 199n14, 207n24); *Anagó*, 139; blackness and, 25–27, 64, 73, 91–92, 103, 111, 129–30, 202n35; "Bregantino Bregantín," 91–92, 95–97; "Chéggue," 91; class and, 17, 26, 60; class discourse and, 32, 61, 73, 141, 162, 171; "Los Compadres" ("The Pals"), 92–95; Cuba as audience, 17; *Cuentos negros de Cuba* (*Afro-Cuban Tales*), 26–27, 30, 51, 91–102, 107, 112, 131–42; Teresa de la Parra and, 30, 69, 200n18; difficulty in categorizing, 24; education, 4, 30, 51, 64, 69, 145–46; as ethnographer, 24, 146–49, 150–58, 162, 169–72, 181, 183; Europe as audience, 17; exile in Miami, 28, 174–75, 181, 182–83, 185–86, 187; experimentation and, 24–25, 27, 170; "Eya," 91; family, 24, 30, 69, 129, 204n17; fieldwork and, 199n13; folktales, 51–52, 91–92, 129, 131, 134–35, 142, 153; gender issues and, 24, 27, 147, 150, 155, 156, 158, 160–61, 170; "Hay hombres blancos, pardos y negros" ("Why There Are White, Brown, and Black Men"), 100–102; historical context and, 54, 56; *La lengua sagrada de los ñañigos* (*The Sacred Language of the Ñañigos*), 200n24; "El limo del Almendares" ("The Mud of the Almendares"), 97; "La Loma de Mambiala" ("Mambiala Hill"), 92; methodology, 53, 54–55, 59, 61; *El Monte* (*The Bush*), 27, 31, 51–60, 147–51, 152–57, 161–65, 168–71; morality and, 58–59, 92; narrative structuring devices, 55–58; national culture and, 173–74; "Nena en sociedad" ("Baby in Society"), 69; Fernando Ortiz and, 24–25, 30–32, 51, 61, 154–55, 181, 194n4; Paris and, 30, 64, 69, 103, 111, 145; paternalism, 58–60, 61; personal narrative and, 158, 160–62; *Por qué... cuentos negros de Cuba* (*Why... Afro-Cuban Tales*) 26, 100–102; "La prodigiosa gallina de Guinea" ("The Prodigious Guinea Hen"), 138–42; racial hierarchy and, 98, 101–2; Signifyin(g) by, 106–7, 130, 134–35, 137, 138–42; *La sociedad secreta abakuá narrada por viejos adeptos* (*The Abakuá Secret Society Narrated by Old Experts*), 31, 181, 200n24; Surrealism and, 69, 200n17; "Taita Hicotea y Taita Tigre" ("Papa Turtle and Papa Tiger"), 134–38; *testimonio* and, 181–82; as translator, 51, 91, 129–30, 155–58, 168–69; use of African-derived language, 94; use of informants, 53, 62, 156–57, 160–62, 164, 168, 171, 181–82 (Omí–Tomí [Teresa M.] and, 160–61); use of silence, 165–69; use of spatial framework, 25, 32, 55–56; use of temporal framework, 32, 97–98, 134–35, 145; "Walo-Wila," 91, 92; wordplay and, 26–27, 91, 106, 112–13, 130, 134, 141–42; *Yemayá y Ochún*, 183–86

Cabrera, Raimundo, 24, 30, 69, 129, 203n17. *See also Cuba y América*

Cahier d'un retour au pays natal (*Notebook of a Return to the Native Land*) (Césaire), 20, 67

Cahiers du Sud, 63

Calesero (coachman-slave), 97, 98–100, 202n38

"Caminando" ("Walking") (Guillén), 126

"Camino de Harlem, El" ("Harlem's Road") (Guillén), 113

"Caña" ("Sugar Cane") (Guillén), 122

"Canción negra sin color" ("Black Song without Color") (Arozarena), 1, 3

Carnival, 140, 142, 202n1

Carpentier, Alejo, 4; Afro-Cuban music and, 63, 66–67, 71, 75–76; Afro-Cuban religion and, 76–79; avant-garde and, 68–69, 71–74, 75–76; ballets, 200n16, 200n20; blackness and, 72, 73–74, 102–3; Lydia Cabrera and, 24–25, 181; comparative approach, 91–102; "De lo real maravilloso americano" ("On the American Marvelous Real"), 85–87; Robert Desnos and, 66–68; *Documents*, 66; *Écue-Yamba-Ó*, 2, 26, 72, 73–84; as ethnographer, 17, 72–73, 77, 78; exile in Paris, 63, 68, 73; exile in Venezuela, 207n2; family, 68; Haiti and, 80, 85–87; hybrid texts, 73–74; Jacqueline texts, 199n14; as journalist, 68–69, 199n14; "Lettre des Antilles," 80; literary *Afrocubanismo* and, 2; the marvelous real, 85–87 (conflict between Old and New worldviews, 86–87); member of Grupo Minorista, 68; "La musique cubaine" ("Cuban Music"), 66–67; national culture

Carpentier, Alejo—*continued*
  and, 72, 173–74; nationalism vs. avant-garde, 69–71, 188; the primitive and, 72–74, 75–76; Fernando Ortiz and, 181, 201n27; *El reino de este mundo* (*The Kingdom of This World*), 26, 73, 84–90; representation of Haitians, 79–80, 201n26; role in revolutionary government, 174, 207n2; "La Rue Fontaine," 63; Santería and, 181, 199n13; Surrealism and, 66, 68–69, 73, 77, 86; use of photographs, 77–78
Carteles, 63, 71, 86, 199n14
Cassou, Jean, 63, 71
Castellanos, Israel, 198n5
Castro, Fidel, 173, 175, 181, 184, 208n4. *See also* Cuban Revolution
Cecilia Valdés o la Loma del Ángel (*Cecilia Valdes or El Angel Hill*) (Villaverde), 5, 99
Césaire, Aimé, 20, 67; *Cahier d'un retour au pays natal* (*Notebook of a Return to the Native Land*), 20, 67
Céspedes, Carlos Manuel de, 7
Chacón y Calvo, José María, 37
Chamoiseau, Patrick, 23, 133–34, 204n21
Chatterjee, Partha, 5–6, 190n9
"Chéggue" (Cabrera), 91
Choteo (Cuban improvised wordplay), 104–7, 113–17, 125–26, 202n1; connections to Afro-Cuban culture, 104
Civilization and barbarism, 38, 196n17
Clifford, James, 16–17, 20, 66, 152, 192nn34, 35, 66; *Writing Culture: The Poetics and Politics of Ethnography*, 192n35
Club Atenas, 11, 97, 191n19
Coachman-slave. *See Calesero*
Coevalness, 14–15, 16, 201n29
Collares (ritual necklaces), 45, 197n23
"Color cubano" (Cuban color), 23
"Compadres, Los" ("The Pals") (Cabrera), 92–95
Comparsa (Afro-Cuban carnival band), 12, 71, 139–40, 191n21, 204n23
Confiant, Raphaël, 23, 133–34, 204n21
Congó (Bantu), 8, 169, 206n15
"Conquista del blanco, La" ("The Conquest of the White Man") (Guillén), 113
Contact zone, 17, 20–21, 23, 60, 150, 170–71, 205n6

Contrapunteo cubano del tabaco y el azúcar (*Cuban Counterpoint: Tobacco and Sugar*) (Ortiz), 25, 30, 33, 39, 48–51, 61–62
Convulsion cubana, La (*The Cuban Convulsion*) (Garrigó, Márquez Sterling, and Figueras), 12
Coronado, Jorge, 191n28
Coronil, Fernando, 49
Corps. Un (*A Body*), 68
Cotera, María Eugenia, 21, 148, 206n19, 207n20
Créolité, 23
Creolization, 23
Criminology, 18–19, 34–36, 39, 194n7, 195n11, 195n14, 198n5
Crisis de la alta cultura en Cuba, La (*The Crisis of High Culture in Cuba*) (Mañach), 37
Cuba: colonial history, 7, 9, 12–13, 24, 37; demographics, 9, 147, 204n3, 207n1; diaspora, 28, 173, 207n1; Haitian influence, 6–7; national culture, 34, 70; national narrative, 5, 6, 13, 25, 35, 173–74, 176; in the nineteenth century, 6–7; North American influence, 8–9, 10, 36, 74–76; North American occupation, 8–9, 10, 18. *See also* Cuban Independence; Cubanness; Cuban Revolution
"Cuba, negros, poesía" ("Cuba, Blacks, Poetry") (Guillén), 123
Cuban Anthropological Society, 18, 34
Cubanidad negativa (negative Cubanness), 13, 37, 41, 191n24
Cuban Independence, 7–10, 34; lateness relative to region, 4, 7, 13; North American intervention in, 8–9, 10, 18; Revolutionary rhetoric and, 176
Cubanness, 1, 13, 15, 20; Fernando Ortiz and, 29, 35, 60
Cuban Revolution, 27–28, 173–74; 26 of July Movement, 173; center of national narrative, 174. *See also* Cuban revolutionary government
Cuban Revolutionary government: antiracism and, 28, 175–76; Alejo Carpentier and, 174, 207n2; ethnography and, 174; folklore and, 176–77, 208n4; Nicolás Guillén and, 174, 207n2; Independence and rhetoric, 176; intellectual and literary production under, 173, 208n4
Cuba y América, 30, 69, 204n17

Cuentos negros de Cuba (*Afro-Cuban Tales*) (Cabrera), 26–27, 30, 51, 91–102, 107, 112, 131–42; "Bregantino Bregantín," 91–92, 95–97; "Chéggue," 91; "Los Compadres" ("The Pals"), 92–95; "Eya," 91; foreword by Fernando Ortiz, 51–53, 91, 95, 129, 154–56, 181; French edition, 51, 64, 69, 111, 197n26, 203n7; "El limo del Almendares" ("The Mud of the Almendares"), 97; "La Loma de Mambiala" ("Mambiala Hill"), 92; "La prodigiosa gallina de Guinea" ("The Prodigious Guinea Hen"), 138–42; "Taita Hicotea y Taita Tigre" ("Papa Turtle and Papa Tiger"), 134–38; traditional folktales compared, 107, 129; "Walo-Wila," 91, 92, 131–34

de Andrade, Oswald, 196n16; *Manifesto Antropófago*, 196n16; *Manifesto da Poesia Pau Brasil*, 196n16
de Certeau, Michel, 16, 192n33
"Declaración del Grupo Minorista" (Minorista Manifesto), 68, 199n15
Decline of the West, The (Spengler), 191n25
De Costa Willis, Miriam, 204n1
de la Fuente, Alejandro, 11, 175
de la Parra, Teresa, 30, 69, 200n18
"De lo real maravilloso americano" ("On the American Marvelous Real") (Carpentier), 85
Deloria, Ella Cara, 24, 205n9
de Melo, Alfredo Cesar B., 32
de Miomandre, Francis, 63, 69
Department of Anthropology and Anthropometric Exercises, University of Havana, 18, 29, 195n8
Desnos, Robert, 66–67, 68, 71
"Diálogos imaginarios" ("Imaginary Dialogues") (Martínez Furé), 176–77
Dianteill, Erwan, 207n23
Diario de la Marina, 107, 111, 203n15
Dirks, Nicholas, 198n8
Diversion, 105–6, 133
Documents, 20, 66, 69, 77–78, 199n10
"Dos niños" ("Two Children") (Guillén), 124
Douglas, Ann, 147
Drewal, Margaret, 202n4
Duno Gottberg, Luis, 22, 195n13

Écue-Yamba-Ó (Carpentier), 2, 26, 72–85
Edwards, Brent Hayes, 20, 22, 67
Ellis, Keith, 116
Engaño de las razas, El (*The Lie of Races*) (Ortiz), 30
Estudios Afrocubanos (*Afro-Cuban Studies*), 29, 30, 32, 52, 155, 194n3, 201n31, 206n12
Ethnographic scenario, 148–52, 156, 160, 163–65, 167, 170
Ethnography, 15–20, 21–22, 201n29; in Cuba, 17–18; development of, 15–16, 19, 21–22, 148–52; ethnographic authority, 27, 148–58; "ethnographic literature," 22; "ethnographic spirit," 21; European avant-garde movement and, 66; experimentation and, 4, 21–22; feminist, 205n8; fieldwork and, 16, 19; gender and, 27, 146, 147–48, 150, 192n35, 205n9; informants and, 47, 179; limits, 27, 152, 169–70; link to colonialist and imperialist expansion, 15–16; participant observation, 26, 35, 152, 192n34, 205n10; personal narrative and, 158–59; the primitive and, 15–18, 38, 43–44, 66, 83–84, 149, 195n14; relation to arts, 19; relation to literature, 4, 21, 174; self-awareness and, 16–17, 192n35; Surrealism and, 66; Universal Exhibitions and, 66; use of informants in, 35. *See also* Anthropology; Autoethnography; Criminology; Eugenics
Eugenics, 18–19, 34–36, 193n37, 195n14
Europe: as audience for Cuban writers, 12–14, 36–38, 51, 68, 71, 92, 196n16; as model, 6, 13–14, 36, 37
"Eya" (Cabrera), 91

Fabian, Johannes, 16, 201n29
Facundo: civilización y barbarie en las Pampas argentinas (*Facundo: Civilization and Barbarism*) (Sarmiento), 196n17
Fernandes, Sujatha, 208n3
Ferrer, Ada, 7, 10
Fetishism, 42–43, 44, 56, 59, 195n7. *See also* Afro-Cuban religious practices
Figueras, Francisco, 12, 37; *La convulsion cubana* (*The Cuban Convulsion*), 12
Filiation, 13–14
Fischer, Sibylle, 7
"Floating signifier," 72

Folklore, 2–3, 44, 129, 149–50, 176–77, 189n5, 206n19, 208n4
Folktale, 91–92, 97, 107, 128–30, 134–35, 159; Lydia Cabrera and, 51–52, 91–92, 129, 131, 134–35, 142, 153
Forewords. *See* Prefaces
France, 19, 24, 63–71; African colonization, 64–65, 67
Francisco (Súarez y Romero), 98
Frazer, James, 44, 195n9; *The Golden Bough*, 44, 195n9
Freyre, Gilberto, 193n41, 205n10

Gallegos, Rómulo, 110
Gallimard publishing house, 51, 63, 111, 197n26
García-Carranza, Araceli, 199n13
García Caturla, Alejandro, 199n13, 200n20
Garrigó, Roque E., 12; *La convulsion cubana* (*The Cuban Convulsion*), 12
Gates, Henry Louis Jr., 26, 104–6, 137, 163, 203n12
Giacometti, Alberto, 20
Glissant, Édouard, 13–14, 102, 105–6, 133, 134–35
Glosario de afronegrismos (*Glossary of Black-African Vocabulary*) (Ortiz), 30, 198n1
Golden Bough, The (Frazer), 44, 195n9
Gómez, Juan Gualberto, 10, 191n18
Gómez de Avellaneda, Gertrudis, 5, 99; *Sab*, 5, 99
González Echevarría, Roberto, 73, 76, 126
González Mandri, Flora, 24, 194n44
González y Contreras, Gilberto, 1–4, 6, 14, 15, 21, 189n3; "La poesía negra" ("Black Poetry"), 1–4, 6
Gordon, Deborah 192n35; *Women Writing Culture*, 192n35
Graff Zivin, Erin, 72
Grafos, 131
"Grito de Yara," 7
Grupo Minorista, 68, 199n15; "Declaración del Grupo Minorista" (Minorista Manifesto), 199n15
"Guerrita del '12" (Little War of 1912), 11
Guillén, Nicolás, 4; "El Abuelo" ("The Grandfather"), 124–26; "Balada de los dos abuelos" ("Ballad of the Two Grandfathers"), 124; blackness and, 107, 109, 112, 117, 123–24, 188; "El blanco: he ahí el problema" ("The White Man: That's the Problem"), 113; Lydia Cabrera and, 24–25; "Caminando" ("Walking"), 126; "El camino de Harlem" ("Harlem's Road"), 113; "Caña" ("Sugar Cane"), 122; *choteo* and, 106, 113, 115–17, 125, 126; "Color cubano" (Cuban color), 23; "La conquista del blanco" ("The Conquest of the White Man"), 113; "Cuba, negros, poesía" ("Cuba, Blacks, Poetry"), 123; Cuban texts and, 106–8; "Dos niños" ("Two Children"), 124; exile, 207n2; historical context and, 112; hybridity and, 22–23, 117, 123; literary *Afrocubanismo* and, 2, 107–8; "Llegada" ("Arrival"), 127; mixture of high and popular cultures, 27, 106, 107, 112–13; *Motivos de son* (*Son Motifs*), 26–27, 106–9, 111–18, 123, 128, 203n5; musical form and, 107–8, 113, 116, 117–18, 120–22; national culture and, 106–8, 173–74; "Negro bembón" ("Big Lipped Nigga"), 113–17, 128; "poesía criolla" (Creole poetry), 117, 128; "poesía mulata" (mulatto poetry), 117; role in Revolutionary government, 174, 207n2; "Rumba," 122–23; "Secuestro de la mujer de Antonio" ("The Kidnapping of Antonio's Wife"), 118–23; "Sensemayá," 126; Signifyin(g) by, 26–27, 106–7, 109, 115, 117–18, 122, 124–28, 141–42, 203n12; "El son de los que protestaron contra el son" ("The Son of Those Who Protested the Son"), 108; "Sones y Soneros," 108–9; *Sóngoro cosongo*, 23, 26–27, 107, 112, 117–23, 127, 130; "Tú no sabe inglé" ("You Don't Know No English"), 128; use of dichotomies, 123–24, 126; use of local dialect, 108–9, 112, 113, 115; use of *son* form, 107–9, 113–18, 122; Ramón Vasconcelos and, 107–9; *West Indies, Ltd.*, 26–27, 107, 112, 123–28; "West Indies, Ltd.," 126–28, 138; wordplay and, 26–27, 106–7, 113, 141–42
Güiraldes, Ricardo, 110
Guirao, Ramón, 2, 31, 111, 122–23, 203n15

Haiti, 6–7, 80, 85–87; colonial history, 87; and Cuba compared, 80; as exotic, 201n31; revolution in, 6–7, 80, 85, 87, 90, 201n30; as hemispheric other, 87
Hall, Stuart, 72
Hampa afrocubana: Los negros brujos (*Afro-Cuban Underworld: Black Witches*) (Ortiz), 25, 30–36, 38–48, 68, 191n22, 201n27, 206n12
Harlem Renaissance, 143–44, 149, 204n2

"Hay hombres blancos, pardos y negros" ("Why There Are White, Brown, and Black Men") (Cabrera), 100–102
Hemenway, Robert, 204n4
Hernández, Graciela, 160
Herskovits, Melville, 205n10, 206n18
Hewitt, Nicholas, 198n3
Hoffman-Jeep, Lynda, 148–49, 151, 171, 204n1
"Homiculture," 18, 193n38
hooks, bell, 157
Hurston, Zora Neale, 157–60, 163–67, 170–72, 201n31; academic training, 144–45, 150, 153–54; Franz Boas and, 144, 150, 153–55, 157, 204n2, 205n9; comparison to Lydia Cabrera, 144; as ethnographer, 27, 146, 148–49, 150–53, 158, 160, 163–64, 169–72; experimentation and, 27, 170; folklore collection, 150, 157–60, 163–64, 207n21; funding, 149, 157, 204n2, 204n4, 206n17; gender issues and, 24, 27, 147, 150, 155, 158–60, 163, 170; Hoodoo and, 167; as insider-outsider, 148–50; *Mules and Men*, 27, 144–45, 147, 150–51, 153–54, 157–60, 163–67; relationship to community studied, 144–45, 147, 149; southern origins, 144–45, 147, 149, 153–54, 159, 171; *Tell My Horse*, 201n31; *Their Eyes Were Watching God*, 163, 205n5; use of informants, 159–60, 164; use of silence, 165–67; "Why Women Always Take Advantage of Men," 163
Hybridity, 21–25, 26, 53, 193n41, 195n13; in work of Alejo Carpentier, 74; in work of Fernando Ortiz, 39, 53

"Ideales de una raza" ("Ideals of a Race"), 111, 203n15
Imagined community, 5–6, 15
Indagación del choteo (*Investigation of the Choteo*) (Mañach), 104–6
Independence. *See* Cuban Independence
Independent Party of Color (Partido Independiente de Color, or PIC), 10
Indigenismo (indigenism), 14, 191n28
"Insider-outsiders," 148–50, 171, 204n1
Instrumentos de la música afrocubana, Los (*Instruments of Afro-Cuban Music*) (Ortiz), 30
Insularismo negativo. *See* Cubanidad negativa; Negative insularity
Intertextuality, 26

Jameson, Fredric, 21; *The Political Unconscious*, 21
Jirousek, Lori, 151

King, Louis Eugene, 206n18
Kutzinski, Vera, 22, 99, 112

Lachatañeré, Rómulo, 194n3; "El sistema religioso de los lucumís" ("The Lucumí Religious System"), 194n3; *Manual de Santería* (*Santería Manual*), 194n3; *¡¡Oh!, mío Yemayá!!*, 197n26
Landes, Ruth, 24, 205n9
Lane, Jill, 99, 195n7
Lang, Andrew, 44
"Légitime défense," 67, 199n11
Leiris, Michel, 20
Lengua sagrada de los ñáñigos, La (*The Sacred Language of the Ñáñigos*) (Cabrera), 201n24
León, Argeliers, 197n24
"Lettre des Antilles" (Carpentier), 80
Levine, Suzanne Jill, 200n17
Leys Stepan, Nancy, 18
"Limo del Almendares, El" ("The Mud of the Almendares") (Cabrera), 97–99
"Llegada" ("Arrival") (Guillén), 127
Lo cubano en la poesía (*Cubanness in poetry*) (Vitier), 203n5
"Loma de Mambiala, La" ("Mambiala Hill") (Cabrera), 92
Lombroso, Césare, 18, 36, 38–39, 51, 53, 195n14
Lucumí (Yoruba): cultural practices, 134, 161, 194n3, 204n18, 206n15; language, 8, 94, 131, 139, 169
Ludmer, Josefina, 156
Luis, William, 5, 97–99

Maceo, Antonio, 8
Machado, Gerardo, 63, 68, 199n15
Magic Island, The (Seabrook), 86, 201n31
Malinowski, Bronislaw, 16, 148, 152, 170, 195n10, 205n10; *Argonauts of the Western Pacific*, 148
Mañach, Jorge, 37–38, 104–6, 202nn2, 3; *La crisis de la alta cultura en Cuba* (*The Crisis of High Culture in Cuba*), 37; *Indagación del choteo* (*Investigation of the Choteo*), 104–6, 202nn2, 3
Manifesto Antropófago (de Andrade), 196n16
Manifesto da Poesia Pau Brasil (de Andrade), 196n16

Manual de Santería (*Santería Manual*) (Lachatañeré), 194n3

Manzano, Juan Francisco, 98

Marcone, Jorge, 203n11

Marcus, George, 192n35; *Writing Culture: The Poetics and Politics of Ethnography*, 192n35

Márquez Sterling, Manuel, 12; *Alrededor de nuestra psicología* (*Concerning Our Psychology*), 12; *La convulsion cubana* (*The Cuban Convulsion*), 12

Marronage, 179, 201n31

Martí, José, 9–10; "Mi raza" ("My Race"), 10; "Nuestra América" ("Our America"), 9–10

Martínez, Prudencio, 8

Martínez Furé, Rogelio, 176–77, 188, 208n4; "Diálogos imaginarios" ("Imaginary Dialogues"), 176–77

Marvelous real, the, 85–87, 90

Mason, Charlotte Osgood, 149, 157, 204n2, 204n4, 206n17

Mauss, Marcel, 20, 198n9

Mead, Margaret, 205nn9, 10

Mestizaje, 22, 23

Mestre, Arístides, 18

Metropole, 19, 20, 33, 64

Minstrelsy (blackface performance), 65

Mintz, Sidney, 15

Molloy, Sylvia, 200n18

Montané, Luis, 18

Monte, El (*The Bush*) (Cabrera), 27, 31, 51–60, 147–51, 152–57, 161–65, 168–71; informants, 53, 156–57, 160–62, 164, 171, 181–82 (Omí-Tomí (Teresa M.), 160–61); preface, 53–54, 154, 156–57, 181–82; structure of, 25, 54–58, 164–65; *Monte, el* (center of Afro-Cuban religion), 33, 54–57, 59, 96, 164–65, 182

Montejo, Esteban, 178–80, 187. *See also Biografía de un cimarrón*

Moore, Robin, 11–12, 71, 99–100, 202n38

Morejón, Nancy, 116

Morúa Delgado, Martín, 10–11, 98

Morúa Law, the, 11

Motivos de son (*Son Motifs*) (Guillén), 26–27, 106–9, 111–18, 123, 128, 203n5; "Negro bembón" ("Big Lipped Nigga"), 113–17, 128; "Tú no sabe inglé" ("You Don't Know No English"), 128

Mulata (mulatta), 98–100

Mules and Men (Hurston), 27, 144–45, 147, 150–51, 153–54, 157–60, 163–67; introduction by Franz Boas, 153–55, 157

Mullen, Edward, 35

Muñoz-Basols, Javier, 85

"Musique cubaine, La" ("Cuban Music") (Carpentier), 66–67

"Myth of racial democracy," 11

Nairn, Tom, 12

Ñáñigo. *See* Abakuá

Nation: as concept, 6, 12–13; and national anxiety, 13, 18, 26, 53; and national culture, 13–15; and national future, 23; and race in the national space, 18, 27; as strategy, 6, 13

National narrative, 5, 6, 13, 20, 25, 35, 173–74, 176. *See also* Nation; Fernando Ortiz

Negative insularity, 37, 41, 191n24, 202n3. *See also Cubanidad negativa*

Negrista poetry, 31, 111–12, 122–23, 203n5

Négritude, 20, 67

"Negro bembón" ("Big Lipped Nigga") (Guillén), 113–17, 128

Negro de nación (African-born slave), 74

Negro Francisco, El (*Black Francisco*) (Zambrana), 5

Negrophilia, 65. *See also* Blackness

Negros curros, Los (*Black Dandies*) (Ortiz), 195n12

Negros esclavos, Los (*Black Slaves*) (Ortiz), 30, 195n12

Nina Rodrigues, Raimundo, 43, 196n22

Niña Zoila, 191n22

Nineteenth-century literature, 5, 6–10

Novás Calvos, Lino, 57

Novelas de la tierra (novels of the land), 110, 112

Novela-testimonio. *See* Testimonio

Nuestra Señora de Regla (Our Lady of Regla), 184–85. *See also* Orichas

¡¡Oh, mío Yemayá!! (Lachatañeré), 197n26

Orichas (Afro-Cuban gods), 44–45, 55, 77, 93–96, 164–65, 183–86, 202n36; Babalú-Ayé, 78; Changó (*oricha* of lightning and thunder), 56, 93, 95, 161; Elegguá (*oricha* of the crossroads), 57; Ochosi (hunter *oricha*), 133; Ochún (*oricha* of fresh water), 78, 93, 95, 183–86; Olokun (*oricha* of the ocean depths), 132, 134, 185; relationship to Catholic saints, 78, 184–86, 207n22; Yemayá (*oricha* of the ocean), 93, 95, 183–86. *See also* Santería

Ortiz, Fernando: *La africanía de la música folklórica de Cuba* (*The Africanness of Cuban Folkloric Music*), 30; Afro-Cuban culture and, 29–30, 38, 42–43, 47, 61–62, 173–74; Afro-Cuban religious practices and, 30, 32, 40, 45–48, 59–60, 196n19; anxiety and, 38, 39–40, 53; *Archivos del Folklore Cubano* (*Archives of Cuban Folklore*), 29, 30; *Los bailes y el teatro de los negros en el folklore de Cuba* (*Black Dance and Theatre in Cuban Folklore*), 47, 197n24; Miguel Barnet and, 174–75; blackness and, 25, 29, 33, 35, 39–40, 51; *brujería*, 39–47; Lydia Cabrera and, 24–25, 30–32, 51–52, 61, 154–55, 181, 194n4; Alejo Carpentier and, 181; comparative approach, 43–45, 47; *Contrapunteo cubano del tabaco y el azúcar* (*Cuban Counterpoint: Tobacco and Sugar*), 25, 30, 33, 39, 48–51, 61–62; criminology and, 35, 38–39, 40, 195n11, 201n27; Cuban national culture and, 30, 34, 48, 60–62, 173–74; Cubanness, 29, 35, 60; education, 29, 34, 194n5; *El engaño de las razas* (*The Lie of Races*), 30; *Estudios Afrocubanos* (*Afro-Cuban Studies*), 29, 30; as ethnographer, 6, 30, 35, 47, 50; Europe as audience, 36–38, 51, 196n16; as founder of Cuban anthropology, 4, 29–30, 34, 52, 60–61, 154, 207n12; *Glosario de afronegrismos* (*Glossary of Black–African Vocabulary*), 30, 198n1; *Hampa afrocubana: Los negros brujos* (*Afro-Cuban Underworld: Black Witches*), 25, 30–36, 38–48, 68, 191n22, 201n27, 206n12; historical context and, 40, 42–43, 45, 49–50, 56, 61; hybridity and, 22–23, 25, 39, 195n30; *Los instrumentos de la música afrocubana* (*Instruments of Afro-Cuban Music*), 30; Césare Lombroso and, 36, 38–39; morality and, 46; national narrative and, 25, 30, 34–35, 51, 60–62; *Los negros curros* (*Black Dandies*), 195n12; *Los negros esclavos* (*Black Slaves*), 30, 195n12; polyethnicity, 39–40, 60; positivism and, 25, 32, 38, 42–43, 45; preface to *Cuentos Negros*, 51–52, 53, 91, 95, 129, 154–55; *Surco* (*Track*), 29; transculturation, 23, 39, 48, 50, 62, 176–77; use of dichotomies, 32, 36, 38, 48–49; use of informants, 35, 47, 191n22, 197n24, 201n27; use of spatial framework, 25, 32, 35, 38–39, 40–43; use of temporal framework, 25, 32, 35, 38–39, 40–43, 57

Ortiz Herrera, María Fernanda, 29

Palmié, Stefan, 15, 192n32
Palo Monte, 8, 12, 56, 58–59, 137–38, 196n19; origin, 206n15. *See also* Afro-Cuban religious practices
Pancrazio, James, 89, 90, 201n34
Paravisini-Gebert, Lizabeth, 87
Paris, 20, 63–71, 145, 198n3
Patakíes (religious tales), 56, 93, 95, 197n26
Pavloska, Susanna, 65, 163, 166
Peláez, Amelia, 69
Pérez Firmat, Gustavo, 29, 48, 50, 125
Performance, 105, 151–52, 202n4, 203n11; in texts studied, 115, 126–27, 141, 157, 163–65; "speakerly text" and, 163
Periphery, 33
Plantation system, 7, 8, 15, 33, 110
Platt Amendment, the, 9, 10, 36
Play (textual improvisation), 26, 112–13, 141–42, 202n4
"Poesía criolla" (Creole poetry), 117, 128
"Poesía mulata" (mulatto poetry), 117
"Poesía negra, La" ("Black Poetry") (González y Contreras), 1–4, 6
Political Unconscious, The (Jameson), 21
Polyethnicity, 39
Por qué . . . cuentos negros de Cuba (*Why . . . Afro-Cuban Tales*) (Cabrera), 26, 100–102; "Hay hombres blancos, pardos y negros" ("Why There Are White, Brown, and Black Men"), 100–102
Positivism, 25, 32, 38, 196n18; in work of Fernando Ortiz, 25, 32, 38, 42–43
Pratt, Mary Louise, 5–6, 17, 130, 152, 158, 193n36, 205n6
Prefaces, 22, 36, 51, 153–56
Primitive, the, 14, 15, 21, 43; Afro-Cuban practices as, 15, 21, 43; in avant-garde sense, 19–20, 26, 64–66, 71, 72, 74; blackness as, 65, 70–71, 74, 79, 201; ethnography and, 15–18, 38, 43–44, 66, 83–84, 149, 195n14; in work of Alejo Carpentier, 26, 72–74, 81–83, 86–87, 90, 102

"Prodigiosa gallina de Guinea, La" ("The Prodigious Guinea Hen") (Cabrera), 138–42

Quiroga, José, 58, 169

Racial determinism, 18, 190n15. *See also* Eugenics
Rama, Angel, 4
Ramos, Domingo F., 18, 193n38
Raza cósmica, La (*The Cosmic Race*) (Vasconcelos), 193n41
Regla de Ochá. *See* Santería
Reino de este mundo, El (*The Kingdom of This World*) (Carpentier), 26, 73, 84–90
Relation, 14, 102
Renda, Mary, 201n31
Republic of letters (*ciudad letrada*), 4, 24, 189n7
Respall Fina, Raimundo, 175, 181–83; "Abriendo Monte" ("Brush Clearing"), 175, 181–83, 175
Revista Bimestre Cubana, 52, 189n3, 206n13
Revista de Avance, 68
Rivera, José Eustacio, 110
Rodríguez-Mangual, Edna, 24, 32, 61, 151, 156, 164, 181, 194n44, 202n35
Rojas, Rafael, 13, 37
Roldán, Amadeo, 200n20
Rosaldo, Renato, 16–17, 206n16
Routon, Kenneth, 208n3
"Rue Fontaine, La" (Carpentier), 63
Rumba, 63, 122–23, 140
"Rumba" (Guillén), 122–23
Russ, Elizabeth, 49

Sab (Gómez de Avellaneda), 5, 99, 190n8
Said, Edward, 67
Santería, 8, 12, 76–78, 181, 196n19; Lydia Cabrera's research into, 30–31, 58–59, 161–62, 164–65, 183–86, 199n13, 207n24; origin, 204n18, 206n15; Fernando Ortiz's research into, 47–48, 181, 196n19; in work of Lydia Cabrera, 56, 137–38, 186. *See also* Afro-Cuban religious practices
Sarmiento, Domingo Faustino, 196n17; *Facundo: civilización y barbarie en las Pampas argentinas* (*Facundo: Civilization and Barbarism*), 196n17
"Savage slot," 16, 21, 31
Seabrook, William, 86, 201n31; *The Magic Island*, 86, 201n31

"Secuestro de la mujer de Antonio" (The Kidnapping of Antonio's Wife") (Guillén), 118–23
"Sensemayá" (Guillén), 126
Serra, Ana, 208n4
Serra, Rafael, 8, 10
Signifyin(g), 26–27, 104–6, 109, 112; by Lydia Cabrera, 106–7, 130, 134–35, 137, 138–42; by Nicolás Guillén, 106–7, 109, 115, 117–18, 122, 124, 126–28, 203n12
Signifying Monkey: A Theory of African–American Literary Criticism, The (Gates), 105–6, 137
Silence, 165–69, 180, 207n25
"Sistema religioso de los lucumís, El" ("The Lucumí Religious System") (Lachatañeré), 194n3
Sklodowska, Elzbieta, 73, 80, 179, 201n26
Slavery: and arrival of Africans to Cuba, 15, 40, 42–43, 50, 55; Cuban national origins and, 7, 10, 110; end of, 8, 9, 34, 190n14, 192n31; France and, 64–65; in Haiti, 6–7; Middle Passage, 132, 135, 185; Esteban Montejo and, 178–80; nineteenth century and, 5, 7, 99; in work of Lydia Cabrera, 33, 96–98, 101–2, 135–36; in work of Alejo Carpentier, 74–75, 85, 87–90, 201n33
Sociedades de color (colored societies), 11. *See also* Cabildos
Sociedad secreta abakuá narrada por viejos adeptos, La (*The Abakuá Secret Society Narrated by Old Experts*) (Cabrera), 31, 181, 201n24
Solar (tenement house/*cabildo*), 198n11, 201n28
Sommer, Doris, 5–6, 180, 188, 190n8, 208n25
Son, 12, 26, 71; working class and, 107; in work of Nicolás Guillén, 107–9, 113–18
"Son de los que protestaron contra el son, El" ("The Son of Those Who Protested the Son") (Guillén), 108–9
"Sones y Soneros" (Guillén), 108–9
Sóngoro cosongo (Guillén), 23, 26–27, 107, 112, 117–23, 127, 130; "Caña" ("Sugar Cane"), 122; "Llegada" ("Arrival"), 127; "Rumba," 122–23; "Secuestro de la mujer de Antonio" (The Kidnapping of Antonio's Wife"), 118–23
Space (physical and textual). *See* Spatial framework
Spatial framework: as used by Fernando Ortiz, 25, 32, 35, 38–39, 40–43; as used by Lydia Cabrera, 25, 32, 55–56

Spengler, Oswald, 191n25; *The Decline of the West*, 191n25
Stephens, Michelle, 72
Stocking, George, 19
Súarez y Romero, Anselmo, 98
Sugar, 6–7, 30, 48–51, 74–75, 122; mill, 74–75, 77
Surco (*Track*), 29
Surrealist movement, 19–20, 66–69, 198n7, 199n11; Alejo Carpentier and, 66, 68–69, 73, 77, 86
Swearingen, Martha, 207n23

Taíno (Arawak) population, 14, 50–51, 192n30
"Taita Hicotea y Taita Tigre" ("Papa Turtle and Papa Tiger") (Cabrera), 134–38
Tallet, José Z., 122–23, 203n15
Taylor, Diana, 151–52; *The Archive and the Repertoire*, 151–52
Teatro vernáculo (comic theatre), 99–100
Tell My Horse (Hurston), 201n31
Temporal framework: as used by Fernando Ortiz, 25, 32, 35, 38–39, 40–43, 57; as used by Lydia Cabrera, 32, 97–98, 134–35, 142
Testimonio, 177–82, 188
Their Eyes Were Watching God (Hurston), 163, 205n5
Time (historical and textual). *See* Temporal framework
Tobacco, 30, 48–51
Transculturation, 23, 39, 48, 50, 62, 176–77
Translation, 129–30, 168–69
Trickster figure, 128, 131, 135, 137, 139–41
Trío Matamoros, 118, 122, 203n13
Trouillot, Michel-Rolph, 7, 15–16, 19, 23, 31; "Savage slot," 16, 21, 31
"Tú no sabe inglé" ("You Don't Know No English") (Guillén), 128

Universal Exhibitions, 65, 66, 198n6
University of Havana, 18, 29, 194n5, 195n8
Urrutia, Gustavo, 111

Vasconcelos, José, 193n41; *La raza cósmica*, 193n41
Vasconcelos, Ramón, 107–9, 203n5
Villaverde, Cirilo, 5, 98, 99; *Cecilia Valdés o la Loma del Ángel* (*Cecilia Valdes or Angel Hill*), 5, 99
Virgen de la Caridad del Cobre, La (Our Lady of Charity of El Cobre), 78, 116, 184, 186. *See also* Orichas
Visweswaran, Kamala, 205n8
Vitier, Cintio, 203n5; *Lo cubano en la poesía* (*Cubanness in poetry*), 203n5
Vodou, 86–87, 201n31
Voix pas claire (the unclear voice), 133–34
Volontés, 67

"Walo-Wila" (Cabrera), 91, 92, 131–34
"Wandering signifier," 72
Webb, Barbara, 89
West Indies, Ltd. (Guillén), 26–27, 107, 112, 123–28; "El Abuelo" ("The Grandfather"), 124–26; "Balada de los dos abuelos" ("Ballad of the Two Grandfathers"), 124; "Caminando" ("Walking"), 126; "Sensemayá," 126; "West Indies, Ltd.," 126–28, 138
"West Indies, Ltd." (Guillén), 126–28, 138
"Why Women Always Take Advantage of Men" (Hurston), 163
Women Writing Culture (Behar and Gordon), 192n35
Woodson, Carter, 143, 204n2
Wordplay, 21, 26, 104–7, 113
Wright, Richard, 205n5
Writing Culture: The Poetics and Politics of Ethnography (Clifford and Marcus), 192n35

Yemayá y Ochún (Cabrera), 183–86
Yoruba. *See* Lucumí
Yúdice, George, 177

Zambrana, Antonio, 5; *El Negro Francisco* (*Black Francisco*), 5

Emily A. Maguire is associate professor of Spanish at Northwestern University.

www.ingramcontent.com/pod-product-compliance
Lightning Source LLC
Chambersburg PA
CBHW020835160426
43192CB00007B/661